From SHAKER LANDS
and SHAKER HANDS

From SHAKER LANDS and SHAKER HANDS

A Survey of the Industries

M. Stephen Miller

University Press of New England

HANOVER AND LONDON

Published by University Press of New England,
One Court Street, Lebanon, NH 03766
www.upne.com

Library of Congress Cataloging-in-Publication Data

Miller, M. Stephen.
From Shaker lands and Shaker hands : a survey of the industries / M.
Stephen Miller.
      p. cm.
Includes bibliographical references and index.
ISBN-13: 978-1-58465-629-6 (pbk. : alk. paper)
ISBN-10: 1-58465-629-8 (pbk. : alk. paper)
1. Shakers—Industries. I. Title.
BX9784.M55 2007
338.0088'2898—dc22   2006033933

THIS BOOK

IS DEDICATED

TO THE SHAKERS,

PAST AND PRESENT.

THIS IS,

IN EVERY SENSE,

THEIR BOOK.

WATERVLIET, NEAR ALBANY, N.Y.

PREPARED IN VACUO.
BY D. M. B. CO.

Shaker Village.

WATERVLIET, NEAR ALBANY, N.Y.

CONTENTS

FOREWORD

Gerard C. Wertkin

During the mid–nineteenth century, when the Shakers were at their height in population and community development, eighteen Shaker villages graced the rural landscape in New York, Connecticut, Massachusetts, New Hampshire, Maine, Ohio, and Kentucky. Most were reasonably prosperous by the standards of the day, with economies based principally on agriculture. In each village, Shaker Brethren and Sisters, assisted by the older children, also engaged in some form of light industry or manufacture. In this colorful, authoritative volume, Dr. M. Stephen Miller explores the economic life of the Shakers, leading readers through a fascinating and relatively unknown terrain. Recognized today for their distinctive traditions in art and design, the Shakers deserve to be better known for the quality and diversity of their work. This handsome book fills a major need and is a welcome addition to the growing literature on the Shakers.

Although it was a spiritual calling and a social ideal that united them, the Shakers have always been a practical people. Much of the daily life of the communities centered on the seasonal demands of their farms, the operation of their mills, and the requirements of their industrial endeavors. Indeed, the Shakers regarded work itself as an act of worship, and even the leadership—the Elders and Eldresses of the Ministry—was expected to engage in hand labor. This was in keeping with the words of Mother Ann Lee, the Shaker founder, who encouraged Believers to seek perfection in everything that they did. As a result, nineteenth-century Shakers were widely regarded as skilled farmers, purveyors of reliable agricultural products and other high-quality merchandise, and innovators in marketing and technology. Among the products with which they were widely associated were packaged garden seeds, herbal medicines, woodenware, chairs, brooms, foodstuffs, and "fancy" goods.

Economic success, although by no means universal throughout the United Society of Believers in Christ's Second Appearing—as the Shakers are more formally known—was in part the result of a progressive spirit that imbued many aspects of Shaker life. Unlike religious communities such as the Old Order Amish, with whom they are often compared, the Shakers were quick to embrace new technologies. Moreover, they were remarkably inventive themselves. The freedom from want that was provided to them by the communal environment—and the collaborative spirit that this environment fostered—permitted gifted Shakers to experiment. The United States Patent Office issued more than thirty patents to members of the Shaker Society, to say nothing of their many innovations and improvements for which patents were not sought. This surprising inventiveness often spurred the development of community industries within the Society. An example of this was the manufacture at Sabbathday Lake, Maine, of Brother Hewitt Chandler's harvesting machine. It was patented in 1865 and marketed as the "Improved Shakers' Maine Mower."

The Shaker villages were a natural magnet to the utopian socialists and reformers of the nineteenth century, who saw in the communal economic system of the Shakers validation of their own untested plans for the reformation of society. As early as 1817, the British social reformer Robert Owen offered their example as proof that his own vision of the "new moral world" was capable of practical realization. In 1845, Karl Marx's collaborator, Friedrich Engels, justified the feasibility of a more radical socialism on the basis of the Shaker economic experience (while rejecting the Believers' theology).

As a central tenet of its religious ideology, the United Society sought "separation from the world," an idea that implied a high degree of communal self-sufficiency. Although never entirely independent—thus providing the incentive for profitable business ventures—the Shakers did attempt to satisfy the internal needs of their villages themselves. It was often from these efforts that an industrial or commercial enterprise developed. For example, the chair factory at New Lebanon, New York—another of the Society's best-known and long-lived industries—evolved from the need to provide seating within the community.

In similar fashion, the Shakers' medicinal herb business developed from three aspects of communal life: the lack of traditionally trained physicians of their own, an interest in other reform movements in medicine such as Samuel Thomson's "botanic" approach to the treatment of a variety of diseases and disorders, and a general openness to alternative solutions to everyday problems.

Another example of this evolutionary model arose from the need to process the laundry of a large community. This not only resulted in the granting of a number of United States patents to the Shakers for improved washing machines, but it led to the manufacture of an industrial washing machine at Canterbury, New Hampshire. A gold medal was awarded for this, the Shaker Washing Machine, at the Centennial Exposition in Philadelphia in 1876.

Among the reasons why successful community industries were developed and sustained within the Shaker Society was the effectiveness of the Shaker leadership. To be sure, some leaders comported themselves poorly in office, but figures such as David Meacham, who oversaw the early development of the medicine business, and Robert Wagan, who reorganized the chair business—in both instances at New Lebanon—were not only beloved Brothers, Trustees, and Elders, but excellent businessmen. "D. M." was printed on seed envelopes decades after Meacham's death in 1826, and Wagan's name was still associated with the chair business in the 1940s, sixty years after his death.

Some Shaker industries flourished in partnership with non-Believers. Two outstanding examples of this were the medicinal products produced by the New Lebanon Shakers and marketed worldwide by A. J. White of New York and London, and the pickles, condiments, and other preserved food products that were distributed for the Sabbathday Lake Shakers by E. D. Pettengill & Co. of Portland, Maine.

The openness to change that marked many aspects of Shaker life permitted shifts within the industrial life of the Society, as necessary. Beginning in the mid–nineteenth century, a slow but unremitting decline began to affect the Shaker communities, a trend that accelerated in the twentieth century. One by one the villages closed, and those that remained open were largely populated by women. As farming and other soil-dependent pursuits were reduced in scope or discontinued, Sisters' industries—the production of cloaks, fancy goods, preserved sweets, woven poplar boxes, and a wide variety of sewing notions intended for sale in their village stores—became increasingly important economically. Today, only Sabbathday Lake remains as an active center of the Shaker faith. True to their trust, the little family of Believers in Maine sustains not only the religious heritage of the Society but its traditions of shared work and consecrated industry as well.

PREFACE

FOR MORE THAN fifty years, the Shakers have surely received the most attention of any religious sect in America. Yet, even from the time that their first members arrived on these shores in 1774, Shakers elicited and excited interest that was entirely out of proportion to their numbers. I believe that in order to understand this phenomenon there are two separate, yet linked, circumstances to be considered. On the one hand there is *the story*: a small band of British immigrants, led by a charismatic woman, Ann Lee, and committed to a radical Christian belief system, grow to nearly five thousand members, live a successful communal life in eighteen largely self-contained villages, have a significant and enduring impact on American society—and, once again a small band of Believers—continue to live their version of the Christlife today in a single community in Maine. On the other hand there is *the response* to that story: an often curious and adoring public who continue to be fascinated by the Shakers' legacy. This is why today the Shakers are sometimes referred to as "America's darling sect."

Every year, for more than three decades, books have been published about the many facets of Shaker life. As of this writing there are five books that are devoted solely to their architecture. Other books deal exclusively with Shaker textiles, music, inspirational drawings, writings, photographic images, basketry and small crafts, herbs and gardens, recipes, and—above all else—furniture and design. In addition there are a number of books on Shaker history and many more directed to the interests of children. Yet, with all these publications, scant attention has been paid to the *economic life* of the Shakers.

The earliest examination of Shaker industries came about in 1930 when the New York State Museum in Albany, New York, opened an exhibition called "The Community Industries of the Shakers." This two-year exhibition was followed in 1933 by the museum's publication of *Handbook No. 15*, bearing the same title as the exhibition. Dr. Edward Deming Andrews, who served as temporary curator of history at the Museum, wrote it. The handbook was 322 pages long and included dozens of black-and-white illustrations of Shaker products, along with some of the buildings in which they were produced. Dr. Andrews relied heavily on his extensive manuscript collection for the numerous references in the book. Since works from the New Lebanon, New York, community dominated his collection, it is not surprising that this community was prominently represented—in both the exhibition and the book. The museum also had a number of artifacts from the nearby community of Watervliet that were displayed. Although there were many necessary omissions in Dr. Andrews's efforts, such as examples of any of the industries at sixteen other Shaker villages, the exhibit and the book were important early landmarks in the study of Shaker material culture and economic activity.

In 1974, Faith Andrews published *Work and Worship: The Economic Order of the Shakers*. This continued the work that she and Dr. Andrews, who had died ten years earlier, had pursued together for more than half a century. The book is a grab bag of subjects including an expanded look at Shaker industries, many lovely photographs (the book was published by the New York Graphic Society), a list of Shaker "inventions and improvements," and various other aspects of their history. Dover Publications republished it in 1982, in softcover, as *Work and Worship Among the Shakers: Their Craftsmanship and Economic Order.*

The next treatment of Shaker economy took place a little more than fifty years after the first exhibition. In 1983 and 1984, the New York State Museum again served as the venue and the exhibition, with an accompanying monograph, was titled "Community Industries of the Shakers: A New Look." In addition to showing the variety of Shaker products, it included a number of pieces of furniture and some of the machinery and devices used in the various industries. Selections from this exhibit were displayed at the museum again in 1999, a display that included much more of its general Shaker collection.

The last large-scale look at the Shakers' community industries took place in 1988 at Hancock Shaker Village in Pittsfield, Massachusetts. This exhibit was called "A Century of Shaker Ephemera: Marketing Community Industries 1830–1930," and was seen by more than seventy thousand people. It was cocurated by June Sprigg, curator of collections, and me. The focus here was on the use of ephemera—generally printed paper that is intended for one-time or short-term use—to market the products of the Shaker villages. Because of space limitations, 131 objects were chosen for display. These came from six institutions with Shaker collections as well as from my personal collection. One of the major goals of the exhibit was to elicit an appreciation for the "usefulness" of ephemera in illuminating this area of Shaker life. An annotated catalog of the same title was written (with Ms. Sprigg's help), photographed, and published by me in 1989.

Considering that so many aspects of Shaker life are so richly represented on bookshelves, while at the same time recognizing the impossibility of fully understanding that life without living it, a larger-scale and more comprehensive look at their economic life is long overdue. The purpose of this book is to survey the economic underpinnings of this movement—the industries *and* their marketing strategies—that allowed and continue to allow the Shakers to live "the life" that is the subject of the essays that follow.

M.S.M.

ACKNOWLEDGMENTS

MY FIRST DEBT of gratitude goes to the "dream team" of contributors who agreed without hesitation to join me in this venture: Gerard Wertkin, Steve Paterwic, and the Shakers at Sabbathday Lake, Maine. Steve's and Gerry's knowledge of and sensitivity to their subjects are peerless, while the Shakers, simply put, "live the life." Magda Gabor-Hotchkiss, Jerry Grant, and Sharon Koomler—well known and well respected in the world of Shaker studies—were exceptional "readers" and rounded out my team. Magda also answered numerous questions and compiled the index.

The Shaker Family contributed a statement of their faith that has not been seen in print in a generation. Beyond that they made me welcome each time I visited at Sabbathday Lake, and their professional museum staff—Lenny Brooks, Director, Michael Graham, Curator, and Tina Agren, Librarian—extended every courtesy to me including the rights to reproduce images of objects from their collections. Michael, in particular, gave me hours of his time, patience, and knowledge.

When I first undertook this project I needed somebody to point me in the right direction. William Drenttel, of Winterhouse Studio, Falls Village, Connecticut, materialized as that person. He then helped me to develop a "Proposal to Publish," which, in turn, led me to University Press of New England. Thank you Bill.

John Landrigan, former acquisitions editor at University Press of New England, accepted this proposal. I am most grateful for this vote of confidence.

The following institutions and individuals granted me access to their collections and rights to reproduce images of objects from them, and were essential to making this book stronger and more comprehensive than it otherwise would have been: Canterbury Shaker Village, Canterbury, New Hampshire, Scott Swank, President, Sheryl Hack, Director of Programs and Collections, Renee Fox, Librarian, and Jennifer Carroll-Plante, Curator of Collections; Fruitlands Museums, Harvard, Massachusetts, Michael Volmar, Director; Hamilton College, Clinton, New York, Randy Ericson, Couper Librarian, Burke Library; Hancock Shaker Village, Pittsfield, Massachusetts, Larry Yeardon, President, Christian Goodwillie, Curator, and Magda Gabor-Hotchkiss, volunteer librarian; the staff of the New York State Museum, Albany, New York; and the Shaker Museum and Library, Old Chatham, New York, Sharon Koomler, Director, and Jerry Grant, Director of Research.

Three individuals whom I first came to know as dealers in Shaker ephemera, but with whom I developed close personal relationships, are David Newell, the late Milton Sherman, and Scott De Wolfe. David was my earliest contact and my first mentor. His wisdom and careful eye continue to influence me. Milt had a formidable intellect and helped shape my own collecting goals. Scott has been a steadfast friend for more than fifteen years and a great source of knowledge about Shaker printed matter. He embodies the qualities of integrity, intelligence, and energy. Without all three friends to guide and to help me there would not *be* a Miller Collection today.

Doug and Connie Hamel have been trustworthy dealers in Shaker artifacts for more than thirty years, and Will and Karel Henry have conducted Shaker-only auctions since 1982. I am grateful to both sources for some of the fine material that appears here.

Two people have helped to lead me through the technical intricacies of color photography for this book with saintly patience: David L. Farrington, West Hartford, Connecticut, and Russell Selzer, Avon, Connecticut. I am indebted to them both.

Collectors of paper matter need conservation specialists to support their activities: ephemera and conservation *must* go hand in hand. My collection has benefited from the professionalism of Debora Dyer Mayer, Sarah Dove, and especially Stephanie Ewing-Darcy. The results of their work will be found throughout this book.

In addition to the people already named above, and at the risk of inadvertent omissions, I would like to thank these friends for their support during the long process of bringing this book to completion: Jean Burks, Carol and Burt Cunin, Diana Granitto, Bill Helfand, Howie Levenbook, Erhart Muller, John and Lili Ott, Amy and Steve Silverman, Maggie Stier, and the members of the Boston Area Shaker Study Group and the Shaker Seminar.

Some of my family was also involved in this project: my son Rick designed the map of the long-lived Shaker communities; my grandson Jordan sat patiently to model a Shaker sweater; and my wife, Miriam, provided unconditional love, support, and computer expertise. While my mission is to do honor to the Shaker legacy, past and present, little would have been possible—and none worthwhile—without Miriam.

A NOTE ON THE ILLUSTRATIONS

Unless noted otherwise, all objects illustrated are from the collection of M. Stephen and Miriam R. Miller. All dimensions are given in inches, height by width (by depth or diameter, where appropriate) to the nearest eighth inch. "R-" refers to the listing in Mary L. Richmond's *Shaker Literature: A Bibliography*, and "v." is used to denote a variant of that description. NIR means "not in Richmond" and is used for objects that presumably would have been listed if she had been aware of their existence.

The printing techniques that are included with each listing fall into three general categories: letterpress, where ink is transferred from a raised surface; intaglio, where ink is transferred from an incised surface; and lithography, where ink is transferred from a flat surface. It should be noted, however, that it is often difficult—and for our purposes not necessary—to distinguish between a wood engraving, which, like letterpress, is a relief process, and a metal plate (copper or steel) engraving, which is an intaglio process.

WATERVLIET, NEAR ALBANY, N.Y.

PREPARED IN VACUO.
BY D.M.B. CO.

Shaker Village.

WATERVLIET, NEAR ALBANY, N.Y.

From SHAKER LANDS
and SHAKER HANDS

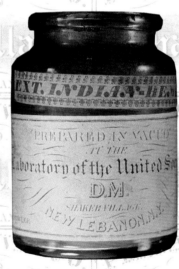

WATERVLIET, NEAR ALBANY, N.Y.

PREPARED IN VACUO.

BY D.M.B. & CO.

Shaker Village.

WATERVLIET, NEAR ALBANY, N.Y.

Introduction

THE FABRIC OF Shaker communal life was and is a unified whole, the warp and weft formed of a tightly woven grid of spiritual, social, and economic threads. The pattern of this cloth was first laid out during the closing decades of the eighteenth century. Some may argue that over the ensuing 225 years this fabric has lost some of its shape, while others might contend that during this time its colors have faded a bit. The truth is that Shaker life today remains "organic," a unified whole, and present-day Believers feel completely in "union" with their founding members. It remains an article of their faith that a member of that first generation of Shakers would readily recognize communal life today, no matter what small alterations in appearance have occurred over the centuries.

Every attempt to examine some single aspect of Shaker life, then, exposes a central paradox: How can one thread of the fabric be teased out for a closer look without distorting the whole? How, for example, does one approach Shaker architecture without considering their social organization; explore Shaker dietary habits without taking into account their own rules of governance; discuss Shaker styles of dress without considering their concepts of modesty and simplicity? And how, finally, can *any* single facet of Shaker life be detached from their religious convictions, the faith that guides and controls every aspect of their lives?

And yet, *and yet*, by examining the single strand of Shaker economic life—the products from their lands and hands that were produced to support their communal life—this is precisely what I will be doing in this book. For the past seventy-five years, non-Shakers have tried to understand the Shakers by studying isolated aspects of their complex culture. This volume is one more chapter in the history of this effort. True Shaker life, however, is greater than the sum of its parts. "The life," as Shakers refer to it, does not yield readily to cursory or piecemeal examination. Perhaps this is why it continues to be studied by the World—the Shakers' term for non-Shakers—with unending curiosity and with a continuing stream of publications.

The Shakers separated themselves from the World in the 1780s for the purpose of living a unique kind of Christian life in a communal setting. This is the essence of Shaker life still. Yet, to most Americans in the twenty-first century who have heard of them at all, "Shaker" stands for the goods that they produced, not the life that they lived. It is easy to see why this is so. Elements of Shaker culture have been borrowed for an array of products that are widely available in today's marketplace: Shaker-style furniture, Shaker-knit sweaters, Shaker-type boxes, and Shaker "Tree of Life" motifs. A modern take on the veritable Shaker hymn "Simple Gifts" is a main theme in Aaron Coplands' ballet score for *Appalachian Spring* and has even been used to advertise a brand of automobiles. Simply put, "Shaker" sells.

Still, all this appropriation of "Shaker" is, in essence, nostalgic. Most of it trades on myths and half-truths. One of the myths is that they are a "simple" people. While it is true that they have always tried to simplify their temporal lives in order to concentrate on living their special vision of the Christlife, they are in many ways a complex people. Some of these complexities will be revealed in the pages ahead.

Another of the myths is that the Shakers, while living apart from the World, were truly independent of it. From their earliest days Shaker communities have never been—nor could they be—entirely self-sufficient. Certain materials could not be produced in their own settlements, which were, in essence, large collective farms. Iron, tin, and copper; glassware and ceramics; cotton cloth and thread; food staples such as sugar and salt; coffee and tea, and so much more all had to be acquired from the World. So while the Shakers lived apart from the World, they were never isolated from it. The truth is that from the start they were dependent on business interactions with the World.

While it is tempting to look on the current attractiveness of "Shaker" with a measure of skepticism or bemusement, the fact is that "Shaker" has always sold. The difference is that up to the latter part of the twentieth century nearly all those products were grown or fabricated by the Shakers themselves. Without an economic base for their communities, there simply would not have been communities.

The records of commercial transactions during the last decade and a half of the eighteenth century are sketchy at best, but it seems reasonable to assume that the Shaker economy in the beginning was in step with that of their rural neighbors. That is to say, it was based largely on a barter system. The Shakers traded whatever soil-based products exceeded their own needs to other farmers or merchants in the World, for goods that they were deficient in or could not produce. In the 1780s and 1790s the Shakers were mainly producing the standard farm-yield of the northeastern United States: eggs, milk, butter, and cheese; fresh meats; wheat, rye, oats, corn, and potatoes; fresh fruits and vegetables.

The first stirring of an industry within the Shaker communities, at least at New Lebanon and Watervliet, New York, and Hancock, Massachusetts, was the raising, packaging, and selling of garden seeds. This is called an industry because it involved multiple levels of cooperation by many hands. It began between 1790 and 1800. In these early years seeds were sold in bulk, probably put up in small linen sacks. (The Shakers

also raised flax and processed it to make their own bags.) By 1810, every one of the eleven eastern communities (in New York State and New England) had a seed business, all of them dealing exclusively in vegetable seeds. Flower seeds, raised only at New Lebanon, Canterbury, New Hampshire, and Enfield, Connecticut, came much later. Around 1800, the industry expanded and was organized around the concept of primarily retail marketing on a regional, rather than a local, basis.

Seeds were first packaged at this time in small paper envelopes or "papers" that were printed in their own communities. The Shakers were the first to sell seeds in this manner. They then developed a network of small merchants who sold their seeds by consignment. The basis for this arrangement was trust—a core value of the sect. For the first half of the nineteenth century, the garden seed industry was the greatest source of revenue for most of the eighteen Shaker communities—eastern and western. At New Lebanon, for one example, seed production was measured in *tonnage* as early as 1805.

In addition to its critical role in the early prosperity of the communities, this industry established a pattern for economic success that prevailed for some eighty years longer. When a medicinal herb business developed, first at New Lebanon (renamed Mount Lebanon in 1861) in the 1820s, and then at most other communities, it eventually eclipsed seed sales and was, for many, the largest overall revenue producer in the second half of the nineteenth century. New Lebanon and its sister community at Watervliet together put up more than a thousand preparations derived from plant material in the form of dried herbs (roots, barks, and leaves), fluid extracts, "essential" and other oils, syrups, ointments, and tinctures. Members of the Harvard community decided in the early 1860s to cede the garden seed business to their sister community at Shirley and to concentrate their efforts on raising and selling medicinal herbs; these were already a huge success. By midcentury, eighteen *tons* of dried material, from more than 170 plant species, were put up for sale at this community. Business here continued into the early twentieth century, almost until Harvard closed in 1918.

Edward D. Andrews observed in his landmark publication, *The Community Industries of the Shak-*

ers, that "The passion of the people composing this sect for being useful, for doing useful things and for making things useful is evidenced in these soil culture activities." Yet, as the nineteenth century progressed, their passion for the "useful" turned from goods harvested from their lands to items crafted by their hands. This change accelerated after the Civil War, and by the end of the century the turnabout was nearly complete. Some of the reasons for this important shift included: the number of Shaker men, hence farmers, was declining steeply as more sought life in cities and factories; hired hands could not take up this slack, and their employment presented its own set of social problems for the Shakers; southern markets for produce, especially seeds, were largely disrupted by the war; and, finally, the Shakers faced greatly increased competition from purveyors of seeds and medicines in the World.

By the end of the nineteenth century, about three-quarters of all Shakers were women. It was now the Sisters who were largely responsible for the economy of their communities. They made and sold handcrafted items, sometimes with the assistance of Brothers. In addition to selling these goods at gift stores located in their own communities, the Maine and New Hampshire Brethren (and later, Sisters) made sales trips to fairs, expositions, and resort sites—mainly the beaches and the mountains of New England. At the Sabbathday Lake, Maine, community, the fabrication and outfitting of oval wooden sewing boxes or carriers continued through the first half of the twentieth century. In 1923, Brother Delmer Wilson crafted 1,083 of these carriers, but it was the Sisters who outfitted them with sewing notions— pincushions, needle books, thread waxes, and emery bags. The Shakers at Sabbathday Lake continue the gift store tradition today, selling books, postcards, and sweets along with a selection of handcrafted items, herbs from their gardens, and wool from their flock of sheep.

There are two basic ways to learn about the economic life of the Shakers: one may study the manuscript records, or one may examine the products of the industries. The Shakers were meticulous record keepers, and these records are replete with detailed accounts of their commercial activities. They were equally assiduous about preserving these written reports. Unfortunately, over time, fires, carelessness, the sometimes hurried closings of communities, and an often indifferent public have robbed us of many of these records. Nonetheless, hundreds of journals, ledgers, account books, diaries, daybooks, letters, receipts, and other business papers have survived.

Manuscripts are invaluable sources for "who, what, when, where, and how much." Today these documents are scattered in numerous public and private collections, without the benefit of a unified database recording content and locations. They were written by many hands, and some are difficult to read. Manuscripts are also limited in their ability to convey to readers the amazing richness—what might be called "texture"—and diversity of the economic engines that powered all the Shaker communities. Finally, if truth be told, the information they contain is, in and of itself, of limited interest to the general reader.

The second approach—the basis for this book—is to look at the products themselves, along with the wide range of materials needed to bring those products to market: packages made from paper, cardboard, glass, and tin; labels; instructions for use; bills and receipts; and many forms of advertising. This latter group includes almanacs, catalogs, pamphlets, posters, broadsides, display signs, and premiums. All these pieces have "texture." (Manuscript sources are also used here, but only to support the images and their attendant text.) The second half of the nineteenth century witnessed the phenomenal and interrelated growth of the advertising and printing industries, and the Shakers were very much a part of this. In many instances, *only* the marketing materials for a Shaker product survive and not the product itself. This is true for virtually all consumables.

This brings us to a vital subtext of this book: the role that ephemera plays in preserving Shaker (or any other) culture. *Ephemera* is a plural noun that, by custom, also applies to individual pieces. It generally refers to printed paper intended for one-time or short-term use. Were it not for ephemera—hundreds of examples of which are illustrated here—we would have to depend mainly on the manuscript record to tell us about all the goods that were critical to the very survival of Shaker communal life right from the beginning.

Ephemera also reveals the marketing strategies of

the Shakers. The selling of garden seeds is a ready-made example. Once the Shakers made the decision to package seeds in small, individual envelopes or "papers," they needed to design wooden boxes to hold them, box labels to advertise them, receipts to record the distribution of the boxes, catalogs to promote them, ordering lists, billheads to record orders, posters to lead the shopping public to the merchant/consignee, and manuals with planting instructions, recipes, and more. All these bits and scraps, ephemera, are minor miracles of survival since they were intended to perish shortly after use. They all deserve our best efforts to collect and preserve them.

The Shakers, unlike some nontraditional Christian sects such as the Amish, with whom they are sometimes mistakenly lumped, have always embraced advances in technology. This includes developments in the advertising fields. As color papers became readily available, the Shakers printed on them. When multicolor letterpress, followed by direct lithography and finally color lithography, became readily available, they availed themselves of these technologies, using printing houses outside their communities to furnish these materials in order to market their products more effectively. In this and many other ways that will be shown in this book, the Shakers were both progressive and innovative.

There were other, more subtle marketing strategies that the Shakers developed over the course of the nineteenth century. In the early part of the century, the New Lebanon and Watervliet communities used the initials D. M. (for David Meacham, Senior) on their seed, herbal, and medicinal products. Brother David was a highly regarded Trustee (or business manager and liaison with the World), and his name carried with it an implied guarantee of quality, purity, freshness, and honest weight. At New Lebanon, "D. M." was still in use more than sixty years after his death in 1826. (This strategy anticipated by about a century the *Good Housekeeping* "Seal," which was introduced in 1909.) Toward the end of the century, the name of Trustee D. C. Brainard was similarly used on a variety of products made at Mount Lebanon, and the name of Elder Robert Wagan, founder of the chair industry, was used as "R. M. Wagan & Co." sixty years after his untimely death in 1883.

The use of the term "Genuine Shaker" was another marketing technique that stood as an assurance of quality. The term came into use around the middle of the nineteenth century, clearly in response to the intrusion of non-Shaker goods into traditional Shaker markets. For example, by the time of the Centennial Exhibition in Philadelphia, that market was peppered with imitations of the chairs that were made for sale at Mount Lebanon. Beginning in 1876, all Shaker stools and chairs bore a gold transfer decal certifying their origin. In a similar manner, one finds the words "Genuine Shaker" applied to other products as diverse as garden seeds, brooms, applesauce, sewing baskets, rug beaters, and woolen cloaks.

Nevertheless, by the end of the century, it was factors besides simple competition that led to the Shakers' waning presence in the marketplace. Many of these factors are addressed in historian Steve Paterwic's essay that follows. Suffice it to say here that problems with leadership and manpower were primary.

It is likely that purchasers of Shaker crafts in the first half of the twentieth century expected their purchases to outlive the movement itself. Of course this did not happen. The Shakers are still here, and so are many of these products. These pieces were meticulously made using the finest materials available. When wood was needed, the Shakers had the patience and experience to carefully select and properly season it. When fabric was called for, they bought the finest imported silks and wool broadcloths. (Although the Shakers produced and wove silk and wool for their own clothing, it seems that they purchased them from the World for lining sewing baskets or making cloaks for sale.) Their beliefs have always informed their work. Some call this "consecrated labor." Work, for Shakers, is a form of worship.

Fabricating these products was so costly and labor-intensive that Worldly manufacturers could easily undersell the Shakers with similar goods. Yet it was the Shakers' reputation for quality and for the development of products that were unique in the market, combined with an interest in handcrafted versus machine-made goods and a slowly gathering sense of nostalgia for "olden ways"—fueled by the likes of Wallace Nutting and the Colonial Revival movement—that influenced a small but important segment of the buying public to continue seeking Shaker-made crafts to buy.

Two examples of Shaker products that originated with them and were never imitated are poplarware goods and oval, swing-handled, and outfitted sewing baskets or "carriers." For the former, the Shakers developed a method for weaving thin strips of poplar wood into a cloth, wrapping this around cardboard forms of various shapes, trimming these containers with kid leather, and lining the interiors with silk. Canterbury made poplarware until the mid-1950s, and Sabbathday Lake, switching from poplar to cloth coverings, almost to the end of the twentieth century. Several communities became known for their oval, handled bentwood carriers, usually outfitted with sewing implements, but Sabbathday Lake led the others in this enterprise.

This book is divided into two main parts: "Products of the Land" and "Products of the Hands." The first part is the larger one, accurately reflecting the preeminence of the soil-based industries until well into the nineteenth century. Three areas of commerce, originating in the fields, farms, and orchards, were dominant: garden seeds, medicinal herbs and preparations, and food products. The evolution of the garden seed industry at one community, New Lebanon, New York, will be used to illustrate the development of the Shakers' first major enterprise. Although this industry actually began at several Shaker villages at about the same time, more remnants survive from New Lebanon's business than from all the other communities combined, making it an especially useful model for displaying the many facets that comprised the whole.

Medicinal herbs and, to a far lesser extent, culinary herbs were important to most Shaker communities, although only a few were largely dependent on this business for their economic base. Harvard, Massachusetts, Canterbury, New Hampshire, and New Lebanon and Watervliet, New York, were the largest producers of herbs and herbal preparations; at some point in each of their histories they derived most of their annual income from these sales. These activities are the focus of the second portion of "Products of the Land."

Food products and preparations fill the third chapter of the first part. As with garden seeds and herbs, all communities offered fresh and prepared fruits and vegetables for sale. Apples and their by-products were, by either weight or volume, one of the Shakers' most important cash crops. Every one of the eastern communities put up applesauce for sale, and most also offered the fresh or dried fruit along with apple cider, vinegar, and butter. Since New Lebanon was the largest of the communities for most of its history, one of the last to close, and readily accessible to early collectors, such as Dr. Andrews and his wife, Faith, it has yielded the largest trove of food-related ephemera.

The "Products of the Hands" part examines those items crafted in the various Shaker shops, mills, and sewing or weaving rooms. On the whole, far less material of this nature was produced, because each piece required a great expenditure of time and investment in materials. At the beginning of the second half of the nineteenth century, it was Shaker Brothers who were mostly responsible for handcrafted items to be sold: chairs and stools, storage boxes of all kinds, brooms and brushes, dippers, measures, sieves, cooperage (pails, tubs, barrels), rulers, oval boxes, and the like. Near the end of the century, as the Brothers' numbers diminished, the focus of handcrafted items was sewn, knit, and woven goods made by the Sisters. Both groups of objects will be examined in this portion of the book, along with some activities that are difficult to classify such as postcard production and the hospitality business.

Probably the most widely distributed and the best-known Shaker crafted items were "production" chairs and stools (as distinguished from those made for the Shakers' own use). The chairs were made by the thousands in assembly-line fashion at the South Family factory at Mount Lebanon using precisely machined and interchangeable parts, assembled in standardized sizes and configurations. Thus one could order most chairs with or without arms, with or without rockers, with taped or slatted backs, and in several finish colors—all in eight sizes. They were mostly sold wholesale to large department stores in cities, although an active mail order business was also conducted with individuals. The industry lasted from the 1860s until about 1940, the last of the Shakers' "heavy" industries.

By the end of the nineteenth century, Shaker craft

items were, on the whole, smaller, more delicate, and fancier—more "Victorian." For the most part, they were made by women, for women. After about 1870 this endeavor was known collectively as the "fancy goods" industry. All these wares were the result of labor-intensive handwork. The products of these labors were mainly designed for needle crafts—wooden or poplar-woven sewing baskets and boxes, spool stands, darning eggs, needle cases, pincushions, and so forth. The Sisters also made bonnets, sweaters, cloaks, and knit socks by the thousands. Much of the woodenware has endured over time but textiles, owing to their more fragile nature, have not fared as well.

It may be tempting to infer the size or strength of a particular Shaker enterprise from the volume of material—especially ephemera—that has survived. The reader is cautioned not to fall into this trap. The circumstances surrounding the closings of communities, patterns of collecting, the nature of materials, the vagaries of what is worth keeping and preserving and what is not, and even pure chance all conspire to make any attempt at correlations misleading and, ultimately, useless.

To pursue this subject a bit further, it will become apparent that material examined in this book from the eastern societies far outweighs that from the West, even though, at the height of prosperity, the two groups were of similar size. At least two factors clearly were responsible for this development. The western communities for the most part closed earlier, with the last closing—South Union, Kentucky—coming in 1922. At that date, there were still seven active communities in the East. Also, in 1922, there were few major collectors or institutions to gather up the fragments of past communal enterprises in the West. In fact, one can date the beginning of a broader public interest in the Shakers to an article published by Edward D. and Faith Andrews in *The Magazine*

Antiques in 1928. It was titled "Craftsmanship of an American Religious Sect."

One should not forget, however, that as early as 1905 a historian and collector named John P. MacLean published a bibliography of Shaker literature that contained over five hundred entries, much of it from the West. MacLean also sold Shaker material, and the director of the Western Reserve Historical Society in Cleveland, Ohio, Wallace Cathcart, bought much of it. The Shakers, as well, recognized Cathcart's interest, and they sent him huge quantities of imprints and ephemera. Today the Western Reserve Historical Society is the single largest repository of Shaker printed matter.

The goal of this book is to provide a comprehensive overview of the Shaker industries; yet it is necessarily limited in this goal by the surviving evidence. This evidence may be as seemingly insignificant as a tiny product label or a torn receipt. Or it may be a never opened, never used example of the product itself. The fact is that all of it is important.

Nonetheless, it must be noted that every community devoted a great deal of effort to, and derived substantial revenue from, industries that will *not* be examined in this book, owing to the lack of physical remnants from that industry. This category includes such profitable activities as the tanning of hides and fashioning of braided whips; cattle, poultry, and sheep breeding; blacksmithing (especially nails, horseshoes, and a wide range of forged tools); lumber milling and wool card making; tinsmithing; wool and linen weaving; the making of men's hats and shirts, women's bonnets and hose; and the raising of grain for sale—*lots* of grain.

It bears repeating that without an economic base, the Shaker movement could not have survived, let alone prospered, for most of its 225-year history. Yet it must be kept in mind that, taken together, the totality of the Shaker industries is still only one thread in the amazingly rich fabric of Shaker communal life that is now in its third century.

Who Were the Shakers?

STEPHEN PATERWIC

"MOTHER TAUGHT a way of life." These six words, spoken by Brother Arnold Hadd of Sabbathday Lake, Maine, have special resonance. Mother Ann Lee's "way of life" is the essence of who the Shakers were and still are. It is the key to entering a very special domain and, once inside, understanding what Shakers are and have been all about for more than two hundred years.

Above all else, Shakers have always sought to create an environment in which spiritual seekers could develop their greatest potential. Shakers believed that their Christlife, in some ways very similar to the monastic concept of a Christlife, could best be achieved by living in communities of celibate men and women—societies that had scheduled times for prayer, labor, and recreation. Additionally, their practice of confession of sins helped to keep an individual on the path of spiritual advancement. Community, celibacy, and confession of sins—these are the "three c's" that present-day Believers (the name Shakers call themselves) use to summarize their lives.

Throughout their history, Shaker writers have claimed that their religious movement is akin to all other groups that have sought truth outside traditional, institutional churches. In the Shaker case, these writers have sought some continuity with the remnants of the French Prophets of the late seventeenth and early eighteenth centuries. It was they who may have influenced discontented English Quakers James and Jane Wardley in the mid-1700s. Whether this actually happened, and if so to what extent, may never be known and seems relatively unimportant. Whatever the Shakers' precise origins, it is certain that a young woman from Manchester, England, named Ann Lee came into the group led by the Wardleys and transformed it.

Under the Wardleys, "operations" of the Spirit—ecstatic movements—characterized their worship and earned them the name "Shaking Quakers" or Shakers. Confessing sins before a witness was also a distinctive tenet of the group. Unfortunately, harassment and persecution were constants. In 1770, Ann Lee was imprisoned for "profaning the Sabbath." There she received a revelation. It was this: although God is one Being, Eternal Unity, God is also both male and female. Women as well as men could receive the Spirit of Christ because "In the depths of the human spirit, man's and woman's, put there by God, resides the latent Living Christ, the Christ of all Ages" (Sister Marguerite Frost, *The Shaker Story*). Through prayer and desire, every person could achieve that indwelling union with God. As a consequence, no other relationship should stand between God and humanity. Earthly marriage would need to give way as the soul fully joined itself to the Christ. It was this powerful new testimony that earned the poor and illiterate young woman from Manchester the name Mother Ann.

Fellow Shakers did not see her as a divine being but rather as the first to proclaim this concept of the Second Coming of Christ. As a result of these truths, it was believed that every individual could labor and attain a oneness with God. By prayer, witness, and prophecy the little band set out to live a religious life that was in contrast to the practices of all existing churches. The Shaker testimony, however, was not destined to be played out in England. Claiming the gift of divine revelation, Mother Ann and her followers became convinced that the gospel should be preached in America. On May 19, 1774, Mother Ann and seven of her companions left England. On August 6, 1774, the group landed in New York City.

The first years in America found few who showed any interest in the Shaker testimony. This changed in the winter and spring of 1780, when the Shakers were visited by the leaders of a religious revival that had taken place in the border towns of New York and Massachusetts. This "New Light" revival had largely spent itself, but ministers Joseph Meacham, Samuel Johnson, and others decided to investigate reports they had heard concerning the Shakers. They were themselves converted and, as new Shakers, carried their beliefs back to their homes, scattered across New England and upstate New York. Meanwhile, Mother Ann and her associates spent the following four years visiting the new converts and laboring with them. These missionary tours often turned into violent confrontations between the Shakers and angry mobs. In spite of hatred, threats, and physical abuse, Shakerism seemed to thrive as it drew more and more people into the work of the Christlife.

The 1770s and 1780s were rich in religious revivals. The uncertainty brought on by America's breakaway from England, as well as a continued longing for a more intense and personal relationship with God (something perceived to be lacking in the traditional churches), created a milieu that was ripe for religious exploration. The pattern of such revivals included, at first, a great feeling of spiritual conviction, a deep awareness of sin, and both mental and physical excitement. These were accompanied by visions, prophecy, and an anticipation that Christ would soon appear. When the fervor died down, a few seekers who longed for more light remained. These were the people who often became Shakers.

In 1784, both Mother Ann and her brother, Father William Lee, died. Nonetheless, before the decade was out, Shaker leaders were in a position to call the scattered Believers into full Gospel order. New Believers who lived adjacent to one another were directed to join their farms together to form communities. Those who lived at a distance were told to sell their farms and join their Brothers and Sisters in communities that were being formed. A "joint interest" replaced individual ownership of property as each person was directed to bring all his/her possessions and unite in a communal setting. Starting at New Lebanon in 1787, Shaker Societies were formally organized. These were the societies of Watervliet, New York; Hancock, Tyringham, Shirley, and Harvard, Massachusetts; Enfield, Connecticut; Canterbury and Enfield, New Hampshire; and Alfred, Gorham, and Sabbathday Lake in Maine.

It is essential to note that by gathering Believers into relatively self-sufficient communes, separated from "the World," the Shakers began to develop a unique theological, social, and economic system within an emerging American nation. Although their numbers in England may have reached over a hundred for a short time, when they left England in 1774, they were a group of only about thirty, living in and around Manchester. In America in the 1780s, by contrast, Shakers numbered in the hundreds and were found in distant and remote areas. By the time they left England, persecution of Shakers had quieted. In America, however, as they attracted more and more converts, the intensity of persecution grew once again. Thus it was for both spiritual and physical well-being that Believers were called to withdraw from the World.

Another adaptation to their new environment was the structure of Shaker leadership. From 1774 until 1780, Mother Ann was recognized as the leader of the small band of Believers. After the Opening of the Gospel on May 19, 1780, so many people joined that Mother Ann had to rely on James Whittaker and on her brother, William, for help. Both had come over from England with her six years earlier. Calvin Harlow, Joseph Meacham, and other American-born converts also assisted as leaders. James Whittaker succeeded Mother Ann following her death in 1784, and continued her efforts to make a permanent and united church. A great sign of this was the building of the Meetinghouse at New Lebanon in 1785. From this time onward, religious leadership was located at New Lebanon rather than at Watervliet, where the Shakers had first settled.

When Father James Whittaker died in 1787, leadership passed to Father Joseph Meacham and Mother Lucy Wright, both American born. It was under their guidance that the governing and communal living structure of Shakerism was set into place. This structure survives to the present day.

The inclusion of a female in the highest governance of Shaker Society was as revolutionary as it was inspired. Although Father Joseph Meacham was acclaimed as the "Visible Head of the Order" in 1787, he chose Mother Lucy Wright as the leader among the Sisters. Wright had been close to Mother Ann and nursed her in her final illness so she was a natural choice. Yet Meacham did not make this decision rashly. He explained that he had received a revelation, or "gift," that he should share the leadership role with a woman. Another leader, Childs Hamlin, said he had received a gift of his own at the same time, thus seconding this revelation. From the beginning, therefore, Mother Lucy was seen as divinely chosen and the one with the strongest connection to Mother Ann. This helped dispel some of the dissension caused by having a woman lead a religious organization that included men.

It is no accident that two years before the formal gathering of the communities the Meetinghouse was completed at New Lebanon. Capable men and women from various places were called by Shaker leaders to take up residence there. They were then sent out as missionaries to gather Believers into the pattern of living that had been established at New Lebanon. These local leaders formed a ministry that included two or three communities in one geographic area called a bishopric. In this manner, the First Bishopric consisted of the Shaker villages in New Lebanon and Watervliet, New York. New Lebanon, home of this ministry, had supervision over all the other bishoprics and was often referred to as the Lebanon Ministry and later the Central Ministry. The Second Bishopric was centered at Hancock, Massachusetts, and included Tyringham, Massachusetts, and Enfield, Connecticut. The Eastern Bishopric consisted of Harvard and Shirley, Massachusetts, with the former as the primary community. The New Hampshire Bishopric was centered at Canterbury, and the Maine Bishopric was centered at Alfred. This structure was in place in the East in some form until the last of the regional ministries, that being in Maine, was dis-

solved in 1927. In the West, the Ohio Bishopric was located at Union Village and the Kentucky Bishopric (most of the time) at Pleasant Hill.

On the local level, communities were made up of units called families. Shaker families comprised twenty to more than one hundred members. The most important one was called the Church Family (or simply, the Church) because it included the Meetinghouse that was used by the entire community. (In Ohio and Kentucky, this family was called the Center Family.) The Church Family was also known as the Church Order, and during the earliest years of Shaker ingathering it served as the spiritual and temporal model for other families. If a society was large enough, the Church Family might have branched into a First and a Second Order.

All the other families belonged to the Order of Families and were located on adjacent properties. At the time of the first gatherings, these families were known by the name of the leading Elder, often the original owner of the farmstead. In 1814, the Order of Families was dissolved, and from then on Shaker families belonged either to the Church Order or to the newly established Gathering or Novitiate Order. Families became known thereafter by their directional location from the Church Family. At Enfield, Connecticut, for example, the Church, North, and East Families comprised the Church Order, while the Gathering Order was made up of the South and West Families.

Two Elders and two Eldresses led each family. Their primary duty was spiritual leadership, and they lived with "their" family in a large communal dwelling house. Office Deacons or Trustees were appointed to handle all contact and commerce with those outside the community, the World. These men and women, generally two of each, lived in an office building convenient to the main road. Finally, duties within the family that required supervision were assigned to family Deacons. Again, two men or two women ran the shops, farm operations, orchards, kitchen, laundry, and so forth.

The first generation of Shakers represented country people from various economic levels, although most were from small to medium-size farms. In common with their rural neighbors, almost all of them were related to each other by either blood or marriage. These earliest Shakers have often been seen as a strong and fervent group who freely devoted their considerable talents to the cause and consequently carried the Shaker gospel beyond the turmoil of the death of the founders and into an era of great numerical and financial prosperity. Certainly, the fact that so many of them were related was a major reason for the great success of the earliest communities. As they joined their farms and pooled their goods, their leaders were their own relatives. This may account for why so many of the first Believers remained faithful. Many of those who had been children at the time of the first gatherings would in turn be the leaders up to the 1830s, thus giving Shakerism, in the East, two strong generations.

Even in the earliest years, however, some people did leave the Shakers, especially the young. At the same time that so much energy was being put toward gathering communities into order, no attention was being paid to missionary work. In fact, Shaker leaders intentionally stopped proselytizing in 1785 so that all their attention could be directed toward building up the new communities. As 1800 approached, it became clear that the original organizational scheme of Father Joseph Meacham was incomplete. No provision had been made to allow for the admission of new members. This was badly needed now because, in addition to the losses, there had been no new converts for well over a decade.

The Ministry at New Lebanon started a Gathering Order, the North Family, in 1800. While it had its own Elders and Eldresses, the Church Family closely supervised the North Family until 1814, when it became a separate entity. Eventually, this family had two other branches in the nearby town of Canaan, New York. When the Gathering Family was first organized, it was thought that New Lebanon could serve as the entry point for new members coming to New Lebanon, Watervliet, Tyringham, and Hancock. This idea was soon abandoned, and the Ministry directed every community to establish a Gathering Order of its own. By 1810, all Shaker Societies had shifted people in order to make one of their families the home for young Believers. The addition of a Gathering Order completed the operational model of Shakerism that lasted until the 1870s.

In Shaker communal life,

"order" signifies several things. The word is found over and over in both sacred and secular writings. The most general use of the term applies to naming the group of people living as Shakers, as in references to the Shaker order or simply "the order." Gospel order or full Gospel order meant the organization of communal life into an orderly pattern. The ministry stood at the head of this order followed by Elders, Trustees, Family Deacons, and regular members. All Shakers lived in families that were either of the Church Order or the Gathering Order. The former were considered the Senior Order or fullest members, and they alone signed a Church Order covenant. Those in the Gathering or Junior Order who were there to try out the life signed a probationary covenant, although they were led and trained by fully covenanted members.

There is yet another use of the term "Shaker order" that appears in the Society's more than two-hundred-year history. This often vague usage generally means the pattern of Shaker life as lived in accordance with the current rules. Throughout Shaker history these rules have been codified four distinct times: in the *Millennial Laws* of 1821 and 1845, *Rules and Orders* of 1860, and *Orders for the Church of Christ's Second Appearing* of 1887. This last, with minor modifications, is still in force today. Unfortunately, historian Edward Deming Andrews published only the 1845 version in *The People Called Shakers* in 1953. Since then, these laws have been endlessly quoted although, in truth, the 1845 laws were never followed or given even token observance after the Era of Mother's Work. These laws were an attempt to reawaken interest in spirit manifestations but simply did not work. Sadly, the number of secondary sources quoting the 1845 laws as normative Shaker behavior remain very much in evidence in spite of Shaker efforts to debunk this myth for at least the past three decades.

One extremely important role of the Gathering Order was that it had charge of all missionary efforts to the World. On the local level, this meant taking charge of the "public meeting" that took place on Sunday mornings and was open to non-Shakers as well. Elders from the Gathering Order generally preached at this service. While in smaller societies all families attended Sunday meeting together, in larger societies the Church Family had a separate service in the afternoon at the Meetinghouse. Thus, the Elders of the Gathering Order were better known to the World than the Elders from the other families. This was reinforced by the missionary work of this group of Elders.

Any hint of religious revival in surrounding areas would draw Shaker missionaries out to "testify" concerning the Gospel of Christ's Second Appearing. During the first quarter of the nineteenth century, this often resulted in a stream of converts who both renewed and enriched an established community. The most spectacular example of this occurred in 1805, when Shaker missionaries were sent from New Lebanon to Ohio and Kentucky, where religious revivalism had reached a fevered pitch. The direct result of their efforts was the establishment of six new permanent communities. Three of these—Pleasant Hill and South Union, Kentucky, and Union Village, Ohio—were as large as or larger than any of the eastern communities. The three smaller societies that were added were all in Ohio: North Union, White Water, and Watervliet (not to be confused with Watervliet, New York).

Meanwhile, established communities grew ever larger. When the number of new Believers grew too large in any one place, new families were added. When the distance of new converts from an established community was too great, a new community was formed. In this manner Sodus (later Groveland), New York, was founded in 1826.

Efforts made by missionaries, positive impressions made on those attending public meeting, and contacts made by Shakers as they visited the World on business helped gather hundreds. The number of Shakers in 1800 was approximately fourteen hundred. By 1825, the total had multiplied threefold. By this time, the Shakers had begun to record their history

and attempted to codify their theology in a series of published works. The most important of these were the *Testimony of Christ's Second Appearing* (1808), Dunlavy's *Manifesto* (1818), and *A Summary View of the Millennial Church* (1823). It was a time when the first generation of Shakers, those who had known Mother Ann, were advanced in age or deceased. As a result of the influx of converts, it was also a time of newfound prosperity and stability. With increasing acreage under cultivation, newer and larger buildings replacing the original rudimentary structures, and increasing commercial contact with the World, Shakerism seemed to have achieved its ideal of a heaven on earth.

One significant influence the Shakers had on the World, from the beginning, was the production and sale of a large variety of commodities. Most of these were what one would expect from communities that were, in effect, vast cooperative farms: poultry and meat, eggs, cheese, butter, milk, grains, tanned hides, field produce, and orchard fruits. They also supplied many manufactured goods such as brooms, baskets, boxes, sieves, measures, and swifts. This was all in addition to their two largest industries: packaged garden seeds and medicinal herbs. All in all, the name "Shaker" became synonymous in the public's mind with high-quality products as much as with a unique religion and a radical, communal lifestyle.

By the early 1830s, Shakers who had been in their twenties when the gospel opened in 1780 were now in their seventies. Just as America had been transformed in the fifty years following the Revolution, so too had Shakerism. More than four thousand Believers, living in eighteen prosperous societies, stretching from Maine to Kentucky, marked its success. Shakers who had witnessed the spiritual and economic growth of the previous decades no doubt received a great deal of satisfaction knowing that the Society of Believers had come so far and accomplished so much. The early dreams of establishing a place where a Christlife could be fully experienced seemed a more lasting reality. Unfortunately, success and stability were also leading to a greater sense of self-satisfaction and complacency. Prosperity was quietly undermining religious fervor and, unknowingly, the seeds of a future spiritual crisis were being sowed.

Meanwhile, promising teenagers such as Giles Avery and Orren Haskins at New Lebanon; Harriet and Wealthy Storer at Tyringham; Thomas Damon and George Wilcox at Enfield, Connecticut; and Joanna Randall and Harriet Prouty at Shirley; and scores of others from every community stood as worthy models for young people. They showed dedication to the faith and seemed ready to take their rightful places as burden bearers as Shakerism moved toward midcentury. Still, as the first generations of Shakers took part in worship or knelt in the dining room, another ominous trend should have been apparent: there were more and more children and teenagers in their communities.

From the earliest years, Shaker communities had a balance of older and younger members. The children present in any community were generally accompanied by at least one believing parent. Often, large, extended families joined; these included aunts, uncles, and even grandparents. This model for accession started to diminish in the 1820s, and Shaker leadership took a gamble that would prove to have dire consequences. To make up for the lack of adult converts, the Society began to take in more children without their parents. Almost at once, the numbers of children coming into the Shaker communities threw off the balance that had existed, and caretakers, housing, and schooling had to be provided on a much larger scale. So great was this influx that attempts were made at some communities to establish a separate Children's Order.

The idea behind this new direction was as logical as it was humane. Most of the leaders, at that time, had grown up in the community from childhood themselves. Therefore, it was natural for them to think that other children growing up in community would choose to remain as well. These children would be "ready-made" members who would require no special missionary efforts to gather in and no extra training to integrate into the existing societal framework as adults. In addition, these children could be given tasks that contributed to the Society's welfare.

From the 1820s until the 1860s, thousands of children passed through the Shaker communities. The Shakers expected youngsters to attend worship services at an early age, but they were not eligible to sign a covenant until turning eighteen. In truth, most Shakers signed this document at age twenty-one, and some lifelong members never signed at all. In the mid-1850s, those under the age of twenty-one accounted for 50 percent of the membership at Tyringham. Although this is an extreme example, it was not uncommon for 30 to 40 percent of a community to be composed of preadults. This increase in the number of members under the age of twenty-one masked for decades the lack of adult converts. Shaker families still seemed full, and New Lebanon, for example, had almost six hundred members in 1860. Since a high percentage of these were children, and at best only 10 percent of them stayed into adulthood, there was a constant and disruptive flow of people into and out of the families.

This had once been the case only for the Gathering Order, where it was only natural that there would be an ebb and flow as people came to inquire about, and try, the Shaker life. By the early 1830s, however, large numbers of young adults began leaving when they came of age. Since most Shaker families had children, this coming and going interfered with a sense of order. Some of the young ran away or were sent away almost as soon as they entered. Others lived as Shakers for twenty or thirty years before leaving. Much energy was spent in providing training in trades or occupations that the community needed, only to have whole groups of promising young people leave.

With the policy of accepting children so firmly in place, missionary efforts to the World diminished. Efforts had to be expended at home in a cycle that demanded the maintenance of the structures of Shakerdom: home, farm, and business. By the later 1830s, less time seemed to be available for the religious aspects of the Christlife. Shakerism seemed to be in a free fall, with forces propelling it away from the direction that would have been recognized by the first parents. This was the near crisis state of affairs when a small number of girls and women at Watervliet, New York, began to have visions and receive "gifts" from the spirit world. The year was 1837, and the Era of Manifestations, or Era of Mother's Work, had come upon Shakerism.

The visionary aspects of early Shakerism had never been completely forgotten, and there is ample evidence to show that some members continued to communicate with those who had died. Dreams, in particular, had led some Shakers to predict that a religious renewal would soon take place. Still, it was not until the manifestations at Watervliet began that the work started in earnest. In fact, the period between 1837 and 1850 actually saw two separate revivals, back-to-back. In every community new songs and dances were introduced that were said to have been divinely inspired; that is, they came directly from Mother Ann, Father James, or other beloved deceased members. The call was for ever greater humility, simplicity, purity, and commitment, all leading to a blessed life of everlasting glory in the next world.

Shaker life for the next decade and a half after 1837 was overcome by a religious zeal that it has not known since. Hundreds of Believers worshipped outdoors atop the highest point in each community (holy hills or feast grounds), communities received mystical names, and the presence of visitors from the heavens was commonly accepted. By contrast, visitation from the World's people was limited and even discouraged, further eroding opportunities for new conversions. By the mid-1850s, the time of Mother's Work was largely over, but for some the manifestations would never quite end. Visions, gift songs, and special dreams continued to inspire certain Believers until recent times. For the movement as a whole though, at midcentury larger issues loomed that would eventually overwhelm it.

After the visions faded, thoughtful leaders were faced with a crisis in membership. The wholesale addition of children had not led to many conversions, and young people were leaving at an alarming rate. Many adults also joined at this time, but most were not suited to the life, and they often left after just a short stay. Significantly, the numbers of women in the communities began to far exceed the numbers of men. The economic base of all Shaker communities had been male-dominated, labor-intensive, soil-based industries. The growing imbalance between the sexes gained greater relevance as the years passed.

Finally, the Civil War, which devastated the nation and caused economic hardships at Sabbathday Lake, New Lebanon, Shirley, and both Enfield villages, was totally ruinous for the two Kentucky commu-

nities. In the eastern societies the problems were cumulative results of the loss of southern markets for Shaker goods, debts created by incompetent or dishonest Trustees, or bad investments. At South Union and Pleasant Hill in Kentucky, the communities were caught in the literal, direct crossfire of the war. Resources and cash to cover debts, as well as the cost of rebuilding, came from the more prudent and prosperous societies.

By the 1870s, the fifty-year-old practice of taking in so many children was showing its unfortunate consequences on a large scale. The old and the very young were now the largest segments of the communities. Only a handful of Shakers aged twenty-five to fifty remained to do the bulk of the work and to fill leadership positions. The numbers of children began to diminish because there were fewer adults to care for them, and more and more communities decided against the practice of adopting children without their parents. With fewer children being taken in and still greater numbers of them leaving, compounded by the loss of aged members, the populations of villages at this time declined rapidly. Had this situation appeared in the 1840s, it is possible that other decisions could have been made and other strategies developed for attracting young people to the Shaker life. The year 1875 exemplifies this condition perfectly. That winter, many significant Church Family buildings at Mount Lebanon burned to the ground, and less than two months later the first of the eighteen communities—Tyringham—closed. In that pivotal year, the headquarters of the faith was in ashes, and the trend of closing down communities was initiated.

From a high of between 4,000 and 5,000 members in the 1840s, the Shakers numbered only 2,415 in 1875. There were only 887 males in all eighteen communities. If full complements of Elderships and Trusteeships were maintained in the fifty-eight existing families (and this was far from the case), then 232 or 26 percent of the men would have been involved in formal leadership. These numbers do not include the ministry positions or various Family Deacons. The remaining men, perhaps totaling around 550, included the very young and the very old. These were the ones who, from Maine to Kentucky, had to care for the farms, gardens, orchards, craft shops, and more. It must be noted, however, that communities did not always rigidly adhere to their own ideal model of organization. Shakerism has survived for more than two centuries in part because of its ability to be flexible and practical.

For a while, the Shakers were determined to uphold the economic structure of Shakerism by hiring more and more outside labor. At the same time, very few "old-time" members were comfortable with the increasing numbers of hired people living in their midst. Periodically a family would stop hiring outsiders and its members would try to do all the work themselves. In even the strongest families, ultimately, the choice came down to either hiring out or closing down. Clearly, Shaker order was threatened.

Another response to the decline in membership was the redoubling of missionary efforts. Beginning in the late 1850s, Shaker proselytizers again went out to the World. Their efforts, however, were unlike those of earlier missionaries. These Believers often spoke at other Protestant churches, as their guests, or in large city concert halls. Their appearances may have been more like entertainment than anything else. Shakers would face the audience and conduct a service or do a few dances and songs. The missionaries spoke of religion, of course, but also of communal living. This latter was calculated to appeal to educated citizens, who were often more interested in reform movements than in religious experiences. Yet very few converts were gained this way.

One more notable effort at expansion was the publication of a Shaker newspaper, beginning in 1871. *The Shaker* began its thirty-year run at Watervliet, New York, and changed its name several times in the ensuing years. At the end it was called *The Manifesto*. Publication of the paper moved to New Lebanon in 1873, where it was edited by the North Family Elders Antoinette Doolittle and Frederick Evans. This family was notably progressive and, after some serious religious controversies and clashes with more conservative members, most notably Elder Harvey Eads of South Union, the paper was taken over by the Canterbury Society in 1882. As a result of this move, Canterbury became the best-known Shaker Society and for the next twenty-five years reaped the benefits of this position. Hundreds of people came to try the Shaker life there. Although relatively few stayed, this influx ensured that Canterbury would not decline as rapidly as other villages. Indeed, it endured for almost all of the twentieth century, closing finally in 1992.

As the influence of Canterbury grew, so too did that community's efforts to reform certain aspects of Shaker life, including music. Choral music from members trained in harmony, as well as the introduction of organ music, transformed Shaker worship in the 1870s. Once organ music was introduced, the traditional dances and marches began to fade out. They did not, however, die out completely, as popular myth would have it. Again, just as visionary aspects of Shakerism never ceased to find a home in some Shaker hearts, so, too, did the dances and marches continue in some communities. They may not have been performed during the public meetings, but they did continue. There is strong evidence, for example, that the Believers at Watervliet, Ohio, danced in worship right up to the dissolution of their village in 1900. Oral tradition kept alive by the present Shakers indicates that dancing was the norm at Alfred, Maine, until its doors were closed in 1931. This would make perfect sense, since that community in particular cherished the early Shaker songs and often sang them.

Another innovation of the 1870s was the decision to allow every Shaker family to act as a Gathering Order and bring in converts as it could. Each community still had a separate Gathering Order, and this Novitiate Family, as it was also called, was the official place where those inquiring about Shaker life were directed. Yet all Shaker families began to take in people who, following meetings with individual members of those families, seemed to be attracted to the life. The older pathway into the community via the Gathering Order did not seem to be working, but this change helped to blur the distinctions between individual Shaker families.

In 1873, Elder Henry Blinn of Canterbury visited nearly all the existing Shaker communities outside New England. A year and a half later, newspaper correspondent Charles Nordhoff visited all the major communities and most of the smaller ones. If Blinn and Nordhoff had made a similar visit in 1900, they would have found a much-changed Shakerism. Four societies had closed by the later date: Tyringham, North Union, Groveland, and Watervliet (Ohio), and one new one was opened, Narcoossee, Florida, in 1896. In the fifteen extant communities in 1900, there were a total of 794 Shakers, a decrease of 67 percent in just twenty-five years. Of this number, only 202 or about 25 percent were men, and of these nearly one-fourth were over the age of seventy.

In contrast to male membership, ten societies—two-thirds of the total—had at least a dozen women aged twenty-one to seventy in 1900. Canterbury, with 50, had the largest number of women in this category, slightly ahead of Mount Lebanon with 48. In every society, women dominated the numbers, accounting for 75 percent of all Shakers.

The four communities of Ohio and two of Kentucky comprised what are called the western Shakers. In 1875, this group accounted for 39 percent of all Shakers. By 1900, only four societies remained there and their combined membership had dropped to only 20 percent of the Shaker total. Of the 161 members then living in Ohio and Kentucky, nearly 28 percent were older than seventy years and only 47 percent were between the ages of twenty-one and seventy.

Two of the western societies, Union Village and Pleasant Hill, were heavily in debt, in spite of the sale of North Union (soon to be Shaker Heights) for $316,000 in 1889. Union Village alone had accumulated an astounding debt of $140,000 (or the equivalent of nearly $3 million today). The fact that this debt was eventually retired, and that the community lasted for another ten years, is a great tribute to Trustees More Mason and James Fennessy. It also speaks well of the productive capacity of the land. For many decades, large tracts were leased out here in lieu of hiring laborers to work them for the Shakers.

As numbers fell off each year in the Shaker West, the main goals became keeping the land as productive as possible and paying off all debts. Except for South Union, which did not close until 1922, the western societies barely survived into the twentieth century. Union Village, Ohio, once the largest community in the West, closed in 1910. By that time, all its Trustees and Elders had been sent there from Mount Lebanon. After its sale, the remaining members were cared for, until 1920, by a cadre of young Sisters sent west from Canterbury.

From the time of Joseph Meacham and Lucy Wright, a formal, structured religious leadership had been an essential feature of Shakerism. During the 1890s, however, this leadership became fragmented, mirroring what was happening in the communities at large. When Central Ministry Elders Giles Avery and Daniel Boler died, only one man, Joseph Holden, was appointed as leader of the Elders lot. Since the Hancock Bishopric had previously been dissolved owing to a lack of suitable leaders, Holden moved to the Hancock community in 1893. The Central Ministry Sisters stayed at Mount Lebanon, but never again was authority as concentrated there as it had been from the beginning.

Hancock had only a few men in 1900, but it was financially stable and had a very strong Trustee in Ira Lawson. He assisted Elder Joseph Holden in temporal matters and himself became a member of the Hancock Ministry in 1899. Around the time of his unexpected death in 1905, a young Sister at Hancock, Frances Hall, became an assistant to Holden. Although she did not become a member of the Central Ministry until 1939, her presence (along with Holden's residence) ensured that Hancock, even with its small population, would outlast all but two other communities.

The Shakers had always been large landowners and loved to buy property. It was a form of wealth that they understood, and it did not conflict with any part of their belief system. In addition to expansive communities, they owned large woodlots, often in places far removed from their homes. Yet, owing to the presence of both slavery and the plantation system, Believers—with the sole exception of South Union—generally avoided investing in land in the South. (While Kentucky was a border state with divided loyalties, sympathizers in the Southern cause surrounded South Union.) Yet, as the nineteenth century came to a close and the question of slavery was settled, the promise of relatively cheap land, high agricultural yields, and a mild climate made the South now seem quite attractive, and a plan was hatched by the Trustees of Mount Lebanon and Watervliet, New York. They reasoned that if large farms could be purchased in Florida, perhaps their communities could be relocated there. Another advantage was that property taxes would be lower. (While legally exempted from paying these, the Shakers always voluntarily did so anyway.) With this daring initiative, the two communities hoped that their fortunes just might be reversed.

Accordingly, in 1896, the Church Families of Mount Lebanon and Watervliet purchased land slightly to the south and east of present-day Orlando, Florida, and a pioneer band of Shakers was sent south to the village of Narcoossee. Once it was actually established, however, very few members seemed interested in leaving their homes in New York State and moving there. The Florida settlement lasted until 1924 and greatly strained the finances of both sponsoring communities. In order to keep the Church Family at Mount Lebanon afloat after the debacle in Florida, the Sisters had to redouble their efforts in the fancy goods and cloak industries. The sale of traditional soil-based products (garden seeds, medicinal herbs and preparations, fresh or prepared fruits and vegetables, condiments, and sauces) had nearly ceased at all the remaining communities by that time. Handmade products now provided the main source of communal revenue.

Elder Joseph Slingerland of Union Village, in 1898 and without full authority, undertook a similar venture in White Oak, Georgia. It may have been his hope that one strong new community would consolidate the remaining weak ones in Ohio and Kentucky. In any event it failed in only a few years and further depressed fortunes in the Shaker West.

Still another plan for self-revival was the modernization of buildings, especially the Church Family offices where visitors from the World came in contact with Shakers. Both Hancock and Union Village made extensive and expensive renovations to their Trustees offices to give them a contemporary appearance. At Mount Lebanon, one of the unused buildings was transformed into Ann Lee Cottage. This was set up to accommodate summer visitors, members of a more educated class who might be interested in joining the Shakers after living among them for a few months. Ironically, this later became the home of the remaining Church Family Shakers after their property was sold to the Lebanon School for Boys (now the Darrow School). Needless to say, the hope for this type of convert proved futile too.

Whatever special talents the members had were used to keep the communities going. At the North Family of Mount Lebanon, a gifted teacher named

Sister Ada Grace Brown started a private school for girls in 1905. At Sabbathday Lake, Brother Delmer Wilson supervised the great sawmill and turned out thousands of sewing boxes that the Sisters then outfitted for sale. On a widespread basis, Shaker cooks and young girls in their charge opened their families up to visitors by serving meals. The Church Family at Pleasant Hill had a restaurant and hotel in their Trustees' office. The North and Church Families at Enfield, Connecticut, served dinners, as did the North Family at Mount Lebanon and the Church Family at Alfred. Each year, teams of Sisters from Canterbury, Sabbathday Lake, and Alfred traveled to resorts along the Maine coast and into the mountains of New Hampshire to sell fancy goods. These mainly consisted of a variety of sewing notions and homemade sweets. Every surviving community also had a store in a portion of its office, and here the Shakers sold both fancy goods and a variety of food items to the carriage trade.

Although children no longer formed the overwhelming percentage of the community populations as in the past, around 1900, nearly all societies still had relatively large numbers of them. What each community did to cultivate its young ultimately determined its own longevity. For example, when Mount Lebanon's large, youthful, and vibrant Upper Canaan Family moved to Enfield, Connecticut, in 1897, its members were faced with open hostility from members of Enfield's North Family. Instead of a gracious welcome, they encountered intrafamily feuding that eventually destroyed this community's last and best chance for survival.

In contrast, in some communities, those in charge of the young people made a special effort to make Shaker life more attractive to them. Music lessons, both vocal and instrumental, literary clubs, and dramatic productions became a mainstay of Shaker childhood, especially for girls. Every holiday was celebrated with parades, pageants, and parties. Societies for young Sisters were started at Hancock (the Royal True Blues), Canterbury, Alfred (the Beacon Light Society), and at Mount Lebanon's North Family (the Self Improvement Society). At Canterbury, during the terms of Eldresses Dorothy Durgin and Dorothea Cochran, scores of gifted young Sisters were so attracted to the life that they stayed for the remainder of their lives. At Sabbathday Lake, under the guidance of Sister Aurelia Mace, a group of young women called the Ten Gems of Priceless Worth was cultivated to give their lives to the work of Shakerism. Nine of them remained in the faith. It is clear that the communities that devoted the most attention toward their young were the communities that lasted the longest.

At Harvard, Massachusetts, at about the same time, the decision was made not to have children any longer and to disperse those presently in residence. Already it was the norm here for members to visit outside the community, and Myra McLean, for example—who was eventually the last of the Harvard Ministry—spent more than a year away from the community consulting with a clairvoyant. In the twentieth century, and to some extent even earlier, unorthodox spiritualism was a strong attraction for many Believers. The Harvard community closed its doors in 1918.

One by one, the weaker communities—those that failed to develop their younger members—began to close. By 1925, there were 213 Shakers, a decline of 73 percent in only twenty-five years. Of the 161 Believers living in Ohio and Kentucky in 1900, a mere two were still alive in 1925, and these were now living at Canterbury. A total of only six communities remained, all in New York or New England. Except for Mount Lebanon, which had four families, all the others had but one apiece.

A closer look at the gender and ages of the Shakers in 1925 is even more revealing than total population figures. Of the 213 members, 26 or 12 percent were men, and ten of these were over seventy years of age. The typical family, and there were nine in 1925, had one or two men in the prime of life, although Hancock had no men at all. In contrast, each community had at least a dozen Sisters between twenty-one and seventy years of age. In actuality these Sisters were not evenly distributed, for while Canterbury had 39 in this age range, Alfred had only 18. These groups of Sisters made up the majority of these two communities, and this helps explain the longevity of Shaker life in Maine and New Hampshire.

In the first three decades of the twentieth century, much of the Central Ministry's time, by necessity, was devoted to closing communities. This, in turn, necessitated the sale of property and effects and the shifting of members to other societies. After Eldress Catherine Allen joined the Central Ministry in 1908, great efforts were made to collect and preserve the myriad of written records as she, in particular, believed that Shakerism would not likely continue for much longer than a few more decades at best. The idea that its demise was both inevitable and imminent took hold of the Central Ministry by 1920. The rapid depletion of the communities at Watervliet (down by 75 percent since 1900) and Mount Lebanon (65 percent since 1900) meant that if Shakerism was to survive it would not be at the places where it began and where the Central Ministry still called home. The Church Family properties at both communities were put up for sale during the 1920s. This must have been a traumatic event for the surviving Shakers. To add to the cascade of woes, the Ministry's preoccupation with temporal duties at the remaining communities left a religious vacuum that was not filled in the traditional way.

For example, after Eldress Caroline Helfrich died at Hancock in 1929, her replacement, Fannie Estabrook, decided to no longer hold religious services. She told the family to find other churches outside the community to attend. Not long after, a Congregational minister officiated at Shaker funerals there. At the same time, at Canterbury, radio programs started to replace regular Shaker services, and the last child to be brought up there recalls that very little was ever taught her about Shaker religion. At Sabbathday Lake, following the death of Eldress Elizabeth Noyes (1926) and Elder William Dumont (1930), the remaining Believers chose to follow Canterbury's approach.

Only at Alfred did a society follow the more traditional life. Yet Alfred was not financially strong and had been living on borrowed time for decades. In 1931, the Central Ministry at Mount Lebanon forced the two Maine societies to merge at Sabbathday Lake. The Sisters from Alfred, most of whom were quite fervent and unusually young, took their places at their new home, although they did not dominate the spiritual climate, which took its lead from Brother (later Elder) Delmer Wilson and Eldress Prudence Stickney. In almost every way it truly seemed as though Shakerism had entered its twilight. Outsiders managed the home farms, and buildings that could not be maintained were torn down or left to decay. Watervliet and Mount Lebanon resembled large rest homes for the elderly, and the few able-bodied members, almost entirely women, relied on the production of labor-intensive crafts to help support their communities.

By 1950, only forty-six Shakers remained in three communities—Hancock, Canterbury, and Sabbathday Lake. This represented a 78 percent decrease in twenty-five years. In the seventy-five years since 1875, their numbers had declined by 98 percent! There were only three men now—two at Hancock and one at Sabbathday Lake. The last male died at Canterbury in 1939. Now there were but four children, all at Sabbathday Lake. The year 1950 also saw the passing of Eldress Prudence Stickney there. She had long been enfeebled, but her death made the already pressing need for a capable leader even greater. Since the Sisters who had come from Alfred stood in too strong a contrast to the Ministry Sisters—Eldress Emma King of Canterbury and Eldress Frances Hall of Hancock—Gertrude Soule was chosen by the Eldresses to lead Sabbathday Lake. She had grown up there but then left for the World in 1925, returning permanently only in 1943. The Ministry expected that Sabbathday Lake during her tenure would follow the path that Hancock and Canterbury had chosen—a peaceful but inevitable demise.

Sabbathday Lake was, in fact, well on its way to this demise when a young man named Theodore Johnson visited the community in the late 1950s. Johnson, who held an advanced degree from Harvard and had been a Fulbright Scholar, had read a good deal about Shaker theology and wanted to explore becoming a Shaker. Since he was from Massachusetts, he went to Hancock first but was eventually directed to Sabbathday Lake, the one remaining community that still offered even a semblance of traditional Shaker life.

Shakerism had long suffered a crisis in leadership. So burdened did Eldress Emma B. King feel about her ministerial duties, in fact, that she dissolved the Central Ministry shortly after the death of Eldress Frances Hall in 1957. Soon after, she decided to reconstitute a ministry that would come to terms with, and deal with, the surprisingly large sum of money dis-

covered in a previously unknown bank account held by the late Eldress. Lawyers, and a somewhat puzzled Eldress Emma, along with Ida Crook of Canterbury and Gertrude Soule of Sabbathday Lake—members of the newly constituted ministry—created a trust fund to provide for the remaining members and to set down guidelines for future Shakers who might have access to the funds. Never trained nor particularly suited for matters of this depth, the new ministry actually relied on lawyers to do this work. At their behest the lawyers also took on the daunting task of trying to decide whether or not several men who inquired at Canterbury and elsewhere should be allowed to become Shakers. (One of these was Theodore Johnson.)

Perhaps if there had been more members at Canterbury, or even a younger group there, the lawyers and the ministry might have been more open to this prospect. Those who favored an open-door policy at Canterbury were never the dominant voices there, and at Sabbathday Lake the tradition of following their leaders, no matter what the consequences, had been deeply ingrained in the Sisters. Finally—and this is an extremely important aspect of the situation—many outsiders had a good deal to lose if young men were allowed to join. If Shakerism were to truly end, those who had been lying in wait for decades to do just that could write about its demise. In addition, antiques collectors and dealers would then have access to the valuable material that always found its way outside whenever a Shaker community closed.

Theodore Johnson settled in at Sabbathday Lake, welcomed by the younger members and the Alfred Sisters, especially the unofficial spiritual leader of the community, Trustee R. Mildred Barker. Ever since Trustee Arthur Bruce had been made an Elder at Canterbury in 1899, there had been a blurring of distinctions between the roles, if any, that some leaders had. As twentieth-century Elders had shown, appointment to the eldership did not necessarily denote any great interest in Shaker religion. The directive encouraging members to follow whatever church they wanted allowed Bertha Lindsay at Canterbury to watch television evangelists, in lieu of the religious radio programs that had so enthralled many Shakers earlier. However, some of the Sisters at Sabbathday Lake, along with the Alfred Sisters, chose to follow traditional Shakerism—with Sisters Mildred Barker, Della Haskell, and others as their guides.

In 1961, a new periodical, *The Shaker Quarterly*, opening with the words "Our Still Small Voice . . . ," was published by the Sabbathday Lake community. Acting in tandem, Brother Ted and Sister Mildred revived the public meeting and, in 1966, opened the Meetinghouse for the first time since the 1880s. Religious leaders of other faiths began to have more contact with the community. Even some of its traditional industries—culinary herbs and dyed wools among them—were revived.

Many museums, "professional" historians, and those who would profit from the closing of Sabbathday Lake chose to side with the views expressed by the Ministry Sisters at Canterbury. This proved to be increasingly problematic as the 1970s progressed and the Sisters at Canterbury died, while at the same time more people joined with the Shakers at Sabbathday Lake. Though poor and struggling to stay afloat, the Maine Shakers were united in their intention to survive. This was especially true after 1971, when Eldress Gertrude Soule moved from Sabbathday Lake to Canterbury—of her own volition. For the first time in more than a century, Shaker fortunes—at least at the Maine community—seemed to be on the rise. Was it possible that Shakerism could be saved just as it seemed to approach extinction?

The renewal itself took many forms. Most importantly, over the past thirty years, a number of people expressed interest in joining the Shakers, and some came and tried the life. Most of these individuals were single adult men and women, although there were also two married couples. In addition to lowering the average age in the community, this new life gave hope that Shakerism would survive. With the unexpected death of Brother Ted in 1986, followed by the death of such stalwarts as Sister Mildred Barker in 1990 and Sister Marie Burgess in 2002, the matter of new members became even more critical.

Another essential aspect of communal renewal over the past thirty years has been a develop-

ing network of outside friends. In 1974, a group of sympathetic non-Shakers organized themselves into the Friends of the Shakers. The Friends offer unconditional emotional support as well as financial assistance for special projects. During the past thirty years, tens of thousands of dollars have been used for the preservation of community buildings and for the conservation of the Shakers' highly prized manuscript collection. The Friends gather there for a weekend each May and October to assist the Shakers with seasonal chores. At Friends' Weekend, every August, enthusiastic men and women fill the Meetinghouse with song and give testimonies alongside their Shaker friends.

The present-day Shakers include Brother Arnold Hadd, who joined the community in 1978 and is now the Elder and Trustee. A deeply read Shaker theologian, he is ever willing to help others gain the true meaning of the spiritual aspects of Shakerism. Sister Frances A. Carr, who joined in 1937, is the Eldress and provides a vital continuity with past communal life and history. Both her hospitality and her cooking are legendary. Brother Wayne Smith joined when he was only sixteen years of age. Although the Shakers had not admitted children for many years, his entrance in 1979 marked a brief return to having a teenager about. He is now the community's farmer and an expert on matters of the land. Sister June Carpenter, a college-trained librarian, joined the Society in the 1989. Besides her duties in the library, this deeply religious woman can be found helping out in many ways around the village.

As this small band of Shakers goes about their daily duties and chores in the community, they are fortified by their religious convictions and secure in their belief that the life they live would be recognized by—and is in union with—that of their forebears in the faith. After all, "Mother taught a way of life."

No one can know with certainty how Shakerism will be lived in the years ahead. Those with faith, however, have a firm confidence in the future. Perhaps, in the providence of an all-loving Father-Mother God, the best of Shakerism is yet to come.

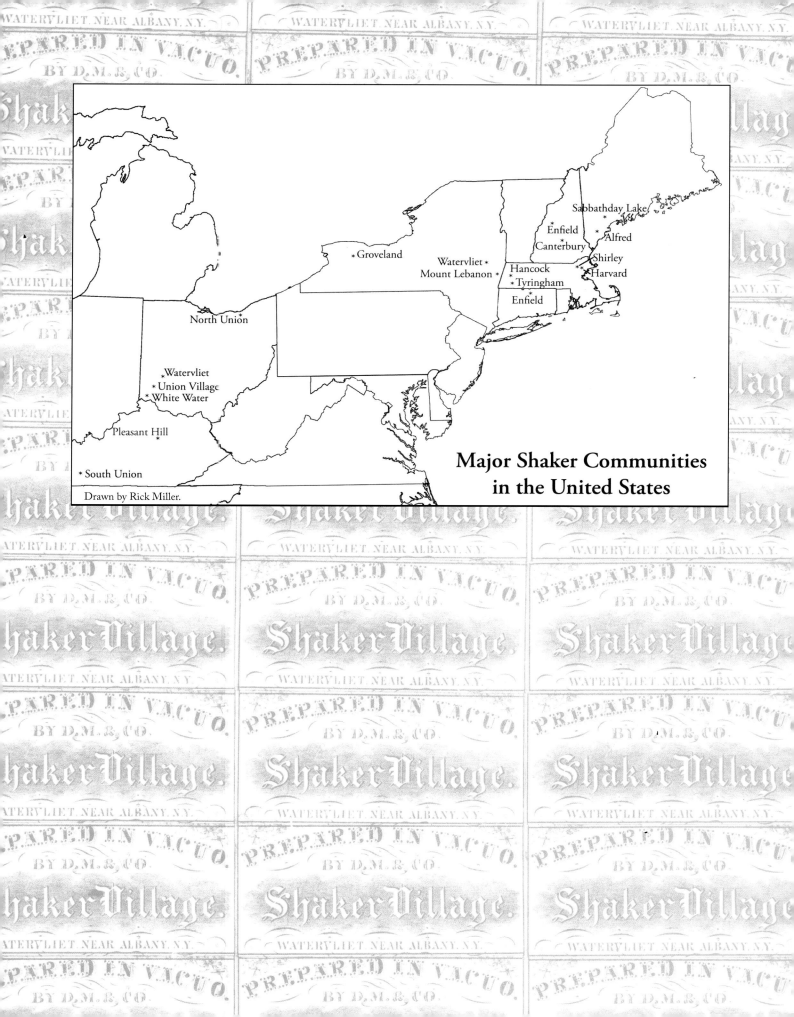

Major Shaker Communities in the United States

Drawn by Rick Miller.

Sabbathday Lake

Enfield
Canterbury
Alfred
Shirley
Harvard

Groveland

Watervliet
Mount Lebanon
Hancock
Tyringham
Enfield

North Union

Watervliet
Union Village
White Water

Pleasant Hill

South Union

Who Are the Shakers?

The Sabbathday Lake Shakers

THE UNITED SOCIETY OF BELIEVERS, commonly called Shakers, has been best described as a Protestant monastic community. We are governed by the life and teachings of Jesus Christ, our model and exemplar. We seek to imitate Him in all things.

We view God as pure spirit. Within that Spirit we believe there are attributes of both maleness and femaleness, and we refer to God as our Father-Mother (see Genesis 1:27).

We believe that Jesus was neither the Christ nor the anointed of God from his birth, but rather became the Christ on the occasion of his baptism by John. For us the sign of the dove descending symbolizes the anointing spirit of God whose voice is heard to say, "Thou art my beloved son in whom I am well pleased." This view in no way affects our attitudes toward the virgin birth or any of the other miraculous occurrences surrounding Jesus' beginnings. For us, these are all signs of God's prior choice of Jesus as the recipient of the anointing spirit. In fact for Believers, Jesus' life, ministry, teachings, and death is our holy rule.

We do not worship Mother Ann Lee. Mother was not Christ, nor did she claim to be. To Mother was given the inner realization that Christ's Second Coming was a quiet, almost unheralded one within individuals open to the anointing of His spirit. She remarked, "I converse with Christ, I feel Him present with me as sensibly as I feel my hands together. My soul is married to him in the spirit—he is my husband. It is not I that speaks, it is Christ who dwells in me." And she further states, ". . . the second appearing of Christ is in His Church."

Central to the teaching of the New Testament is love: the love of God for His creation and the love of mankind for God. This love is the cornerstone of Shakerism. It is a living force that must be rediscovered and acted upon each day. Perfect joy comes only with laying aside one's self in love. Day after day, in the sharing of the common life, the Shaker seeks to lose himself by giving joyfully and freely, expecting nothing in return. Such perfect love is manifested in Universal Brotherhood, equality of all people, and pacifism.

We are not *the* Church, but a part of *the* Church. To be a Shaker is a special calling (see Matthew 19:12), meant only for those who ". . . wish to go the whole way. Go sell your possessions and give to the poor and then you will have riches in heaven and come follow me" (Matthew 19:21). We are called to reveal Christ to the World, a place in which the will and purpose of God are largely forgotten. God calls in many ways, but all men and women, whatever their occupation, whatever their profession, are called to that holiness without which no man shall see the Lord.

In this sacred oneness we seek to emulate Christ and his first Apostles in practicing the same Community of Goods where no one owns anything, but we all own everything. Those who give up material things for the sake of the Gospel are taught by that same Gospel that they may learn to live in joyous confidence that they will lack for nothing. The spirit of Christian poverty is more than the absence of wealth. Anyone who regards all that he has as a trust from God and uses it for His glory is living in the true spirit of Christian poverty.

Mother Ann gave us the motto, "Hands to work and hearts to God." To this end we are all employed in manual labor, each according to his/her ability. All contribute, young and old, with willing hands and hearts. This is not done for personal or monetary gain, but to support our community and to come to the aid of those others in need. In so doing we are able to fulfill the words of Christ. ". . . anything you did for one of my brothers here, however humble, you did for me" (Matthew 25:40).

We are called in this life of holiness and prayer to "give our hearts to God." As such all work has the potential of being worship in that it is not being done for ourselves, but for others and for the upbuilding of God's Kingdom here on earth.

Shakerism continues to have a message as valid today as when it was first expressed. It teaches above all else that God is Love and that our most solemn duty is to show forth that God—who is Love in the World. Shakerism teaches God's immanence through the common life shared in Christ's mystical body. It values human fulfillment highly and believes that we fulfill ourselves best by being nothing more nor less than ourselves. It believes that Christian love is a love beyond disillusionment, for we cannot be disillusioned with people being themselves. Surely God would not have it otherwise, for it is in being ourselves—our real selves—that we are most like Christ in His sacred oneness.

PART I

PRODUCTS
OF THE
LANDS

Garden Seeds

The Garden Seed Industry

THE RAISING AND SELLING of garden seeds was the first of myriad Shaker industries. While the precise time and place of this development cannot be ascertained with any degree of certainty, by 1790 the Shaker Society at New Lebanon, New York, is believed to have initiated a business of selling seeds, in bulk, to neighboring farmers. The Shakers were not the first in this country to engage in the sale of seeds, and so this local activity of theirs seems at first to have attracted little notice, inside or outside their community. It was likely a matter of a cash exchange, or barter, for production that exceeded their own needs.

Around the turn of the nineteenth century, however, the New Lebanon Shakers did something that forever changed the way seeds were sold. Although the details are again rather sketchy, it is certain that the community began to package seeds in individual, small paper envelopes for retail sale. Several other Shaker communities, including those at Alfred, Maine, Watervliet, New York, and Enfield, Connecticut, have also claimed that they were the first to put up seeds for retail sale, but it is impossible to settle this matter more than two hundred years removed.

One more thing is certain: the Believers at New Lebanon developed both the largest and the longest-lived seed industry of any Shaker community, one that lasted for nearly a century. In 1790 the population of the newly independent United States stood at just under four million people. By 1890, only two years after the seed business ended, the national population had swelled to almost fifty-two million. Some of the sweeping changes in the nation during this span are reflected in the evolution of this one industry.

This enterprise, more than any other, was the main economic engine at New Lebanon until the 1850s, at which time medicinal herbs surpassed seeds as the chief source of revenue. It should also be noted that this community was the home of the Central Ministry—the ultimate authority for the entire movement—and that the seed industry here would have logically served as a model for all the other communities. At one time or another, every one of the eighteen long-lived Shaker villages produced garden seeds for sale. And yet far more material has survived from New Lebanon that from all the other communities *combined*.

The garden seed business was a true industry in that it required the use of many hands, working at many levels, in a precisely choreographed cooperative effort in order to succeed. And succeed it did. It was also a year-round operation that took place in four distinct arenas:

(a) In the fields: cultivating, fertilizing, planting, weeding, and harvesting.

(b) In the barns: separating, cleaning, drying, and sorting. Some biennial plants, such as carrots, cabbages, and onions, were "wintered over" here as well.

(c) In the shops: printing seed envelopes, labels, invoices, receipts, advertising material, and other ephemera needed to carry on the business; cleaning old or making new wooden seed boxes; folding, filling, and pasting seed envelopes.

(d) Outside the community: delivering or shipping (and then retrieving) seed boxes; collecting money; negotiating business arrangements.

In addition to all this the New Lebanon community, unlike any of the other Shaker villages, developed, and carried on right up to the end, a very large mail order business. For this and for their retail sales, beginning after 1865, the (now renamed) Mount Lebanon Shakers had seed catalogs printed at commercial printing houses outside their own village. Until that time they printed most of the various items needed to support the industry themselves. Thus the business of garden seeds involved a substantial commitment of all their resources—land, time, manpower, cash reserves, and a large measure of ingenuity. They had no other model to look to, so they innovated as they went.

The earliest records of sales show us that in 1805 New Lebanon processed and sold approximately seven tons of seeds and received $1,240.00 in revenue.[1] All this was the result of offering just twenty-two varieties of vegetable seeds. By way of contrast, thirty years later, New Lebanon listed seventy varieties and printed some 150,000 seed envelopes to package them. Since these "papers" (as the Shakers referred to them) sold for six cents apiece at that time, gross sales would have totaled $9,000.00. The merchants' commission was 25 to 33⅓ percent of sales, so the Shakers would have netted approximately $6,000.00 to $7,000.00 (assuming all their seeds were sold).[2]

Through the 1840s and 1850s business thrived, with income nearly every year exceeding the previous year's. With the onset of the Civil War in 1861, however, the bottom fell out. Although the Shakers were pacifists and found ways to avoid conscription or, failing that, active service, they suffered economic losses as the result of the closure of their southern markets and the general strain of war on the northern economy. In 1860, the New Lebanon Shakers put up more than a quarter of a million seed envelopes. The following year this total dropped to under eight thousand. Some communities, such as Enfield, Connecticut, never recovered from their wartime losses and shut down their seed business a few years later.

By 1867, Mount Lebanon's business had rebounded to about three-quarters of the prewar output, but now two new factors conspired against this labor-intensive industry: competition from seed companies in the World and the steady aging, then loss, of adult male members. The Mount Lebanon Shakers responded to the first challenge by borrowing the marketing strategies of their competitors: more colorful advertising, buyers' incentives such as premiums, and an emphasis on the Shakers' historic reputation for quality. To make up for the loss of their communal labor force they resorted to hiring more non-Shaker day laborers. Nonetheless, in 1883 Elder Giles Avery recorded, "The seed business has failed."[3]

Up to that time most of the family units at New Lebanon had marketed seeds under their own family designation: N. F. for North Family, E. F. for East Family, S. F. for Second Family. In 1883, the business was reorganized into a single entity called the "Shaker Seed Company." Thereafter, presumably to maximize the effectiveness of a reduced labor force, most sales were wholesale. Still, some seeds were put up in individual paper envelopes for retail sale, and some Shaker Brothers continued to deliver them in wooden boxes along well-established seed routes. These envelopes and boxes were fancier and more colorful than earlier versions but, unfortunately, to no avail.

On October 6, 1887, Elder Avery wrote the following entry in his journal: "This evening we have [sic] a meeting of Ministry, Elders & deacons of the Church [Family] at the Trustee's Office to consider the subject of continuing, or discontinuing the seed business. It is decided to throw it up as soon as practicable to do so."[4] In May of the following year he recorded that the remaining seed furniture had been removed from the seed shop in order to ready the building for other uses. This was the last notation made regarding the industry.

The next section of this chapter looks at the many components of the seed industry at New Lebanon (which changed its name to Mount Lebanon in the autumn of 1861, when the Society was granted its own post office). Following that, some of the remnants of the seed industries at eleven other communities—all but one of which are in the East—will be considered.

ABOVE: These three seed envelopes (bags, papers, packages, packets) are the earliest surviving remnants of the industry at New Lebanon. Although the Turnep [*sic*] and Sage varieties appear on a seed listing from 1835, these examples are likely from an earlier time. "D. M." stands for David Meacham, Sr., the first Trustee or business manager at this community, and "N F" signifies the North Family. These packages sold for six or eight cents apiece.

Black ink letterpress on heavy tan and gray paper. From the left, 4¾" × 3¾", 3¾" × 2¾", and 3" × 1¾". New Lebanon, NY.

ABOVE: The earliest wooden boxes used to house and display seed envelopes were simply constructed from clear pine and nailed together; the lid attached with leather or wire hinges. These examples date from the 1840s or 1850s, before the sizes of the bags were standardized. When boxes were retrieved at the end of each selling season, the labels were often covered over with a newer, cleaner example for the next year.

Black ink letterpress on white and off-white paper, pasted on pinewood. Box sizes 6¼" × 17" × 8½" and 7¾" × 21" × 10½". New Lebanon, NY. Courtesy of The Shaker Museum and Library, Old Chatham, NY. # 1325 and # 765.

ABOVE: The first *Gardener's Manuel* [*sic*] was published in 1835 (and again in 1836). It was written by Charles F. Crosman, the head gardener, and printed by a company in Albany, New York. In the same manner that seed envelopes were marketed to small, noncommercial growers, these pamphlets were intended to help develop family "kitchen gardens." Sixteen thousand copies were printed, and they sold for six cents each.[5]

Black ink letterpress on white paper, 7" × 4¼". New Lebanon, NY, R-482.

RIGHT: Beets, of many varieties, were a very popular root vegetable in the first half of the nineteenth century. This style of seed envelope, in two sizes, soon evolved into the smaller, standard-size ones shown in the illustration on page 30. The orange color, format of planting instructions within a decorative border, and family of origin seen in these examples were retained until the early 1880s. Between 1836 and 1840, the Shakers printed 930,400 of these on their own label press, as many as 30,000 in one day in 1847.[6]

Black ink letterpress on stiff orange and tan paper, 3¼" × 4½" and 5½" × 8½". New Lebanon, NY.

The second and last *Gardener's Manual* was published in 1843, three years after Brother Crosman had left the Shakers.[7] It is a much more elaborate affair than its predecessor, with brightly colored covers and many recipes for cooking, pickling, and preserving vegetables in addition to advice on field culture. Its list of offerings was expanded to seventy-three varieties. The introduction firmly states, "These pages contain no suggestion or instruction, but what may be practical." We shall see many times over in this book that practicality is almost synonymous with the Shakers.

LEFT: Black ink letterpress on stiff yellow paper, 7" × 4¾". New Lebanon, NY, R-485; RIGHT: Black ink letterpress on white paper, 7" × 4¾". New Lebanon, NY, R-485.

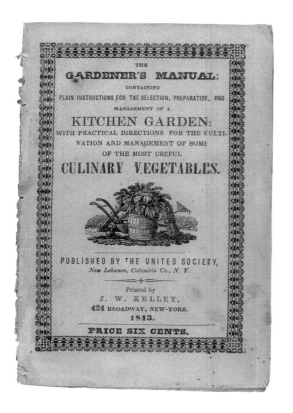

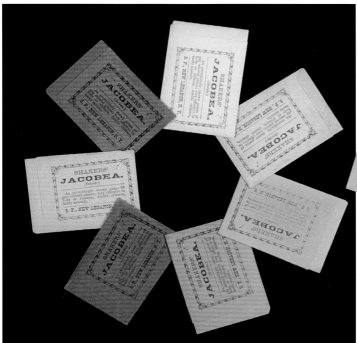

ABOVE: The vast majority of seeds sold by all the communities were for vegetables, but after about 1850 New Lebanon began to offer a modest number of flower and other ornamental varieties. This may have been its response to a growing interest in the World (and among the Shakers themselves) in alternative forms of medicine, some of which utilized material from flowering plants for therapeutic purposes. Jacobea, for example, is a form of ragwort that is a diaphoretic — a sweat producer — and this was an essential property in the practice of nontraditional medicine advocated by Samuel Thomson. For flower seeds alone New Lebanon's Second Family used a rainbow array of colored papers.

Black ink letterpress on stiff variously colored papers, 1¾" × 2¾". New Lebanon, NY; black ink letterpress on stiff variously colored papers, 1¾" × 2¾". New Lebanon, NY.

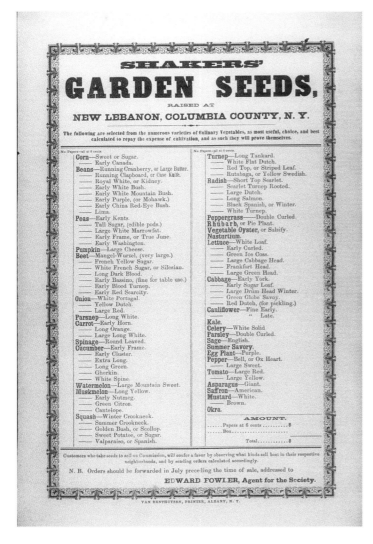

LEFT: It seems odd that New Lebanon did not publish its first seed list until the 1830s, because Alfred, Canterbury, Hancock, and Shirley were doing this before 1820.[8] These broadsides were sent to customers, who entered the numbers of packages of each variety wanted, in ink, and returned them to the Shakers, who would promptly ship the order. This list, dating from the mid-1840s, is a reduced one, including only the "most useful, choice, and best [varieties] calculated to repay the expense of cultivation, and as such will prove themselves." Nasturtium is included as a culinary vegetable rather than an ornamental flower; it was commonly eaten as a salad green then.

Black ink letterpress on off-white paper, 14½" × 9". New Lebanon, NY, R-279.

SHAKERS' GARDEN SEEDS.

FOR SALE HERE.

ABOVE: The earliest-known surviving seed poster or display sign, this probably dates from the 1840s. It would have been hung on a merchant's wall or in a window and reflects the way the Shakers were viewed by the World's people: simple, solid, bold, and straightforward. It also suggests, in its appealing lack of sophistication, the fact that they were probably still unchallenged in the seed business by competition from the World.

Black ink letterpress on heavy white paper, 17½" × 23¼". Probably New Lebanon, NY, NIR.

ABOVE: The first known use of two-color printing for the seed industry is this display sign from around 1860. The community's name changed to Mount Lebanon late in 1861, so this must have been issued shortly before that. Although there is no commercial printer's name present, the sign was surely produced outside the community, because there is no evidence that the Shakers had typefaces or borders of this style.

Red and blue ink letterpress on white paper, 10½" × 15". New Lebanon, NY, NIR.

These envelopes, along with the type of box that housed them, date from the Mount Lebanon period, beginning with the selling season of 1862. Both styles lasted for a little more than twenty years, although the designs varied slightly over that time. Except for flower varieties, the seed packages of this period uniformly used heavy tan or orange-colored paper. The boxes were still assembled from pine boards, only now they were machine dovetailed, with the edges of the top fitted with splines to prevent warping. They generally were given a protective coat of red paint.

LEFT: Black ink letterpress on stiff orange paper, 1¾" × 4". Mount Lebanon, NY; BELOW: Black ink letterpress on red paper, pasted on wood with red paint, 3¼" × 23¼" × 11½". Mount Lebanon, NY.

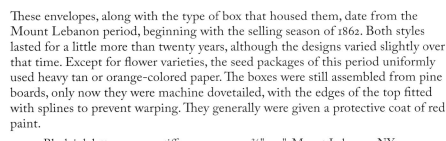

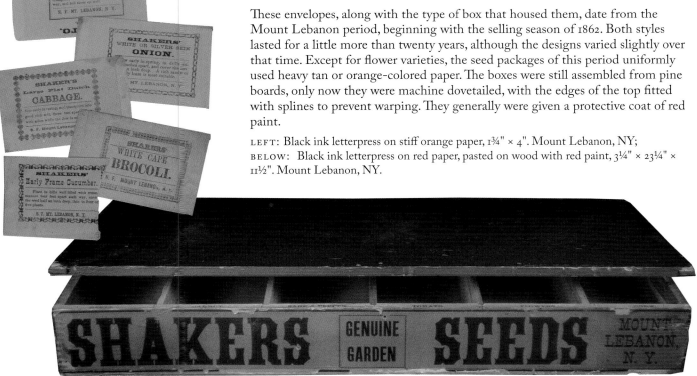

The Shakers could not raise melons to harvest their seeds as far north as Mount Lebanon and so resorted to buying these and other seeds from the World. This apparently created problems of quality control, so back in 1819 New Lebanon, Hancock, and Watervliet agreed that, with the exception of melon seeds, all those sold by the Shakers had to be grown by the Shakers.[9] This may explain why the design of these packages differed from those of all the rest.

An "exploded" view of a melon seed envelope illustrates how all were made. Stacks of rectangular sheets of paper were printed on the community press, and their sides were trimmed with a Shaker-made offset chisel to shape them. Each sheet was folded in half. The tabs on the left and bottom were then folded under and pasted to form the three sides of the envelope. Once it was filled with seeds, the right flap was folded and pasted, and the package was ready for the market. The photoengraving of a melon is from the Mount Lebanon catalog of 1874.

ABOVE LEFT: Black ink letterpress on thin orange paper, 5" × 3¾" and 2½" × 3½". Mount Lebanon, NY; ABOVE RIGHT: Steel, lengths 8¼" and 5". New or Mount Lebanon, NY. Courtesy of The Shaker Museum and Library, Old Chatham, NY. # 3085 and # 3086; BELOW: black ink letterpress (with wood or metal engraving) on white paper, image size 4" × 4½". Mount Lebanon, NY, R-261v.

MELON — Melon — *Zandia* — Melonen.

Culture. — Melons thrive best in a warm, rich, sandy loam, and in a sheltered exposure. If the soil is heavy, dig large holes two feet in diameter and eighteen inches deep; fill with stable manure; cover this with soil three inches deep; on this plant the seeds. When out of the reach of insects, thin to two or three plants in a hill. Melons should not be planted near pumpkins or squashes, as they will mix.

Green Citron Melon.

MUSK VARIETIES.

Fine Netted Nutmeg. — A popular variety. Fruit roundish. Flesh thick, and excellent flavor.

Pine Apple. — A dark green oval melon. Medium size. Rough netted; flesh thick, juicy and sweet.

Green Citron. — A large, roundish fruit, flattened at the ends, and rough netted. Melting and fine flavored.

Jenny Lind. — Size small, but very delicious. One of the earliest.

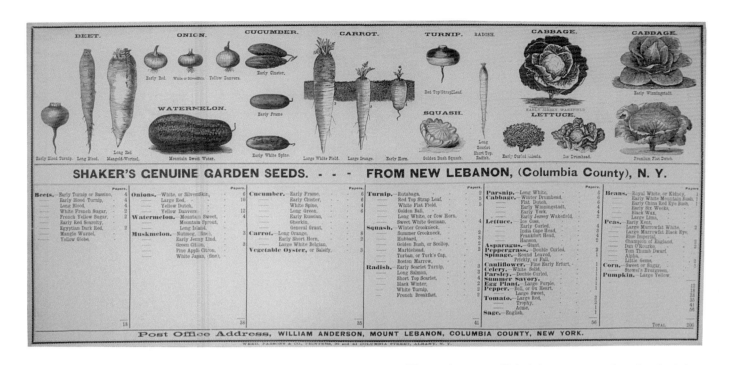

SHAKER'S GENUINE GARDEN SEEDS. - - - FROM NEW LEBANON, (Columbia County), N. Y.

Post Office Address, WILLIAM ANDERSON, MOUNT LEBANON, COLUMBIA COUNTY, NEW YORK.

ABOVE: This is the type of label that was pasted under the lid of the box shown in the illustration on page 30. When this box was placed on a merchant's counter, the lid was likely left open so that the bright yellow paper and the illustrations of vegetables could attract the eye of would-be customers. The listing on the lower half of the label was filled in by the Shakers by hand, in ink, before the box was left on consignment. This allowed for a quick and accurate calculation of the merchant's commission when the box was retrieved.

Black ink letterpress (with wood or metal engraving) on yellow paper, 11¼" × 22¾". Mount Lebanon, NY, R-280.

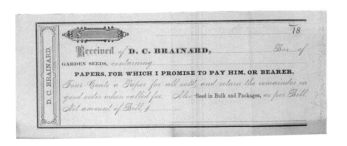

LEFT: An array of printed materials, ephemera, was needed to support this industry, and as far as we know the Shakers produced most of it themselves. Every seed box that was left on commission required a receipt signed by the merchant. The topmost example, dated 1862, records 217 "papers" or seed envelopes inside just one box. The middle receipt is dated 1878, with a "promise to pay bearer three cents per paper for all not returned when called for"—an unusually high, 50 percent commission. The lowermost receipt is undated but from the early 1880s; it calls for a more usual 33⅓ percent commission.

Black ink letterpress on white paper, 3" × 6¼", 3½" × 7½", and 3½" × 8½". Mount Lebanon, NY.

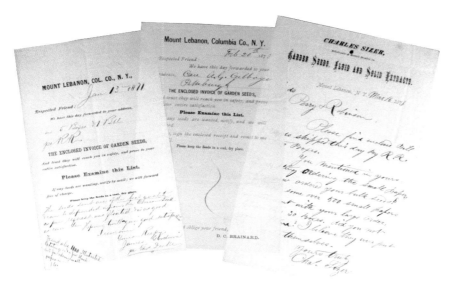

Seeds that were shipped by rail required invoices in order to maintain a "paper trail." The Shakers carried on a large mail order business, especially for bulk or wholesale seeds, throughout most of the nineteenth century. These examples (*left* to *right*) date from 1871, 1873, and 1876. The last one was probably printed commercially. Its message reads in part, "There was some over 500 small papers assorted sent with your large order [of bulk seeds]."

LEFT: Black ink letterpress on white paper, 7¾" × 4¾", 7⅞" × 5", and 8¾" × 5⅝". Mount Lebanon, NY.

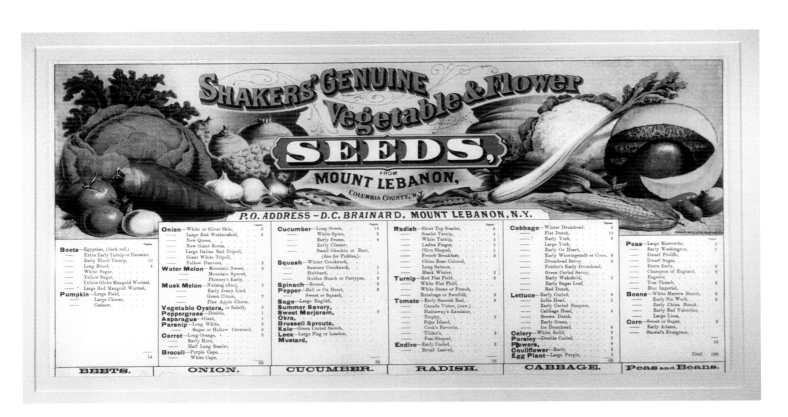

This was the final design for an interior seed box label before the business was reorganized in 1884. For the first time, the Shakers took advantage of color lithography to market their seeds. This now-iconic example features a luscious assortment of fruits and vegetables depicted in gorgeous color. The largest number of varieties offered is for cabbage seeds, twelve, followed by radishes and peas, nine each.

Color lithograph on white paper, 11⅛" × 27⅞". Mount Lebanon, NY, NIR.

A new (but short-lived) era began when the Shaker Seed Company was formed in 1884. No longer were family designations used, but the Second Family, under the leadership of Elder DeWitt Clinton Brainard (1828–1897) was put in charge for the entire village. These were the first seed envelopes to be printed after the reorganization and date to 1885 or 1886. The latter date is more likely, since little business was conducted in 1885. Beets maintained their popularity throughout the century. Of the root vegetables, the Shakers sold more varieties of beets than carrots, turnips, or radishes.

ABOVE: Black ink letterpress on off-white paper, 3⅛" × 4¾" and 3⅞" × 5¾". Mount Lebanon, NY.

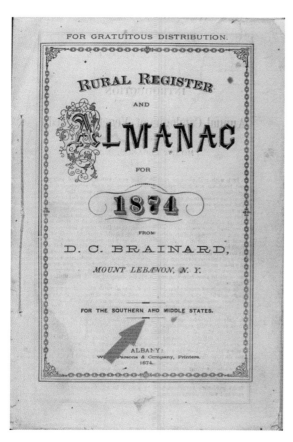

LEFT: New Lebanon's seed business rebounded remarkably well from the disruptions caused by the Civil War. The numbers of seed envelopes printed annually track this recovery well, from a low of 7,900 in 1861 to 136,100 in 1865 and, in 1870, slightly more than a quarter of a million.[10] This 1874 seed catalog, clearly directed to the southern markets, demonstrates Mount Lebanon's commitment to this region. Planting instructions begin in *January*, which is called "an active month in the Gulf States . . . but little can be done in the garden [of the Middle States] this month [although] hot-bed frames and sashes should be prepared."[11]

Black ink letterpress on off-white paper, 9" × 5¾". Mount Lebanon, NY, R-26IV.

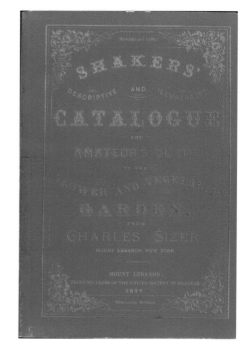

RIGHT: Beginning a year before this 1877 edition, and continuing until 1883, the Society published a series of imprints called "Shakers' Descriptive and Illustrated Catalogue and Amateur's Guide to the Flower and Vegetable Garden." These hefty booklets ran from sixty to eighty-four pages and were filled with wood or metal plate cuts of vegetables and flowers along with detailed descriptions and planting instructions for each. At the back there were sixteen varieties of medicinal and sweet (i.e., culinary) herbs offered.

Gold ink letterpress on heavy blue paper, 8¾" × 5⅝". Mount Lebanon, NY, NIR (but see R-275).

RIGHT: The 1885 edition, now retitled "Illustrated Catalogue of the Shaker Seed Co.," used a two-color cover, red plus yellow resulting in brown, but still only black ink inside. The envelope that was used to mail these booklets is shown in the background. Nowhere in these later publications, or in the manuscript journals of the period, is there any indication that consumers were charged for these catalog/guides, and so it seems safe to assume that they were distributed for free. The covers of some list Washington Jones (1845–1913), a Brother at New Lebanon, as the printer.

Two-color lithograph on heavy tan paper, 9¼" × 5¾". Mount Lebanon, NY, NIR.

LEFT: These envelopes represent the final style of a form that began some eighty-five years earlier. The vivid colors and a technique called "vignetting" (shading) were made possible with color lithography.[12] These envelopes were used only between about 1886 and 1888; hence few have survived. (This was also the time when most seeds were sold in bulk forms.) The example on the left has a pencil notation that reads, "Sowed April 16, 1887." It seems fitting that two of these packages were for cabbage seeds, historically one of the largest groups of vegetables in the Shakers' inventory, at least as far back as 1835. Once again the initials of Trustee David Meacham, who died in 1826, were used as a mark of quality.

Color lithograph and black ink letterpress on stiff white paper, each 4¼" × 2". Mount Lebanon, NY.

RIGHT: There is a tone of quiet desperation evident in the publications of the Shaker Seed Company. In their attempt to compete with Worldly seed merchants whose operations were much larger and more efficient—and some of whom also offered inducements to buyers—the Shakers resorted to giveaways. These ranged from free seeds, for orders large and small, to other premiums such as "free chromos." This is an example of the latter—a small, lushly colored color lithograph of eleven varieties of flowers. Unfortunately, the business failed in spite of these valiant attempts.

Color lithograph on heavy white paper, 9" × 5¾". Mount Lebanon, NY, N.R.

After reorganization in 1884, the Shakers concentrated their efforts on the wholesale mail order business. This fourteen-page pamphlet opens with the statement: "As customary at this time of the year [January], we send you our price list for the coming season." Almost all illustrations and descriptions were omitted, and the focus was the prices of seeds per pound. In the back is a notation that "special prices quoted on hundred lb. lots whenever desired." The inside of the front cover shows two varieties of cabbage with a correction overprinted in red, changing "imported" to "improved," obviously a very important distinction.

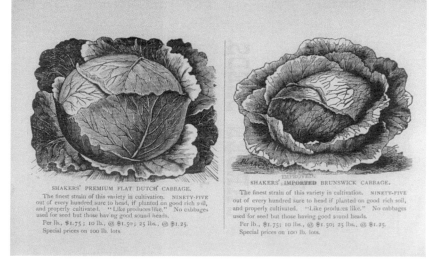

ABOVE LEFT: Black and green ink letterpress on white paper, 7" × 4¾". Mount Lebanon, NY, R-266v; RIGHT: Black and green ink letterpress (with wood or metal engraving) on white paper, 7" × 4¾". Mount Lebanon, NY, R-266v.

Livingston's Beauty Tomato.

DESCRIPTION.

"The color is quite distinct from any sort we are acquainted with, being a very glossy crimson with a slight tinge of purple, the color alone will bring it into favor. It grows in clusters of four or five large fruits, retaining its very large size late in the season. This is an essential point in its favor, as many other good sorts decrease in size at least one-half before the season is

RIGHT: The penultimate seed catalog was issued in 1886. More color illustrations were added to the usual mix of black linecuts, and, for the first time, endorsements were included. Typical endorsements were: "I have grown vegetables extensively for the Philadelphia market for over thirty years and have tried almost every strain of seeds, and don't hesitate to pronounce thine *the best*"; and "The seeds I got of you last spring, did splendidly, especially my Brunswick Cabbage, Cucumbers and Melons, which were the admiration of all my neighbors."

Multicolor letterpress on tan paper, 9⅛" × 6". Mount Lebanon, NY, R-273.

BELOW: The last of the seed box labels is arguably the most attractive, with rich, saturated colors and an inviting wedge of watermelon. In order to conform to the later boxes, which were longer and narrower, the list of contents was shifted to the side. Significantly, this list was now reduced to sixty-two varieties. Companies in upstate New York that sprang up along the Erie Canal from Albany to Buffalo produced this and all the other color lithographs for Mount Lebanon.

Color lithograph on white paper, 8½" × 21¼". Mount Lebanon, NY, NIR.

OTHER COMMUNITIES

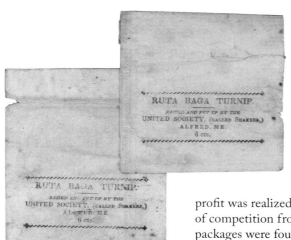

Alfred, Maine, was one of the communities that laid claim to having originated the retail sale of seeds in individual paper envelopes in the 1790s. At the least it had its business in place by 1803. The community eventually developed seed routes that extended as far north as the tip of Maine and into Canada. At the height of prosperity, during the 1830s and 1840s, up to $1,800.00 of profit was realized in a year. Around 1856 the business ended, probably because of competition from the World.[13] It seems extraordinary that until these two packages were found in a Maine attic in 2003, not a single other example came to light from an industry that had lasted for more than seventy-five years.[14]

LEFT: Black ink letterpress on white paper, each 2¾" × 2⅝" (folded). Alfred, ME.

Canterbury, New Hampshire, issued its only known seed list in 1808. As far as we know, this was the earliest seed broadside of any Shaker village.[15] Twenty-six varieties were offered, and cabbages, with four types, predominated. These seed envelopes, of the earlier style, show only the variety and the initials of Trustee Francis Winkley (d. 1848). The business was terminated in the 1830s, apparently the result of competition from other Shaker Societies, but was revived on a much-reduced scale after 1850. This time planting instructions are included on the packages. RIGHT: The receipt is for "One box of Garden Seeds, amounting to Ten Dollars and 8 cents to sell on commission of fifty per cent," and is dated 1854.

LEFT: Black or brown ink letterpress on tan paper, 2⅝" × 2½". Canterbury, NH; RIGHT: Black ink letterpress on tan paper and black ink letterpress and manuscript on white paper, 2½" × 3½" and 2" × 6½". Canterbury, NH.

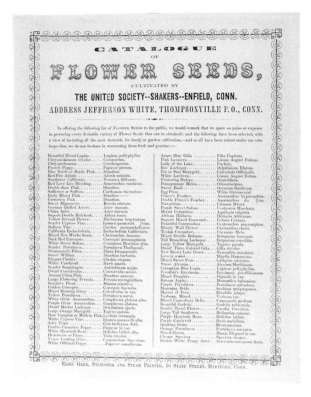

The industry at Enfield, Connecticut, is in some ways the most enigmatic of all. At its height in the mid-1850s, with one hundred acres of seed plants under cultivation, it was said to be second in size only to New Lebanon's. Yet, with the onset of the Civil War, it vanished without a trace.[16] ABOVE LEFT: The broadside that is illustrated offered 210 varieties of vegetable seeds plus 15 of herbs and 10 of grasses, all "put up in papers with directions, stating time of planting, mode of culture, &c., printed on them."[17] RIGHT: *The Catalogue of Flower Seeds* lists 95 varieties and states that [since] "all have been raised under our own inspection, we do not hesitate in warranting them fresh and genuine." With the possible exception of these two flower seed envelopes, which have no community name printed on them (and do not actually appear on *this* list), no seed envelope from this community has come to light. Jefferson White, the head seedsman noted on both lists, was the driving force behind the Enfield industry from 1832 to 1857. The envelope shown here has his signature plus "Shaker Garden Seed" written across the stamp. The stamp was issued the year that he retired as head seedsman and therefore can be logically dated to 1857.

ABOVE LEFT: Black ink letterpress on white paper, 19¼" × 12⅜". Enfield, CT, R-200; ABOVE RIGHT: black ink letterpress on gray paper, 10¾" × 8⅛". Enfield, CT, R-196; BELOW RIGHT: Black ink letterpress and manuscript on yellow paper, 3" × 5⅛". Enfield, CT.

Enfield, New Hampshire, never issued a seed catalog or list. Its seed boxes bore a simply painted name on the front without the benefit of paper labels. This community did sell seeds late into the nineteenth century, and more envelopes from Enfield have survived still filled with seeds than from anywhere else. The routes of distribution seem to have been confined to northern New Hampshire and Vermont, and no conflicts with other Shaker communities are recorded. (This contrasts with Enfield's sister community in the New Hampshire Bishopric, Canterbury which was forced to negotiate routes with Shirley, Massachusetts and Alfred, Maine.) The initials N. D. on each package stand for Trustee Nathaniel Draper, who died in 1838; the significance of the extra letter is not known. As with D. M. at New Lebanon, Brother Draper's initials were used throughout the century. The postcard image shows only the onion seed fields, but without a seed list it is not possible to know if this was a major seed offering or simply the choice of the commercial photographer who took the picture. While onions are easy to grow from seeds, it is difficult to harvest *seeds* from onions. Since they are biennial, the seeds appear only in the late summer of the second growing season, and the time available for the Shakers to gather them, before insects ate them, was short.

Seed Onions, Shaker Horticultural Gardens, Enfield, N. H.

TOP: black ink letterpress on tan paper, 2½" × 2¼" and 3¾" × 3½". Enfield, NH; CENTER: Black paint stenciled on natural pine, 7⅛" × 21⅝" × 9½". Enfield, NH; LEFT: Photoengraving on card stock, 3½" × 5⅜". Enfield, NH.

Scanty information is available about the Hancock, Massachusetts, seed business, but we know that it was active by 1811, the date of an ad that appeared in a Hartford, Connecticut, newspaper and reads, in part: "Received from the Shakers at Hancock, and various other quarters, a supply of Garden Seeds."[18] Hancock's earliest surviving printed list dates to 1813, with thirty-five varieties offered. By 1869 this number had grown to sixty-nine, with an impressive nineteen types of melon seed alone. We know that 122,900 seed envelopes were put up in 1842 but not the number sold. And we know, from the partial interior seed box label illustrated here, that the business extended into the era of Trustee Ira Lawson (active 1862–1899). The two seed lists shown are from 1823 (*left*) and 183_ (*right*). Apparently no seed lists were printed after the 1830s.

ABOVE LEFT: Black ink letterpress on tan and orange papers, 2¼" × 2½" (1), 2¾" × 4" (1), 3⅞" × 4¾" (1), 4½" × 5½" (2). Hancock, MA; LEFT: Black ink letterpress (and black ink and pencil manuscript, *left*) on white paper, 16" × 6¾" (*left*) and 14½" × 7⅞" (*right*). Hancock, MA, R-215v. and R-212; RIGHT: Black ink letterpress on off-white paper, 8½" × 3¾". Hancock, MA. Courtesy of Hancock Shaker Village, Inc., Pittsfield, MA. # 7532, NIR.

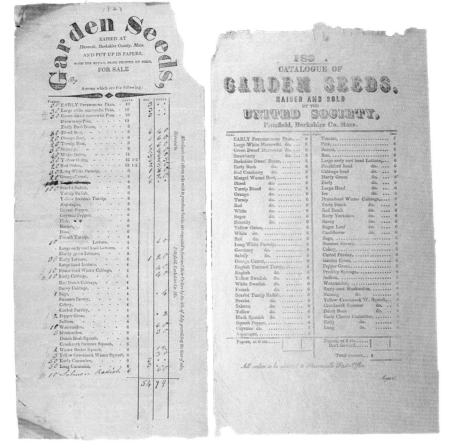

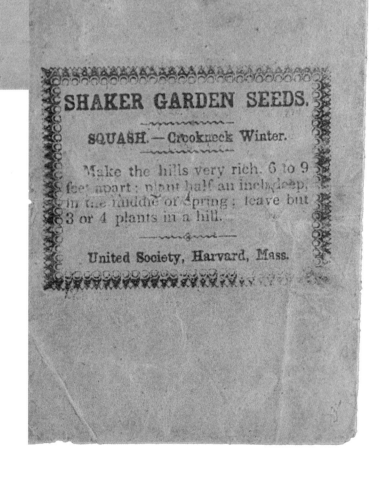

LONG ORANGE CARROT.

Sown in May, or as late as the middle of June, in light mellow soil; esteemed the most valuable of all roots for horses and cattle. See New American Gardener.

Raised and put up by the
UNITED SOCIETY, (called Shakers,)
Harvard, Mass.

SHAKER GARDEN SEEDS.

SQUASH. — Crookneck Winter.

Make the hills very rich. 6 to 9 feet apart; plant half an inch deep, in the middle of spring; leave but 3 or 4 plants in a hill.

United Society, Harvard, Mass.

The earliest date recorded for the seed industry at Harvard, Massachusetts, is January of 1821, although it is likely that retail seed sales preceded this date. Journals show that every subsequent year, until 1863, Brethren undertook journeys to deliver boxes of garden and grass seeds between November and February.[19] The industry ended in 1864 as the community evidently decided to commit its resources to the large and expanding herb business.[20] As evidence of this, in 1850 the community converted its carrot fields into dandelion fields, dandelion (*Taraxacum*) being one of the most important herbs in Harvard's huge catalog.[21] These two seed envelopes are almost all that have survived. The "Long Orange Carrot" probably antedates 1850; the date for "squash" is unknown (but, based on style, appears to be later).

Black ink letterpress on orange and tan papers, 3" × 4" and 2¾" × 4". Harvard, MA.

The industry at Sabbathday Lake, Maine, is traditionally traced back to the 1790s and to Deacon James Holmes and his natural brother, John. Thus this community also claims to have been "first among equals." As the nineteenth century progressed, the Shakers at Alfred and New Gloucester (West Gloucester after 1860, Sabbathday Lake after 1886) found themselves competing with one another to peddle seeds within the borders of Maine. In 1837, the Deacon and Trustee at Alfred drew up an agreement that was accepted by New Gloucester whereby the former was granted exclusive rights to the seed routes in coastal Maine and the latter's territory was restricted to scattered interior regions.[22] Both were allowed to sell in Portland, the largest city and an important seaport. This clearly shows the dominant size and position of Alfred's industry at this time. The seed box illustrated, from New Gloucester, predates 1860; the other dates to between 1860 and 1880, when retail sales ended and only bulk sales took place. The seed box receipt is from 1849, with James Holmes *still* serving as head seedsman. (His brother, John, was expelled from the community in 1830.) No intact seed envelopes from here are known to have survived; the label that is shown below was taken from one envelope and pasted onto the drawer front of a seed chest (or "bunk," as the Shakers refer to it).

TOP TWO BOXES: Black ink letterpress on off-white paper, pasted on pine, 5½" × 14½" × 7⅛". Sabbathday Lake, ME. Collection of the United Society of Shakers, Sabbathday Lake, Maine; CENTER: Black ink letterpress on pale yellow paper, pasted on pine, 5½" × 14½" × 7⅛". Sabbathday Lake, ME. Collection of the United Society of Shakers, Sabbathday Lake, Maine; black ink letterpress and manuscript on white paper, 2¼" × 6¼". Sabbathday Lake, ME; LEFT: Black ink letterpress on white paper, pasted on unidentified wood, 2½" × 1½". Sabbathday Lake, ME. Collection of the United Society of Shakers, Sabbathday Lake, Maine.

The Shakers at Shirley started their seed business in 1805, and it followed a generally conservative trajectory: retail sales only, and seed routes close to their eastern Massachusetts home. Only once, in 1838, did another community—Canterbury—complain about Shirley encroaching on its territory in New Hampshire.[23] Seed lists were issued in every decade beginning in 1810, with the last one dated 1865.[24] For some unknown reason, Shirley ended its business in the mid-1860s, only a few years after its sister community at Harvard did, and thereafter concentrated on other industries such as processed fruits and brooms. The seed envelopes illustrated are of two sizes, both selling for six cents. Printed on each is: "Raised and put up by the United Society, (Shirley, Mass.)." Included here is a package of muskmelon seeds, a variety that the Brethren at New Lebanon once agreed was acceptable to purchase from outside sources because the Shakers could not raise it themselves. The receipt, dated 1847, has the standard commission of "twenty-five" (percent) crossed through, and "forty" (percent) written in. This may indicate a response to competition from the World.

ABOVE RIGHT: Black ink letterpress on tan and orange papers, 2¼" × 3½" and 3¼" × 4". Shirley, MA; LEFT: Black ink letterpress and manuscript on blue paper, 2¾" × 4⅞". Shirley, MA.

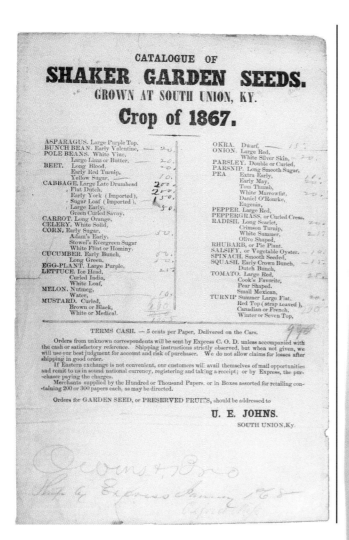

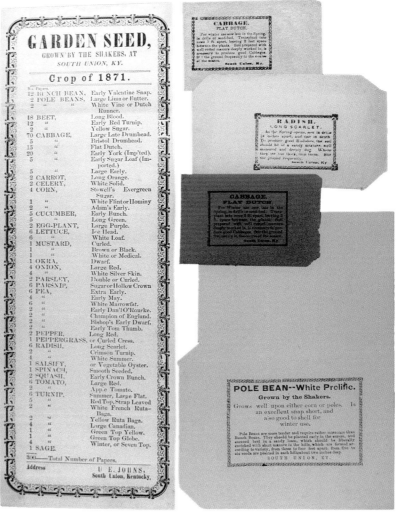

A citation in a secondary source indicates that South Union, Kentucky may have sold seeds as early as 1815 (the community was "gathered" in 1807).[25] Other than seed-selling trips down the Ohio and Mississippi rivers in the 1830s, little else is known about the industry until the first seed list appears, dating from the 1840s.[26] Several more lists survive from 1850 to 1861, but during the war years the community's very survival was challenged. Early in 1864, however, six months after Union forces lifted the Confederate blockade of the Mississippi River at Vicksburg, two South Union Shakers undertook their first river journey south since the war began, bringing 150 seed boxes with two hundred envelopes in each.[27] Two years later the business took off, perhaps fueled by the devastation of local seed stocks and seed merchants. Over the ensuing eighteen years, catalogs were published annually with forty to fifty varieties offered. The single broadside illustrated is from soon after the war and lists sixty types of seeds at five cents each. At the bottom it records a shipment of about twenty dollars worth of "papers" to "Owens & Bro, Oxford, Miss." The other, narrower list was probably intended to be a catalog, pasted inside the lid of a wooden seed box. Brother Urban E. Johns acted as the South Union seed agent for many years before and after the war. Alongside the list is a sampling of the types and sizes of seed envelopes used, although their dates are unknown.

ABOVE LEFT: Black ink letterpress and manuscript and pencil manuscript on white paper, 14" × 8½". South Union, KY; ABOVE RIGHT: Black ink letterpress on white paper, 14" × 4¾", R-400. Black ink letterpress on blue gray, deep blue, and tan papers, 2½" × 3⅝", 3 × 5", and 8" × 6¼". South Union, KY.

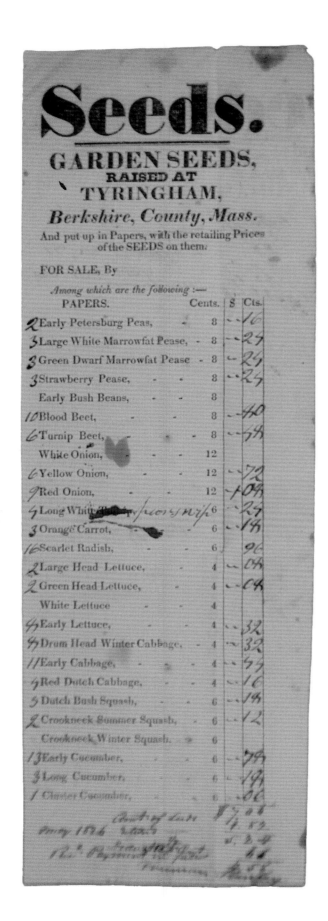

Seeds.

GARDEN SEEDS,
RAISED AT
TYRINGHAM,
Berkshire, County, Mass.

And put up in Papers, with the retailing Prices of the SEEDS on them.

FOR SALE, By

Among which are the following :—

PAPERS.	Cents.	$ Cts.
2 Early Petersburg Peas,	8	16
3 Large White Marrowfat Pease,	8	24
3 Green Dwarf Marrowfat Pease	8	24
3 Strawberry Pease,	8	24
Early Bush Beans,	8	
10 Blood Beet,	8	40
6 Turnip Beet,	8	78
White Onion,	12	
6 Yellow Onion,	12	72
9 Red Onion,	12	108
4 Long White	6	24
3 Orange Carrot,	6	18
16 Scarlet Radish,	6	96
2 Large Head Lettuce,	4	08
2 Green Head Lettuce,	4	08
White Lettuce	4	
4 Early Lettuce,	4	32
4 Drum Head Winter Cabbage,	4	32
11 Early Cabbage,	4	44
4 Red Dutch Cabbage,	4	16
3 Dutch Bush Squash,	6	18
2 Crookneck Summer Squash,	6	12
Crookneck Winter Squash.	6	
13 Early Cucumber,	6	78
3 Long Cucumber,	6	19
1 Cluster Cucumber,	6	06

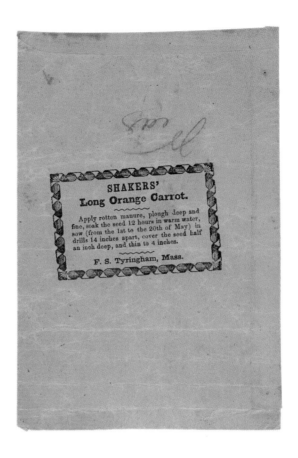

There is almost no information in the surviving manuscript records about any industries, including garden seeds, at the Tyringham, Massachusetts, community. Yet this very small (never more than one hundred members) sister to Hancock is believed to have had a sizable seed business, from at least 1826—the date of the earliest known list—to the 1850s, the date of the last one.[28] The former, illustrated here, offers twenty-six varieties, with the prices ranging from four to twelve cents each; the later listing was expanded to sixty-seven varieties. We also know that the Tyringham Shakers built a five-story seed house in 1854 and designed it to handle every facet of the industry, from printing seed envelopes and lists to preparing the product for market.[29] The seed envelope illustrated here is the only known survivor, and its date is unknown. The initials on the bottom, "F. S.," stand for Trustee Freeman Stanley, who died in 1862. The community was dissolved in 1875, the first of the Shaker villages to close.

LEFT: Black ink letterpress on orange tan paper, 12½" × 4⅛". Tyringham, MA. Courtesy of The Shaker Museum and Library, Old Chatham, NY. # 2790, R-409; ABOVE RIGHT: Black ink letterpress on orange tan paper, 7⅜" × 4¾". Tyringham, MA.

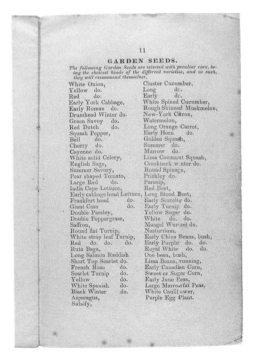

Watervliet, New York (not to be confused with the Shaker village in Watervliet, Ohio, from which there are no remnants of any industry), epitomizes many of the dilemmas discussed above: a very early start in the seed business, a long-lasting and sizable business, and very little physical evidence to show for it. The sole published work devoted to this community has only this to say: "A garden seed business, which had a modest beginning at Watervliet in the 1790s, gradually increased in volume under the administration of Trustee David Osborn[e]."[30] He died in 1834. Edward Andrews had little to add to that description except for noting that Watervliet is a legitimate candidate for the first village to sell seeds retail. The fact that it issued a catalog, with 120 varieties, in the 1870s (illustrated) and another in the 1880s attests to the size and longevity of the industry. Watervliet also included lists of seeds in its medicinal herbs catalogs, such as this one, which was issued in 1845. Its last list, the narrow one pictured here, was published under the auspices of Philip Smith; he succeeded Chauncy Miller as Trustee for one year (March 1885 to March 1886) and closed out the business. This single seed envelope, bearing the initials of David Osborn[e], is one of fewer than a half-dozen examples known to have survived from a business that thrived for the better part of ninety years.

ABOVE LEFT: Black ink letterpress on off-white paper, 16" × 11". Watervliet, NY, R-437; ABOVE RIGHT: Black ink letterpress on off-white paper, 15½" × 5½". Watervliet, NY, R-443; BELOW LEFT: Black ink letterpress on stiff tan paper, 2¾" × 4". Watervliet, NY. Courtesy of Hancock Shaker Village, Inc., Pittsfield, MA; BELOW RIGHT: Black ink letterpress on thin off-white paper, 7¼" × 4¼". Watervliet, NY, R-423.

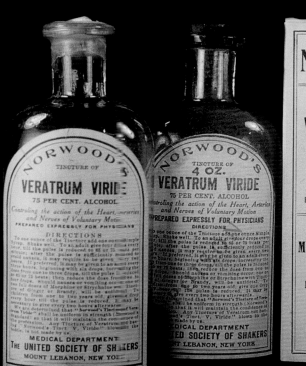

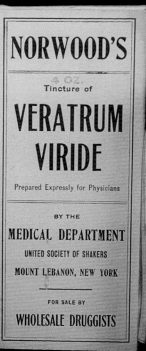

Medicinal Herbs and Preparations

MEDICINAL HERBS AND PREPARATIONS INDUSTRY

THE SHAKERS' MEDICINAL herb industry, including both raw packaged products and the preparations derived from them, was enormous. No matter what yardstick is used as a gauge, this industry's size, scope, and influence was vast. So too was its financial impact on those communities which, over the course of the nineteenth century, adopted it to help support their economy. It will not be possible to explore this subject in its entirety within the space limitations of the next section; instead a selective survey of this important enterprise will have to suffice.

Fortunately, unlike the seed industry in the preceding chapter, from which (except for New and Mount Lebanon) little material remains, a wealth of marketing materials for medicinal herbs, along with a relative abundance of packaged herbs and preparations, survive. Also, since this industry began twenty or more years later, there is more manuscript evidence in the form of records and journals that a researcher can draw on. The challenge then is to *limit* the amount of material illustrated and discussed. The remedies that will be considered vary in size from a tiny toothache pellet—smaller than a BB—to the globally marketed entity called the Shaker Extract of Roots or Mother Seigel's Syrup. In the last quarter of the nineteenth century, this single medicine, manufactured at Mount Lebanon, was the most widely distributed and, most likely, the best-selling remedy in the world.

Edward Andrews's insightful observations, first published in 1933, cannot be improved on today and are worth quoting at length: "The medicinal herb industry was as natural an outgrowth of the Shakers' early interest in gardening and agriculture as was the seed business. Each was a semi-agricultural occupation, a combination of garden and shop activity . . . The Shakers were among the first in this country to see more than the obvious possibilities of gardening, and here, as in many other fields, their habitual genius for recognizing and developing economic opportunities is apparent. The passion of the people composing this sect for being useful, for doing useful things and for making things useful is evidenced in these soil culture activities. It was consistent with their pragmatic philosophy that plants should be utilized in every way possible. Some were useful for food, some for their medicinal qualities, some for seed production; in their roots and leaves, in their flowers and fruits, one or the other useful quality was present."[1]

While everything that Andrews says is true for the "supply side" of the equation, it does not consider the equally important "demand side."[2] In the first half of the nineteenth century, traditional medicine was not really medicine at all; it was much closer in spirit, although certainly not in technique, to today's surgical specialties. "Treatment" was generally aimed at removing the offending agent or part, and since germ theory was still some fifty years distant, bloodletting, purging, excision, and amputation were the orders of the day. This combination of aggressiveness and empiricism did not inspire confidence in the American public. Furthermore, many sick people were excluded from a system that was based mainly in population centers, was expensive, and often did not cure or even help those who did avail themselves.

Into this void flowed nontraditional medicine, based on "natural" or botanical remedies. Although these too were not evidence-based in the contemporary sense, Europeans, European Americans, and Native Americans had used them for centuries or millenniums. They were usually as close as the closest field or forest, cheap, and—often enough—effective. (Their safety was another issue altogether.) The Shakers themselves had depended on herbal remedies for two generations before they developed the cultivation and marketing of them as a major industry. It should also be pointed out that long before Louis Pasteur wrote on the subject (1857–1858), the Shakers instinctively applied many of the basic principles of germ theory to their own daily lives: proper ventilation, asepsis, careful preservation and storage of foods, regular bathing, and regular work and sleep habits.

The vacuum in effective medical practice, both traditional and nontraditional, afforded an opportunity for those individuals who were only too eager to prey on a susceptible public. Amy Bess Miller, another author to whom this present book is indebted, published an important study of Shaker medicinal herbs in 1976. In her summary and conclusion she wrote: "Healing in the eighteenth century was a ready field for the sharper, the quack, and the flamboyant purveyor of nostrums and cure-alls. But the Shakers, whom many regarded as 'religious quacks,' brought herbal medicine to a plane of probity and respectability and, of course, their business in pure herbs accordingly became the source of enormous profit for the order . . . During the seventy-five years when it was at its height [1825–1900], the business at just five Shaker communities (Watervliet and Mount Lebanon, New York; Harvard, Massachusetts; Canterbury, New Hampshire; and Union Village, Ohio) was averaging an aggregate gross of $150,000 annually."[3]

In the survey that follows, the focus will be on the same five villages named above, for they were, year in and year out, the major producers. In actuality, all the Shaker communities were involved in growing and processing medicinal herbs—if not for sale then for their own use. (Culinary herbs will be considered in the section dealing with Shaker foods.) In Maine, both Sabbathday Lake and Alfred sold herbs, and the former also manufactured the Tamar Laxative, which included herbs but was fruit based. In New Hampshire, Canterbury was heavily invested in herbs and medicines while Enfield produced relatively few

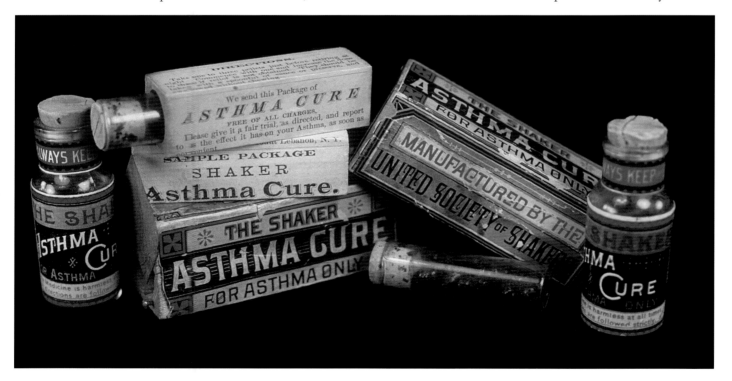

preparations, of which only Brown's Shaker Extract of English Valerian and Shaker Anodyne were important sources of revenue.

The herbal culture among the four Massachusetts societies was confined to processing and packaging the raw product: roots, barks, and leaves in dry and liquid forms. Only Harvard did this on a large scale and, in addition to its own retail business, sold processed herbs in bulk form to other Shaker communities (mostly Canterbury and Watervliet) and to major commercial drug houses (such as J. C. Ayer Company of Lowell, Massachusetts). In the West, only Union Village engaged in the medicinal herb business in a large way, and this involvement will be sampled ahead.

It is essential to note that the development of this industry began everywhere with the simple gathering of local wild herbs for the Shakers' own uses and only later developed into an industry—first at Harvard or New Lebanon, either in 1820 or 1821—when large tracts of land were set aside for cultivating these herbs. As with garden seeds, multiple levels of coordinated responsibilities were required along with a large workforce and, usually, a building or two dedicated to preparing herbs for the marketplace. Some plant material was bought from outside sources, even from abroad, and often one Shaker community sold processed herbs to another.

In the section that follows, the medicinal herb industry will be divided into three areas: packaged herbs, preparations intended for external use, and preparations intended for internal use. In this last category there are three remedies that will be considered separately: Veratrum Veride, Mother Seigel's Syrup, and Seven Barks. Each of these has a distinct history, and all were produced at Mount Lebanon into the twentieth century—the only Shaker-made medicines to survive for that long.

When approaching so vast and varied an enterprise as this, it is easy to overwhelm the reader with numbers—pounds, bottles, packages, and so forth. Another danger is that of trying the reader's patience with repetitive images. And, finally, it is tempting for the author to indulge an interest in pharmacodynamics: the safety and efficacy of these substances. While every effort will be made to resist overdoing any of these, some of each is necessary to demonstrate how integral this industry was to the Shakers' economy. As Andrews made clear, the economic opportunities of a medicinal herb culture were fully in step with the Believers' spiritual belief system. This industry was, one may fairly say, a marriage made between "Shaker heaven" and "Shaker earth."

PACKAGED HERBS

The medicinal herb business at Harvard, Massachusetts, began modestly in 1820, when gathered wild herbs were first offered for sale. By the time Harvard's first "Catalogue of Medicinal Plants and Culinary Herbs, Barks, Roots, Extracts &c." was issued around 1830, many acres there had been dedicated to cultured herbs. Hosea Winchester, whose name appears at the bottom, was appointed as Trustee for the Society in that year (but left the Shakers in 1835). This catalog lists 140 varieties of herbs, and while it gives the prices by the pound, it says that one- and two-ounce packages are also available for a small surcharge. Some herbs, such as "Thorn-apple" [*sic*], are offered in a choice of leaf, root, seed, or extract form. Thorn apple, a type of datura or jimsonweed, had many uses, depending on its form: leaves were smoked to relieve the symptoms of asthma, an extract was used as a sedative and narcotic, and an ointment could be made from its roots for cuts and burns.[4] This broadside/catalog is the only such list known from Harvard until late in the century, for a series of bound catalogs were printed in the interim.

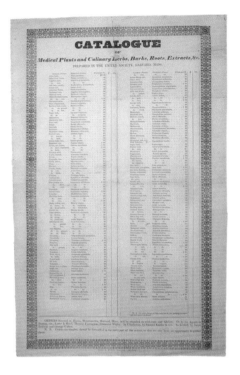

RIGHT: Black ink letterpress on off-white paper, 19⅜" × 11½". Harvard, MA, NIR.

The earliest of the bound catalogs was issued in 1845. The number of herbs that are listed is greater than that on the broadside, but not by a lot. In fact, the number of offerings between 1830 and 1890 remained remarkably constant. Although by this time it was standard practice for the community to segregate the four main culinary herbs—marjoram, sage, savory, and thyme—from the rest of the list, they are all included here (along with parsley, peppermint, spearmint, and wintergreen) with the rest of the medicinal herbs. This is because they were *used* therapeutically. The Shakers recommended that the three mint products, for example, be made into teas to treat nausea, upset stomach, and colic.[5] A glimpse into the industry's marketing strategy is found on the first page, where discounts of from 12½ percent to 25 percent are offered on bulk orders, the latter for orders over one hundred dollars.

LEFT: Black ink letterpress on yellow paper, 6⅞" × 4⅛". Harvard, MA, R-228.

The 1854 catalog was published when the industry was in full bloom. Like its predecessor, it contains both the common and botanical names for each herb along with the pharmacological properties of each. The renowned Harvard College botanist Asa Gray served as a consultant to the Harvard community, further adding to its reputation for quality and dependability. (It should be noted that the only thing that the two Harvards had in common was their name.) In 1849, when their herb house was still under construction, the Shakers reported processing just over five tons of herb material and receiving just over four thousand dollars from their agents. Five years later, with the herb house finished and this catalog in print, eighteen tons of herbs were processed.[5] Over the years, Harvard maintained a network of wholesalers in Boston and other New England cities. Journal entries indicate that about half of the community's sales went through these agents and half came to them directly.

RIGHT: Black ink letterpress on yellow paper, 6¾" × 4⅝". Harvard, MA, R-222.

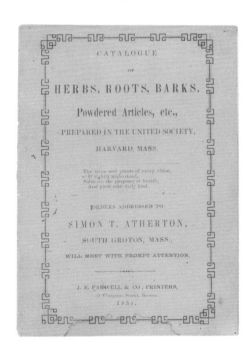

After the herbs (in all their forms—leaves, roots, barks, berries, etc.) had been harvested, they were brought to the herb house to be separated, cleaned, dried, and packaged. This postcard photograph shows the herb house around 1900. Built in 1848–1849, it was the center of industrial activity at Harvard for more than fifty years. The large quantity of wood seen stacked and protected on the left side of the building, usually thirty cords at a time, was used to fuel a large boiler that both dried the herbs upstairs and ran a hydraulic press on the lower level.

Shaker Herb House, Harvard, Mass.

Unlike any other Shaker community, Harvard formed most of its dry herbs into one-pound "bricks." This was done under tremendous pressure. It also boxed roots and barks in similarly sized packages. The five packages shown here, wrapped in blue or gray paper with labels pasted onto their ends, are bricks.[7] Harvard also pressed herbs into one-ounce "cakes," seen on the left in the image of four packages.[8] The other two are cardboard boxes, filled here with Wahoo Bark and Prickly Ash Berries. These boxes are rare survivors of a seldom-used form of packaging.

Harvard changed its postal designation three times in the 1800s, and this is a great help in determining the dates of its products. From 1849 to 1862, it was called South Groton, the name of its new post office. From 1862 to 1871, it was known as Groton Junction for the railroad intersection recently located there. After 1871, it became part of the incorporated town of Ayer. The great herb house, incidentally, burned to the ground in 1920.

ABOVE RIGHT: Photoengraving on white card stock, image size 2⅞" × 5½". Harvard, MA; LEFT: Black ink letterpress on off-white paper, pasted on gray or blue papers, 1½" × 4¼" × 8½". Harvard, MA; BELOW: Black ink letterpress on off-white paper, pasted on gray or blue papers, 2" × 2" × 1". Black ink letterpress on off-white paper, pasted on tan cardboard, 2" × 2" × 1¼". Harvard, MA.

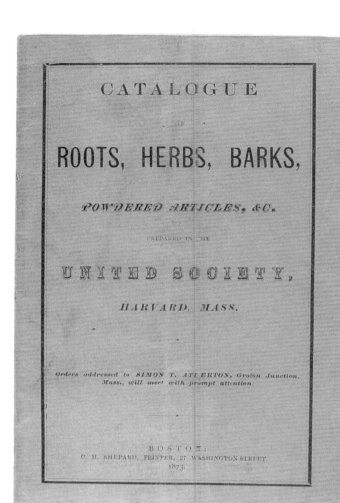

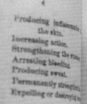

CATALOGUE.

SUBJECT TO THE FLUCTUATIONS OF THE MARKET.

FROM THESE PRICES A LIBERAL DISCOUNT IS MADE TO
WHOLESALE DEALERS AND PHYSICIANS.

Common Names.	Per lb.	Botanical Names.	Properties.
Aconite Leaves,	0 60	Aconitum napellus.	Nar. Dia.
Alder buds,	0 42	Alnus serrulata,	Deo. Alt. Ast. Ton.
Alder bark, black,	0 50	Prinos Verticillatus,	Ast. Ver. Ton.
Angelica leaves,	0 50	Archangelica atropurpurea,	Car. Sot.
do. root,	0 50	do. do.	" "
Ash bark, prickly,	0 50	Xanthoxylum Americanum,	Stl. Aro.
do. do. pulv.,	0 75	do. do.	" "
do. berries,	1 00	do. do.	" "
Ash bark, Mountain,	0 50	Pyrus Americana,	Ton. Ast.
Avan's root,	1 00	Geum Rivale,	Ton. Ast. Sto.
Balm, sweet	0 75	Melissa Officinalis,	Sto. Dis.
Balm, lemon,	0 50	Dracocephalum Moldavium,	Sto. Dia.
Balm Gilead, buds,	1 50	Pupulons balsamifera,	Pec. Bal. Sto.
Bayberry bark,	0 30	Myrica cerefera,	Err. Ast. Eme.
do. do. ground,	0 38	do. do.	" " "
do. do. pulv.	0 42	do. do.	" " "
Barberry bark,	0 50	Berberis vulgaris,	Ton. Ref. Ast.
do. do. pulv.	0 60	do. do.	Ref. Ast.
Beth root,	0 75	Trillium erectum,	Pec. Alt. Ast. Ton.
do. do. pulv.	1 00	do. do.	Ast. Ton.
Belladona leaves,	1 00	Atropa Belladona.	Nar. Dia. Ano. Diu.
Birch bark, black,	0 25	Betula lonta,	Aro. Ton.
Bitter sweet,	0 50	Solanum Dulcamara,	Nar. Her. Deo.
Bitter sweet, false,	1 00	Celastrus scandens,	A-bil. Dis.
Bitter root, Dog bane,	1 25	Apocynum androsæmifolium,	Diu. Ver.
do. do. pulv.	1 50	do. do.	" "
Blackberry root,	0 42	Rubus occidentalis,	Ast. Ton.
Blood root,	0 40	Sanguinaria Canadensis,	Err. Deo. Dia.
Blue flag root,	0 70	Iris versicolor,	Diu. Eme. Cath.
Boxwood bark	0 50	Cornus flida.	Ton. Ast.

This is the last bound catalog from Harvard, published in 1873. In the number and types of medicinal and "sweet" (culinary) herbs offered, it is nearly identical to the first bound edition, published some thirty years earlier. One significant addition is a list of synonyms with the following explanation: "Difficulties having sometimes arisen from the use of the common name being applied to different plants in different localities . . . we have appended a list of synonyms which that seller will please refer to before turning a customer away." (This is not to mention the fact that confusion over the names of some plant matter could be dangerous, even life-threatening.) The last page provides a list of wholesale merchants outside the community—in Boston, Salem (Massachusetts), and Providence—nine in all.

ABOVE LEFT: Black ink letterpress on stiff blue-green paper, 6⅞" × 4⅝". Harvard, MA, R-230; RIGHT: Black ink letterpress on white paper, 6⅞" × 4⅝". Harvard, MA, R-230.

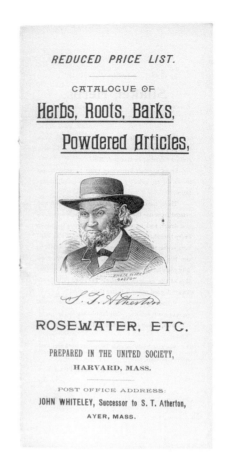

ABOVE: The narrow "Reduced Price List" is the last one the Harvard community issued. John Whitely is listed as Trustee, so we know that it dates to the 1890s. On the inside cover there is a tribute to the business and to his predecessor: "These natural remedies have supplanted and retired from use the debilitating nostrums [i.e., quack medicines] and mineral [i.e., non–plant based] drugs, and have become the welcome friends of every household. Much of the success in this business is due to the intelligence and strict integrity of the late Simon T. Atherton." In the narrowest sense, this is a bound catalog rather than a broadside, yet the format within and the pagination—with the cover counted as page one—are more in keeping with the latter. "Reduced" does not refer to the number of herbs listed, still 165, but to their prices. Most of the varieties are 10–20 percent less than their 1880s prices. One wonders if this was not some form of "going out of business" sale.

Black ink letterpress (with wood or metal engraving) on white paper, 7½" × 3⅜". Harvard, MA, R-231.

ABOVE: This broadside, "Catalogue of Herbs, Roots, Powdered Articles, &c.," is dated 188_ and is typical of the lists issued after the 1873 bound edition. There are three versions of this in the author's collection, each with nearly identical offerings (the number varying from 166 to 172), at the same prices, but with reset type. The copy illustrated has some prices changed, obviously by the Shakers, and an order filled in—both in manuscript ink. The total for this order came to $131.33. These lists were circulated among Worldly merchants and returned to Harvard for the order to be filled. On the back of this one a merchant, "C. H. & J. Price," and the dates "1883" (for order placed?) and "April/May 84" (for order filled?) are recorded in manuscript pencil.

Black ink letterpress (and pencil manuscript, verso) on white paper, 14" × 8½". Harvard, MA, R-232v.

When Simon T. Atherton died unexpectedly in 1888, after fifty years of distinguished service to the Harvard community as a Trustee overseeing the herb and other businesses, Elder Elijah Myrick took over.[9] It was Atherton who borrowed the saying from Proverbs "A good name is better than riches" and used it as his motto for the herb industry. As a personal warranty for Shaker-grown and Shaker-sold quality, in much the way that David Meacham's initials were used in the New Lebanon seed industry, the proverb was a gentle but persuasive marketing tool.

In 1889, when this small broadside was distributed, the herb business was on a downhill slide. Competition aside, there were only about a dozen men at Harvard, and more than half of them were over sixty years of age. The numbers on the Sisters' side were not much better. Then, to add further distress, Elder Myrick himself died suddenly in 1890, and an Elder from Shirley, John Whitely, had to be appointed to fill the void and oversee the herb business. Ten years later *his* health failed, and he died in 1905. Soon after this, the herb industry also expired.

RIGHT: Black ink letterpress (with wood or metal engraving) on off-white paper, 8" × 5⅛". Harvard, MA, R-233.

This is one of the most elaborate display signs that any community had printed to advertise any product. The dark area uses a flocked material—originally green but now darkened—that stands out boldly against an off-white background. Brother Warren Sparrow is listed in the 1850 census as a "nurseryman" and in 1860 as a Trustee. This sign dates from the South Groton period, 1849–1862.

LEFT: Dark green flocked cotton or wool on off-white card stock, 10½" × 8½". Harvard, MA. Courtesy of Fruitlands Museums, Harvard, MA. # S.0095.139.

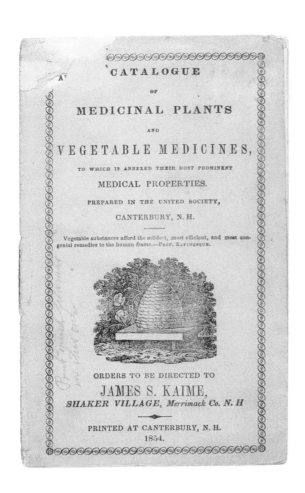

It is tempting to simply skip past the packaged herbs that Canterbury, New Hampshire, sold and to focus instead on its bottled remedies. So much remains from the latter endeavor, so little from the former. The truth, however, is that the Shakers there had a rather large business of dried and processed medicinal herbs. The first of their four catalogs was published in 1835, and the last (illustrated here) in 1854. The interior view of this one shows that the format for listing the products was similar to that of all the communities that put out an herb catalog. There are 146 varieties offered—in several forms—plus 16 extracts, 7 oils, and some ointments, pills, and syrups. Unlike any other community's catalog, this one was actually printed at Canterbury. James S. Kaime, whose name is on the cover, took over the herb business from Thomas Corbett (about whom we shall hear much in the section on bottled preparations) in 1850 and oversaw it for the following thirty years.

LEFT: Black ink letterpress (with wood or metal engraving) on yellow paper, 6¾" × 4". Canterbury, NH, R-172; BELOW: Black ink letterpress on off-white paper, 6¾" × 4". Canterbury, NH, R-172.

CATALOGUE.

Common Names.	Per lb.	Botanical Names.	Properties
Alder buds	$0 25	Alnus serrulata	Deo. Alt. Ast. Ton
Alder, black, bark	0 50	Prinos verticillatis	Ast. Ver. Ton
Angelica, leaves	0 33	Angelica atropurpurea	Car. Sto
do. root	0 50	do. do	" "
Ash, prickly, bark	0 40	Zanthoxylum fraxineum	Sti. Aro.
do. do. pulv	0 50	do. do	" "
do. berries	1 50	do. do	" "
Avan's root	0 50	Geum rivale	Ton. Ast. Sto.
Balm, sweet	0 33	Melissa officinalis	Sto. Dia.
Balm, lemon	0 33	Dracocephalum virginianum	Sto. Dia.
Balm Gilead, buds	1 00	Populus balsamifera	Pec. Bal. Sto.
Bayberry, bark	0 20	Myrica cerifera	Err. Ast. Eme
do. do. pulv	0 38	do. do	" " "
Barberry, bark	0 42	Berberis vulgaris	Ton. Ref. Ast.
do. do. pulv	0 60	do. do	" " "
Beth root	0 75	Trillum erectum	Pec. Alt. Ast. Ton.
do. do. pulv	1 00	do. do	" " "
Bitter sweet	0 50	Solanum dulcamara	Nar. Her. Deo.
Bitter sweet, false	0 75	Celastrus scandens	A-bil. Dis.
Bitter root, dog bane	0 75	Apocynum androsæmifolium	Diu. Ver.
do. do. pulv	1 33	do. do	" "
Blackberry, root	0 25	Rubus villosus	Ast. Ton
Blood root	0 50	Sanguinaria canadensis	Err Deo. Dia
do. do. pulv	0 65	do. do	" " "
Blue flag, root	0 75	Iris versicolor	Cath. Eme. Dia.
Boxwood, bark	0 50	Cornus florida	Ton. Ast
Beckbean, plant	0 50	Menyanthes trifoliata	Cath. Ton. Deo
Buckhorn malefern	0 50	Osmunda interrupta	Ton. Ast Ver
Buckthorn Syrup	0 40	Rhamnus cathartica	Diu. Cath. Ver
Bugle, sweet	0 50	Lycopus virginicus	Sty. Pec Deo. Ton.
Bugle, bitter	0 50	do. Europæus	Nar. Pec. Deo. Ton
Burdock, leaves	0 25	Arctium lappa	Sud. Dia. Ape.
do. root	0 38	do. do	Sud. Her. A-scor.
do. seed	0 30	do. do	Car. Ton.
Butternut, bark	0 25	Juglans cinerea	Cath. Deo.
Cancer root, plant	0 50	Epiphegus virginianus	Ast. Ton.
Catmint	0 25	Nepeta cataria	Dia. Sto. Car.
Caraway seed	0 30	Carum carui	Sto. Car. Aro

3

Common Names.	Per lb	Botanical Names.	Properties.
Cardus, spotted	0 30	Centaurea benedicta	Ton. Dia. Diu.
Cayenne, Afric. gro.	0 50	Capsicum annuum	Sti. Rub. Efr.
do. pure pul. No.1.	1 00	do. do	" "
do. do. No.2.	0 55	do. do	" "
Celandine, garden	0 38	Chelidonium majus	Cath. Diu. Dia.
Camomile, low	0 50	Anthemis nobilis	Ton. Sto.
Cherry, black, bark	0 25	Prunus virginiana	Feb. Ast. Ton.
Cicuta, leaves	0 33	Conium maculatum	Nar. Deo.
Clary	0 33	Salvia selara	Sto. Diu.
Cleavers	0 33	Galium aparine	Diu. Sud.
Cohosh, black	0 50	Macrotys racemosa	Alt. Deo. Nar.
do. yellow	0 75	Flavus pulvus	Alt. Deo. Nar.
do. red and white	0 75	Actæa ruba et alba	Alt. Deo. Nar.
Coltsfoot, leaves	0 50	Tussilago farfara	Exp. Pec. Dem.
do. root	0 50	do. do	" "
Comfrey	0 38	Symphitum officinalis	Pec. Dem
Cow parsnip, royal	2 00	Zizia aurea	A-spas. Ton.
do. root, masterwort	50	Heracleum lanatum	Ner. Car. Diu.
do. seed	0 63	do. do	Car. Aro.
Cranesbill, American	0 50	Geranium maculatum	Sty. Ast. Ton.
do. pulv	1 00	do. do	" "
Culver's black root	1 00	Leptandra virginica	Cath. Deo.
do. do. do. pulv	1 34	do. do	" "
Dandelion, plant	0 25	Leontodon taraxacum	A-bil. Ast. Ton.
do. root	0 42	do. do	" "
Dock, yellow, root	0 38	Rumex crispus	Ton. Deo. Her.
do. broad-leafed	0 33	Rumex obtusifolius	Cath. Deo. Her.
Dragon root	0 38	Arum triphyllum	Dia. Sti. Acr. Nar
Elder, flowers	0 38	Sambucus canadensis	Alt. Sud. Ner.
Elder, dwarf	0 30	Aralia hispida	Dia. Diu. Dem. Ton
Elecampane, root	0 25	Inula helenium	Exp. Ast. Sto.
do. do. pulv	0 35	do. do	" "
Elm, slippery, bark	0 17	Ulmus fulva	Emo. Diu. Dem. Ton.
do. do. extra	0 45	do. do	" "
do. ground	0 25	do. do	" "
do. super. flour	0 50	do. do	" "
Feverfew	0 50	Chrysanthemum parthenium	Ner. Sto.
Fern, sweet	0 25	Comptonia asplenifolia	Sto. Ast.
Fleabane	0 42	Erigeron canadense	Sty. Ton. Ast. Diu.
Flax seed, ground	0 20	Lini usitatissimum semins	Dem. Ema.
Foxglove	0 50	Digitalis purpurea	Nar. Diu

This group of labels for dried herbs, in leaf, root, and pulverized forms, is but a tiny sampling of the number and variety of the offerings in every one of Canterbury's catalogs. Although they look today like small and insignificant bits of paper, each label refers to an herb with a long tradition of uses behind it. Dandelion Root (*upper right*), for example, was a mainstay of the Shakers' business, here and elsewhere. The dried root has properties that differ from those of the flowering portion. It was used in the nineteenth century to stimulate digestion in the stomach and as a tonic (a vague term, common in nineteenth-century parlance, for refreshing or restoring "body tone"). Mandrake Root (*center*) was a powerful cathartic, but in smaller doses it was used for disorders of the liver. The cabinet for labels is one of several examples that have survived. It speaks to the degree of organization that this industry, like all the Shaker industries, demanded.

ABOVE LEFT: Black ink letterpress on yellow or pink papers, each about ⅞" × 2¼". Canterbury, NH; ABOVE RIGHT: Pine and fiberboard with printed paper, 26¾" × 17" × 4¾". Canterbury, NH. Courtesy of Canterbury Shaker Village, Inc., Canterbury, NH, # 1982.94.1.

After Isaac Hill, the editor of a farm journal, visited Canterbury in 1840, he wrote this: "The vegetables [i.e., herbs] were introduced in the shape of dried leaves pressed into a solid cake weighing a specific quantity, in shape like a brick."[10] This is puzzling because, unlike Harvard, New Lebanon, or Watervliet, this community did not have a hydraulic press (although it is likely that it did have a hand-operated one) and there are no known examples of paper herb wrappers, or pressed cakes and bricks, from there. A part of the answer may be in this bundle of sixty or so brown paper envelopes. A hand-written note from Sister Marguerite Frost reads: "These hand-made bags were for many years used by the Shakers at Canterbury, N.H. for the dispensing of herbs and dry medicines."[11] About one and a half times the size of a typical seed envelope, and similarly formed, these bags seem capable of holding an ounce or two but certainly not a pound.

Most of the herbs offered in the Canterbury catalogs were in one-pound quantities. Thus, more of the puzzle remains to be solved. Nonetheless, in 1848, when the community bought additional acreage along the Merrimac River in order to expand its "physic garden," the Shakers there were already packing—after cleaning and processing—9,327 pounds of roots for the medicinal herb trade.

ABOVE RIGHT: Stiff brown paper, string, and blue ink manuscript on white paper, 3¾" × 4¼" × 2". Canterbury, NH.

Anyone who examines comparable artifacts from the medicinal herb businesses at New Lebanon and Watervliet, New York, must be struck by how often it is difficult to tell the two apart. These, the first two Shaker communities to be formed, shared an organizational division known as a bishopric and were separated by only about thirty miles. Brethren and Sisters traveled between them for work and for visits, and not infrequently moved from one to the other. While the manuscript evidence of a shared herb industry is spare, the physical evidence is abundant.

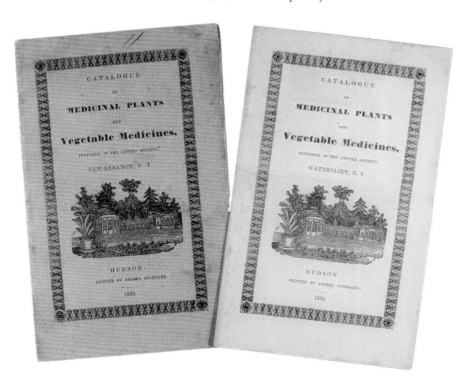

Take, for example, these two *Catalogue[s] of Medicinal Plants and Vegetable Medicines*. Both were issued in 1833, New Lebanon's first but Watervliet's second bound herb listing. Except for the color of their covers and the names of the communities, the catalogs are identical. Since both were products of the same non-Shaker printer, it is not surprising that only the title pages have had their type reset with the different community names. An epigram on this page reads: "Why send to Europe's distant shores / For plants which grow at our own doors?" (Never mind that the Shakers *themselves* sometimes purchased plant material from Europe!)

LEFT: Black ink letterpress (with wood or metal engraving) on green and yellow papers, 6½" × 4". New Lebanon and Watervliet, NY, NIR and R-427.

The one-ounce herb cakes illustrated here came from New Lebanon and Watervliet and differ only in name. Dried herbs were generally used in the form of infusions or teas; a piece of the cake was simply broken off and placed in boiling water. After the herbs were strained, the liquid was poured and sipped. Sometimes the dry material was mixed with grease to make a salve, but hot drinks were the rule.

ABOVE RIGHT: Black ink letterpress on various colored thin papers, each 1⅝" × 3¼" x⅞". New Lebanon and Watervliet, NY.

While no surviving one-pound bricks are known from either community, there are some one-pound "blocks"—sixteen one-ounce cakes packaged together—that have survived from Watervliet. This group includes "Oak of Jerusalem," used to expel worms in children; "Ground Ivy," for treatment of mild lead poisoning (thus useful for housepainters); and "Sweet Balm," used for low fevers and to assist menstruation.[12]

LEFT: Black ink letterpress on tan, blue, and pink papers, pasted on buff paper, 3⅜" × 3" × 6½". Watervliet, NY. Courtesy of The Shaker Museum and Library, Old Chatham, NY. # 99.1.14, 99.1.144, 99.1.130.

These tiny labels were printed at Watervliet and pasted onto the ends of one-pound blocks. To appreciate the large number of offerings, consider that this group represents only those herbs from the first two letters of the alphabet!

RIGHT: Black ink letterpress on various colored papers, each about 1" × 1¾". Watervliet, NY.

These colored wrappers from Watervliet held compressed herb cakes. The actual compressing machine, located in the basement of the herb house there, was probably identical to the one at New Lebanon, illustrated from *Harper's New Monthly Magazine*.[13] "That press . . . has a power of three hundred tons, and turns out each day about two hundred and fifty pounds of herbs, or six hundred pounds of roots, pressed for use."[14]

Black ink letterpress on various colored thin papers, each about 5¾" × 4⅝". Watervliet, NY.

In July of 1857, *Harper's New Monthly Magazine* published a rather extensive article about the Shakers at New Lebanon, written by Benson John Lossing, that included eighteen very detailed engravings. One of the areas that it paid particular interest to was the medicinal herb industry, with eight of the illustrations being devoted to this activity. The article reported that in 1855 about seventy-five tons of roots and herbs were pressed here—presumably using this massive piece of machinery. (Three of these presses had been installed in 1852.) Altogether, fifty acres were dedicated to growing herbs; the Shakers referred to them as their "physic garden."

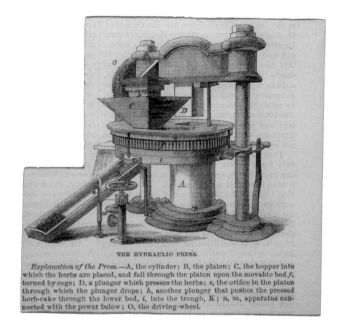

THE HYDRAULIC PRESS.

Explanation of the Press.—A, the cylinder; B, the platen; C, the hopper into which the herbs are placed, and fall through the platen upon the movable bed *f*, turned by cogs; D, a plunger which presses the herbs; *e*, the orifice in the platen through which the plunger drops; *h*, another plunger that pushes the pressed herb-cake through the lower bed, *i*, into the trough, K; *n*, *m*, apparatus connected with the power below; O, the driving-wheel.

RIGHT: Black ink letterpress (with wood or metal engraving) on off-white paper, image size 3½" × 3¼". New Lebanon, NY.

The herb house at New Lebanon was a most imposing structure. Built by the Church Family c. 1832, it had thirteen thousand square feet of floor space. Each area of the building was designed and designated for carrying out a distinct step in the process of preparing harvested herbs for sale. Cleaning, separating, and drying took place on the top floor. Next came "cracking" (or crushing), followed by pressing into compacted one-ounce cakes. This took place in the basement, where the heavy equipment was located. (Vacuum pans for extracts were also located here until a separate extract house was built in 1850.) Finally, the pressed herbs were raised to the first floor by means of platforms and pulleys. Here, in the "finishing room," they were wrapped, bundled, and stored until they were shipped. A small label press was also positioned on this main level. The herb house burned down in 1875, three weeks after the Church Family dwelling house was lost in another huge fire. Both were arsons, committed by a non-Shaker handyman at the community.

BELOW: Black ink letterpress (with wood or metal engraving) on off-white paper, image size 3¼" × 3½". New Lebanon, NY.

THE HERB HOUSE.

CATALOGUE

OF

HERBS,. ROOTS, BARKS,

POWDERED ARTICLES, &c.,

PREPARED IN THE

UNITED SOCIETY,

NEW GLOUCESTER, MAINE.

Orders addressed to CHARLES VINING, West Gloucester, Maine,
will meet with prompt attention.

PORTLAND:
B. THURSTON, PRINTER, FOX BLOCK, 82 EXCHANGE STREET.
1864.

8

	Common Names.	Per lb.	Botanical Names.	Properties.
26	Horse radish leaves,	0 14	Cochlearia Armoracia,	Dia. Acr. Sti.
56	Horse radish root,	0 28	Cochlearia Armoracia,	Dia. Act. Sti.
56	Horsemint,	0 28	Monarda punctata,	Diu. Ton.
36			Humulus Lupulus,	Amo. Ton.
	Hops,			
	Hyssop,	0 18	Hysopus officinalis,	Aro. Sti. Dia. Sto.
	Iceland moss,	0 18	Cetraria Islandica,	Pec. Dem. Ton.
	Indian hemp, root	0 40	Asclepias incarnata,	Diu. Dia.
	Indigo root, wild,	0 35	Baptisia tinctoria,	A-sep. Ton.
	John's wort,	0 18	Hypericum perforatum,	Dia. Ast.
36	Life everlasting,	0 18	Gnaphalium polycephalum,	Sto. Sud.
56	Lily root, white,	0 28	Nymphæa odorata,	Pec. Emo. Ast. Ton.
	do. do. flour,	0 40	do. do.	" " " "
56	Lily root, yellow,	0 28	Nuphar advena,	" " " "
80	do. do. flour,	0 40	do. do.	" " " "
160	Liverwort, noble,	0 80	Hepatica triloba,	Pec. Nar.
44	Lobelia,	0 22	Lobelia inflata,	Dia. Exp. Eme. Nar.
	do. pulv.,	0 35	do. do.	" " " "
	do. seed,	0 80	do. do.	" " " "
	do. pulv.,	1 10	do. do.	" " " "
56	Lovage, leaves,	0 25	Ligusticum levisticum,	Dia. Car. Sto.
100	do. root,	0 55	do. do.	Aro. Dia. Car. Sto.
	Lungwort, maple,	0 40	Variolaria faginea,	Pec. Sto. Dem. Ton.
56	Maidenhair,	0 28	Adiantum pedatum,	Pec. Ver.
	Mallow marsh, leaves,	0 28	Althæa, officinalis,	Dem. Ast.
	do. do. root,	0 28	do. do.	" "
	Mallow, low,	0 14	Malva rotundifolia,	Dem. Pec.
	Mandrake root,	0 28	Podophyllum peltatum,	-bil. Din. Nar.
80	do. do. pulv.,	0 40	do. do.	
56	Marigold, flowers,	0 28	Calendula officinalis,	Sto. Aro.
	Marsh rosemary,	0 28	Statice Caroliniana,	Ast. Ton.
	Mayweed,	0 14	Anthemis Cotula,	Ton. Dia. Sto.
70	Majoram, sweet,	0 35	Origanum marjoranum,	Sto. Aro.
	do. do. gr.,	0 60	do. do.	" "
	Melilot,	0 18	Melilotus officinalis,	Dem. Ton.
56	Moccasin or Valerian,	0 28	Cypripedium acaule,	Ton. Ner. Ano.
	do., flour,	0 40	do. do.	" " "
36	Motherwort,	0 18	Leonurus Cardiaca,	Dia. Ner. Sto.
56	Mountain Mint,	0 28	Origanum vulgare,	Sto. Aro.
56	Mugwort.	0 28	Artemisia vulgaris,	Ton. A-bil. Ner.

Sabbathday Lake, Maine, issued only one catalog of medicinal herbs, and that one was in 1864. Although in its overall size of fifteen pages it is larger than the ones issued by any other community, its contents are remarkably similar to those of other Civil War–era editions. An impressive 155 varieties are offered in one-pound packages, but unfortunately none of them, not even a single printed label, is known today. Since this community did not have the equipment to hydraulically press its own herbs, these offerings may have been bought from other Shaker villages and simply sold here.

LEFT: Black ink letterpress on white paper, 8⅞" × 5⅝". Sabbathday Lake, ME, R-358; RIGHT: Black ink letterpress and pencil manuscript on white paper, 8⅞" × 5⅝". Sabbathday Lake, ME, R-358.

FRESH HERBS,

RAISED, GATHERED, AND PUT UP BY THE UNITED SOCIETY..SHAKERS..ENFIELD, CONN.

Address JEFFERSON WHITE, (SEEDSMAN AND HERB AGENT,) Thompsonville P. O., Conn.

(On or before July, annually.)

Pressed and neatly put up in packages, from 1 oz. to 1 lb. each, as ordered.

To our knowledge, Enfield, Connecticut, put out only this one medicinal herb broadside, but it was a whopper. It measures almost two feet in height—the largest broadside that the Shakers ever used for any purpose. With 221 different herbs, many of which were available in various forms, there are altogether more than three hundred items listed. As usual, there are also four "pulverized sweet herbs," in addition to those that are also used therapeutically: "Rosemary," "Sage," "Savory," and "Thyme." As in the previous case, Enfield may have bought these herbs from other Shaker villages to sell.

Black ink letterpress on white paper, 22¼" × 17¼". Enfield, CT, R-195.

In the Shaker West only Union Village, Ohio—a few miles west of the town of Lebanon—sold bulk and packaged herbs in large quantities. This was a very large community, at times the largest of any Shaker village, East or West. With huge tracts of fertile land at its disposal and a large labor force, garden culture was a natural fit. This single-fold pamphlet tells us that herbs, generally similar to those raised in the eastern communities, were sold in half-, quarter-, and sixteenth-pound packages, and roots or barks by the pound. Brother Abiathar Babbitt (1802–1865) was in charge of the Botanical Department and published this edition. Union Village was also an important wholesale supplier for two drug firms—Dr. Louis Turner, Shaker Medicine Co., in St. Louis and S. D. Howe & Co. in Cincinnati. (We shall see some of their products later.)

RIGHT: Black ink letterpress on off-white paper, 8" × 6½". Union Village, OH, R-412.

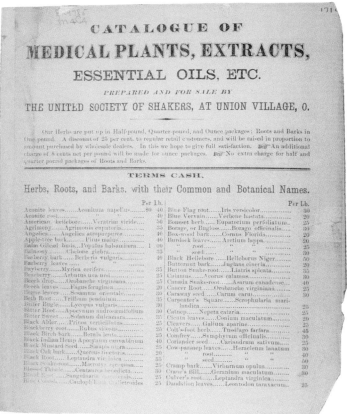

Shirley, Massachusetts, was certainly not known for producing medicinal or culinary herbs, or herbal products, for sale. In fact, this uncut sheet of five "Pure Cayenne [Pepper]" labels may be the only evidence for this activity. It is included here, rather than in the foods chapter, because its active ingredient, capsicum, was an essential element in the botanical medical practice of the extremely influential Samuel Thomson (1769–1843). Dr. Thomson believed that "cold, or want of heat," was the cause of "all disorders which the human family are afflicted with, however various the symptoms," and furthermore advocated the "purification" of the body by means of the release of impure, waste products through *all* orifices, especially by perspiration. Cayenne, of course, causes internal heat along with peripheral dilation (red skin), profuse sweating, and nasal discharge. Since this variety of pepper did not grow in cooler zones, the Shakers imported it from Africa. (Of the sixty-four plant products that were recommended by Dr. Thomson, the Shakers offered at least sixty for sale. Many of them applied his principles to their own health care as well.)

LEFT: Black ink letterpress on stiff orange paper, 9¾" × 7⅞". Shirley, MA.

PREPARATIONS FOR EXTERNAL USE

Among all the communities, New or Mount Lebanon, respectively, was almost alone in producing remedies designed for external or topical use. For convenience' sake these will be divided into those that may be called, in the broadest sense, cosmetics and those intended for palliative (i.e., soothing) application.

Imperial Rose Balm was a thick liquid or lotion made from "soap, alcohol, and [unspecified] chemical oils."[15] The origin of the formula is not known, but the business was initiated and developed at New Lebanon by Benjamin Gates (1817–1909). Brother Gates was an entrepreneurial and indefatigable Trustee of the Society for many years. In the spring of 1861 he traveled to Buffalo and New York City to purchase the necessary chemicals for making what he referred to as a cosmetic and dentifrice. We shall soon see that the idea for this combination was not a new one for this community.

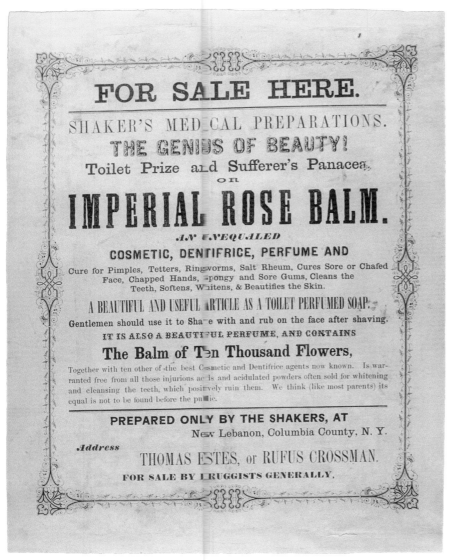

The broadside shown here, printed in 1861 (before the name of the community changed in October of that year to Mount Lebanon), lists a host of widely varied conditions that another product, a "Toilet Prize and Sufferer's Panacea," was capable of *curing*: pimples, tetters (nonspecific eruptive skin disorders such as psoriasis), chapped hands, and spongy and sore gums. It claimed further that the chief ingredient was "The Balm of Ten Thousand Flowers" (also sold, by itself, at Watervliet as a dentifrice or tooth cleanser). Apparently the panacea was bottled in two very differently shaped bottles, the shorter one embossed with the name of "Tilden & Co." on its side. This large drug firm was a neighbor, and sometime rival, of the Shakers in the *town* of New Lebanon (before the community was granted its own post office and became Mount Lebanon).

ABOVE: Black ink letterpress on yellow paper, 12½" × 9¾". New Lebanon, NY, R-317; RIGHT: Red ink letterpress on yellow paper, pasted on pale aqua glass, labels 2½" × 1½", bottle heights 6" and 4". New Lebanon, NY.

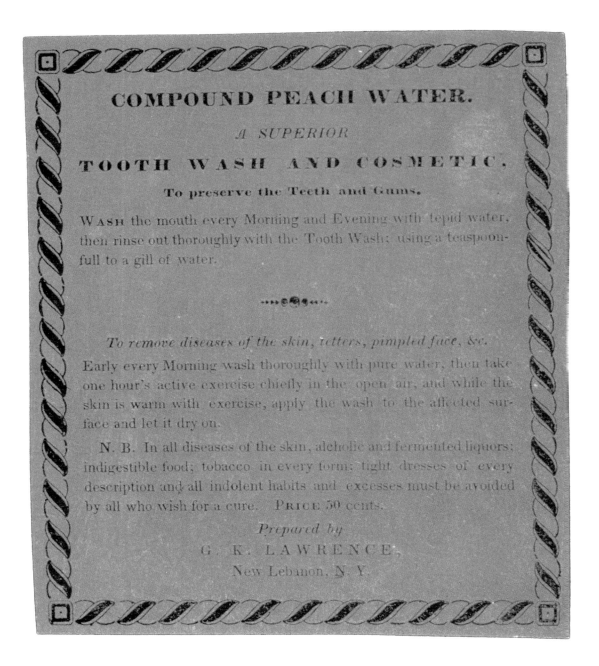

COMPOUND PEACH WATER.

A SUPERIOR

TOOTH WASH AND COSMETIC,

To preserve the Teeth and Gums.

WASH the mouth every Morning and Evening with tepid water, then rinse out thoroughly with the Tooth Wash; using a teaspoonfull to a gill of water.

To remove diseases of the skin, tetters, pimpled face, &c.

Early every Morning wash thoroughly with pure water, then take one hour's active exercise chiefly in the open air, and while the skin is warm with exercise, apply the wash to the affected surface and let it dry on.

N. B. In all diseases of the skin, alcholic and fermented liquors; indigestible food; tobacco in every form; tight dresses of every description and all indolent habits and excesses must be avoided by all who wish for a cure. PRICE 50 cents.

Prepared by
G. K. LAWRENCE,
New Lebanon. N. Y.

This label for a "Tooth Wash and Cosmetic" predates the above example by twenty-five years and is, by far, the earliest label known for any Shaker preparation. Garrett K. Lawrence, who died in 1837, was a trained physician at New Lebanon in the 1820s and 1830s. The label advises users to "Wash the mouth every Morning and Evening with tepid water, then rinse out thoroughly with the Tooth Wash." No examples of the bottle are known, but we do know that the product first appeared in a catalog issued by the community in 1836.

Black ink letterpress on orange paper, 4¼" × 3⅝". New Lebanon, NY.

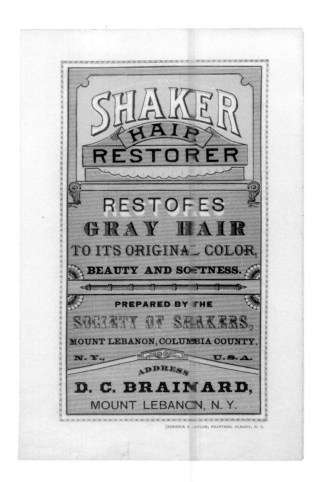

In January of 1885, Brothers Benjamin Gates and DeWitt C. Brainard went to New York City to see the irrepressible A. J. White—about whom we will soon hear a good deal—to discuss putting up a new White product, a hair restorer. A preparation that promised to "[restore] gray hair to its original color, beauty, and softness" was a curious choice for the Shakers to be involved with, but toward the end of the century they were driven to replace the income previously generated by their seed and herb industries.

Over the next fourteen months, the two Shakers made several more visits to White. In the journal that Elder Giles Avery kept, he wrote on March 8, 1886: "We had a meeting this evening . . . to decide what work should be carried on in the coming season as a source of income for the family." Four days later, he recorded part of the response to this meeting: "Second family trying to start their hair restorer business."

Although the Second Family succeeded in getting it launched, the business evidently lasted for only a short time. After an initial burst of advertising, along the lines of "Gray hair may be Honorable, but the Natural Color is Preferable," and "It is not a dye, but when used according to directions it will restore gray hair to its original color," no sales were recorded after about 1890. Nonetheless, the family undertook the enterprise with confidence, for the name of a valued Trustee for the Society appeared once again as an implied warranty. D. C. Brainard served in this capacity until his death in 1897.

ABOVE LEFT: Color lithography on white paper, 9¼" × 5⅞". Mount Lebanon, NY, R-314; ABOVE CENTER: Color lithography on white paper (on cardboard), 8" × 3" × 1¾". Mount Lebanon, NY. Courtesy of Hancock Shaker Village, Inc., Pittsfield, MA; ABOVE RIGHT: Blue ink letterpress and lithography on white paper, pasted on amber glass, 7½" × 2⅝" × 1½". Mount Lebanon, NY; LEFT: Black ink letterpress on white card stock, 3½" × 5½". Mount Lebanon, NY. Courtesy of Hamilton College, Burke Library, Clinton, NY.

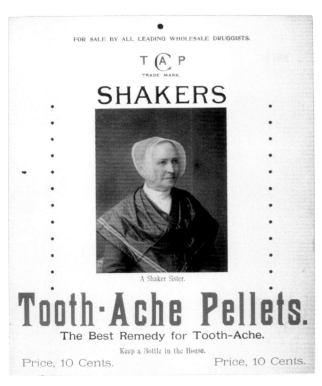

A Shaker Sister.

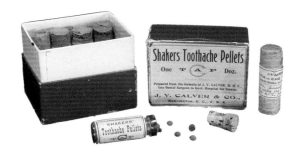

There is a fascinating story behind "Shakers Tooth • Ache Pellets," one that unites Mount Lebanon with a former member and that transcends both time and distance.[16] The story begins in 1850, when James Valentine Calver, along with his parents and eight brothers and sisters, joined the Society at New Lebanon when James was eight. Recent emigrants from England, the family took many, often widely divergent paths over the ensuing years.

James remained at the community until 1871, filling roles such as woodworker and schoolteacher. Nine years after he left, and at the age of forty-one, he enrolled in the Baltimore College of Dental Surgery. After receiving his degree he established a practice in Washington, D.C., and also married. Nevertheless, over the years, he stayed in contact with his former home, and in 1888 he brought the Mount Lebanon Shakers an idea for a palliative medicine for topical application in the event of toothache. The formula that he developed and found to be especially effective contained three active ingredients: pure wood creosote, oil of eucalyptus, and oil of cloves.

Trustee Benjamin Gates, always looking for ways to produce income for his community, took a keen interest in Dr. Calver's remedy. He agreed to manufacture, package, and wholesale it with a percentage of the profits returned to Calver. The product was launched by Mount Lebanon in 1890, but in 1897 Calver took over the production phase from his base in Washington. Following his death in 1913, his wife—herself a chemist—continued manufacturing "Shakers Tooth • Ache Pellets," first in Washington and then in Los Angeles, where she relocated in 1922.

ABOVE LEFT: Black and red ink letterpress with photoengraving on white card stock, 11" × 9". Mount Lebanon, NY, NIR; RIGHT: Black and red ink letterpress on off-white paper pasted on cardboard, 1¾" × 2¼" × 2" (each vial height about 1⅞"). Mount Lebanon, NY; BELOW LEFT: Red ink letterpress and/or wood engraving on white paper, 8" × 9½". Mount Lebanon, NY, NIR; RIGHT: Black and red ink letterpress (with wood or metal engraving) on light green card stock, 7¼" × 12⅛". Mount Lebanon, NY, NIR.

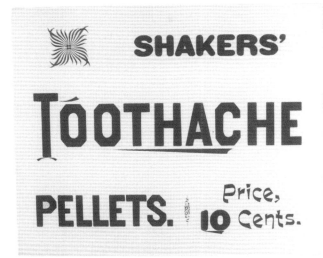

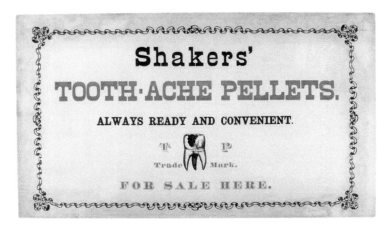

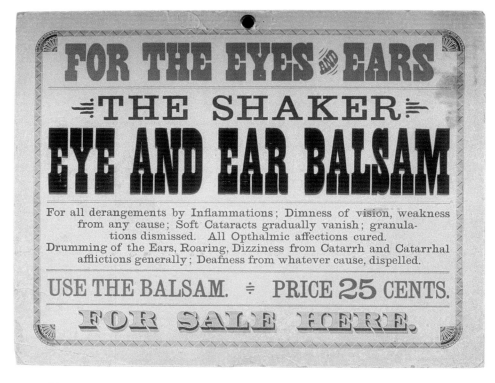

We know little about "Laurus Eye Water" and less about "The Shaker Eye and Ear Balsam." Both New Lebanon and Watervliet sold the former remedy as an emollient, meant to lubricate the inflamed eye and allow for "easy and natural" motion. The Shakers referred to it as a "vegetable mucilage" (which is actually a sticky or gummy substance, the opposite of a lubricant). Watervliet, which first advertised "Laurus Eye Water" for sale in 1837, issued this broadside. New Lebanon, by contrast, did not offer it until its catalog of 1860. It may be presumed that the active ingredient derives from lauric acid, a fatty acid extract of laurel leaves—hence its name.

Black ink letterpress on white paper, 8⅜" × 4⅞". Watervliet, NY, R-433.

This large and attractive display card is all that seems to have survived of the Shaker Eye and Ear Balsam. Richmond's *Bibliography* names Watervliet as its place of origin but offers no reason for this or other information.[17] The brass grommet at the top shows that the card was designed for hanging.

Multicolor letterpress on off-white card stock, 10¾" × 14". Watervliet, NY? R-432.

By far, most Shaker extracts—produced almost exclusively at New Lebanon and Watervliet—were in liquid form and were intended for internal use. (They will be surveyed in the next section.) New Lebanon also put up fifty-eight *solid* extracts, "in lb. and ½ lb. earthen jars" such as the one illustrated. It was especially difficult, however, to control the potency of solid extracts in ointment form. The 1851 catalog issued by both communities states: "Perhaps no other class of medicines presents so many difficulties, and certainly none which have given such universal dissatisfaction on this point as Vegetable [i.e., herbal] Extracts; and some of our best [World's] physicians have nearly abandoned their use on this account." They go on to assure the medical profession, for whose purchase these were meant, of the stringent controls that the Shakers employed in every phase of preparation to assure freshness and purity.[18]

Black ink letterpress (with wood or metal engraving) on off-white paper, pasted on white ceramic, 3¼" × 2⅞". New Lebanon, NY. Collection of the United Society of Shakers, Sabbathday Lake, Maine. #95.1234a.

Hamamelis (extract of Witch Hazel):

Per barrel	$0.65 per gallon.
Five or ten gallons	.75 per gallon.
Per gallon	1.00
Per quart	.40
Per pint	.25
Per half-pint	.15
Price of barrel	1.00 extra.
Price of jug, one gallon	.15 extra.
Price of jug, two quarts	.12 extra.
Price of jug, one quart	.10 extra.

Address, ARTHUR BRUCE,
East Canterbury, N. H.

Witch hazel is still in use today, although not to the extent that it was a hundred years ago. Witch hazel is both a small shrub and the name of the distillate from its leaves and bark. It is a mild astringent—a topical agent that contracts fibers in the skin and constricts the small peripheral blood vessels—made mostly from the shrub variety known as *Hamamelis virginiana*. The plant extract is placed in an alcohol solution in an eight-to-one ratio (by volume). Dried leaves of *Hamamelis* were sometimes used in the late nineteenth century to make a hot tea that was supposed to help a variety of disorders, from amenorrhea to gastric ulcers.[19]

Canterbury manufactured witch hazel for sale beginning in the 1880s. It was relatively cheap and easy to make, requiring only a basic distilling apparatus. This made for an easy and profitable venture at a time when there were only ten Brothers left but still seventy-six Sisters. The Shakers first advertised it in 1893, and by 1900 enormous quantities were being made for sale.[20]

The price list illustrated here is located in the back of an eight-page Canterbury catalog from about 1910 that mainly advertises handmade goods for sale. Not only was witch hazel offered by the gallon; it was also offered by the *barrel*. Elder Arthur Bruce (1858–1938) was one of the last two male members at Canterbury and the last male Trustee. (Elder Irving Greenwood died a year later.) Sales of witch hazel ceased in 1917, but the Shakers continued to make it for their own use into the 1940s.

ABOVE RIGHT: Black ink letterpress on white paper, page size 6" × 4¼". Canterbury, NH, R-154; ABOVE LEFT: Black ink lithography on white paper, pasted on clear glass, heights 8½" and 9". Canterbury, NH.

LEFT: The Shakers left us no information about the manufacture and/or distribution of their Transparent Court Plaster. The product itself is actually *not* a court plaster—a term reserved for a material, backed with adhesive, that we will find in the next item to be considered—but a thick sheet of a cellophane-like substance that adhered to the skin when moistened and covered and protected cuts, scrapes, and burns. A formula given in an 1878 issue of *The Manifesto*, a Shaker periodical, calls for French isinglass (fish gelatin), warm water, glycerine, and tincture of arnica. This would yield a substance that would, in fact, *look* like this product. Since there is no Trustee's name on the folded paper package, we can say only that it dates to the Mount Lebanon era, sometime after 1861.

Black ink letterpress on light yellow paper, 3⅝" × 2¼". Mount Lebanon, NY.

A good deal more is known about the Shaker Soothing Plaster. A. J. White was a Worldly distributor of mostly Shaker-made remedies and will be considered in greater detail later. This product was first advertised in his catalog for 1882, where it sold for twenty-five cents. It last appeared in 1897, the year before White died, for the same price.

The trade card, shown front and back, recommends the Shaker Soothing Plasters for "Backache, Lumbago, Muscular Rheumatism, [and] all pain of lameness in any part of the body . . . they never produce a blister, but merely 'draw' through the skin the underlying inflammation that causes the pain." The essential element was a thin sheet of India rubber, perforated with many small holes to make it flexible, wrapped in woven linen. One would never know any of this from the front of the trade card, for it was simply meant to attract a potential consumer's eye. Trade cards were late-nineteenth-century advertising giveaways that also played into the collecting mania of that era.

CENTER: Black ink letterpress on linen, 5½" × 8⅜"; RIGHT: Blue ink letterpress and color lithograph on off-white thin card stock, 5" × 3⅛". All Mount Lebanon, NY, R-333 (card).

PREPARATIONS FOR INTERNAL USE

Until Mount Lebanon formed a partnership with A. J. White in the mid-1870s, Canterbury may have been the largest maker of proprietary medicines of all the Shaker Societies.[21] The name Thomas Corbett is almost synonymous with the medicinal business there. He was an unusually gifted Brother who, like many of his Brethren and Sisters, developed his talents to their fullest capacity while living communally.

Born in 1780, Brother Thomas moved to the Enfield, New Hampshire, Shaker community with his family when he was ten. In 1894 he moved south to Canterbury, where he lived the remainder of his life. In 1813, when he was thirty-three, he was directed by the Canterbury Ministry to "qualify himself" to become that community's first trained physician. He became apprenticed to a World's physician and studied with several herbalists inside and outside Canterbury. He also took classes at one or two medical colleges. Although he did not receive a formal degree, he was highly regarded by other, trained physicians and always called doctor.

When he returned to Canterbury permanently, he went about laying out and planting a physics garden for the community's own use. Sometime in the 1830s he greatly enlarged the gardens for full-scale cultivation of medicinal herbs—first for simply producing dried and packaged herbs ("simples") and later for processing extracts for complex formulations ("compounds").

In the early 1840s, Corbett—with help from a well-respected physician at Dartmouth College, Dr. Dixi Crosby—modified a formula provided by a physician at New Lebanon and developed what came to be known as "Corbett's Shakers' Compound Concentrated Syrup of Sarsaparilla." The syrup was made up from about ten herbs, chiefly sarsaparilla root (*Aralia nudicaulis*) plus Epsom salts, sugar, and alcohol, all in an aqueous solution. (Several formulas with varying ingredients have been found for this preparation at Canterbury. This is not surprising, since it was made there for at least sixty years.) The liquid, awarded a United States patent in 1886, was mostly sold in aqua-colored bottles, embossed on its sides: "No. 1 Shaker Syrup" and "Canterbury, NH, U.S.A." Although the ending date for production of the syrup is often given as 1895, the example illustrated—alongside its packing box—dates to sometime after passage of the 1906 Pure Food and Drug Act. Conforming to that landmark legislation, the alcohol content, 10 percent, is clearly stated on the label.

Black ink letterpress on off-white paper, pasted on aqua-colored glass, height 7¾". Black ink letterpress on off-white paper, pasted on wood, 9½" × 13" × 7¼". Canterbury, NH.

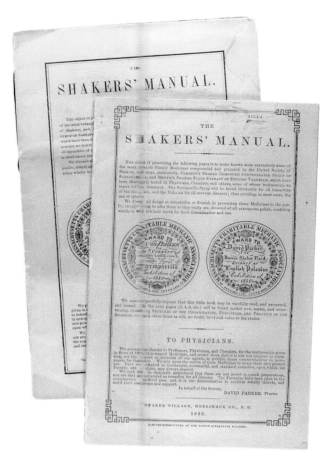

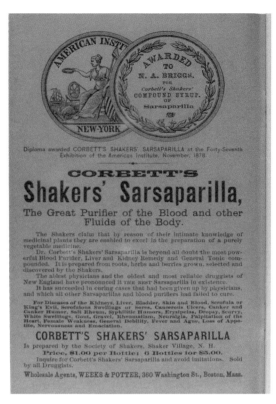

Today we call Corbett's preparation a "panacea" or cure-all, for its label lists fourteen disparate disorders that it claims to be useful for. Its main attribute was "invaluable for all impurities of the blood." This ambiguity was often the justification for *any* cathartic, of which "Syrup of Sarsaparilla" was but one. Nonetheless, it received high marks from many of the World's physicians and was awarded a medal in 1850 (through Trustee David Parker) by the Massachusetts Charitable Mechanic Association, based on the recommendations of three of their physicians.

This was half the reason for these two *Shakers' Manual*(s) — the other being "Brown's Shaker Fluid," put up by their sister community at Enfield, New Hampshire. These "manuals" were little more than eleven and twenty-two pages of endorsements for the two products and were issued in 1851 and 1852.

ABOVE LEFT: Black ink letterpress (with electrotypes) on tan papers, 8⅞" × 5½" (*top*) and 9½" × 6⅛" (*bottom*). Canterbury, NH, R-182 and R-181.

In 1882, the Shakers published Mary Whitcher's *Shaker House-Keeper*, a thirty-two-page "recipe book" that was something of a Trojan horse. While it included many helpful hints on food preparation, its main purpose seems to have been to slip in advertising for medicines, some of which were not even made by the Shakers. The inside cover, shown here, features the second medal that the Shakers received, this one in 1878, for exhibiting at the "American Institute" in New York City. Dr. Dixi Crosby, a friend of the Shakers for about fifty years by now, offered an endorsement for the syrup that *he* had once actually helped to develop!

ABOVE: Black ink letterpress (electrotype) on heavy pink paper, 7" × 4½". Canterbury, NH, R-1428.

Accounts for "Syrup of Sarsaparilla" (in liquid form) show that about five thousand bottles and twenty one-gallon jugs of syrup were sold in 1861, with sales recorded up to 1895. On the other hand, there are no figures for sales of sarsaparilla in lozenge form. This author suspects that the product was manufactured and sold by a non-Shaker firm, licensed by the Shakers. Canterbury had registered a trademark for sarsaparilla lozenges in 1886. On the yellow box a notation reads: "This sarsaparilla in syrup form has been on the market for 50 years." This indicates that the lozenges were marketed at least into the 1890s.

RIGHT: Black ink letterpress on yellow paper, pasted on yellow paper-wrapped cardboard, 3¼" × 4¾" × 2¼". Canterbury, NH. Courtesy of Hancock Shaker Village, Inc., Pittsfield, MA. # 74–58.2.6.

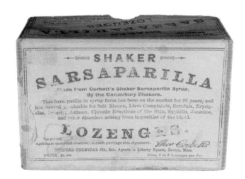

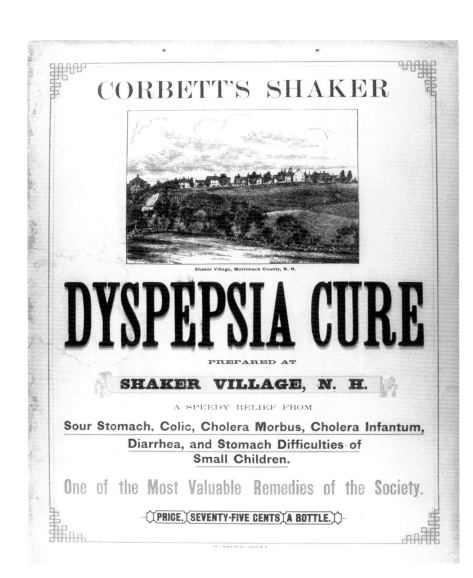

CORBETT'S SHAKER

Shaker Village, Merrimack County, N. H.

DYSPEPSIA CURE

PREPARED AT

SHAKER VILLAGE, N. H.

A SPEEDY RELIEF FROM

Sour Stomach, Colic, Cholera Morbus, Cholera Infantum, Diarrhea, and Stomach Difficulties of Small Children.

One of the Most Valuable Remedies of the Society.

PRICE, SEVENTY-FIVE CENTS A BOTTLE.

CORBETT'S SHAKER
Dyspepsia Cure.

A speedy relief and radical cure of

Sour Stomach, Colic, Cholera Morbus, Cholera Infantum, Diarrhœa, and Stomach Troubles of Small Children.

Dose for an adult, two to four teaspoonfuls every half hour until relieved.

This medicine is prepared wholly from vegetable substances, and is safe in all conditions.

Prepared at
SHAKER VILLAGE, N. H.

Price, 75 Cts. per Bottle.

Thos Corbett

Three other products put up by Canterbury that bore the name of Thomas Corbett were "Dyspepsia Cure," "Wild Cherry Pectoral Syrup," and "Vegetable Family Pills." Although we do not know the formula for the first, we may be quite sure that it included herbs whose primary effect was to act as a laxative. Many herbs have this effect, and catharsis was the standard approach to dyspepsia in the nineteenth century. The Shakers actually referred to this condition as "the national disease of Americans." Fatty meat products, cooked in animal fats, dominated diets at that time and, along with other nutritional factors beyond our scope, surely contributed to disturbed digestion.

ABOVE LEFT: Black and red ink letterpress (with wood or metal engraving) on off-white card stock, 14" × 10⅞". Canterbury, NH, NIR; ABOVE RIGHT: Black ink letterpress on off-white paper, 4½" × 1⅝". Canterbury, NH; BELOW LEFT: Black ink letterpress on off-white paper, pasted on blue paper-wrapped cardboard, 7¼" × 8¾" × 6½" (box). Canterbury, NH.

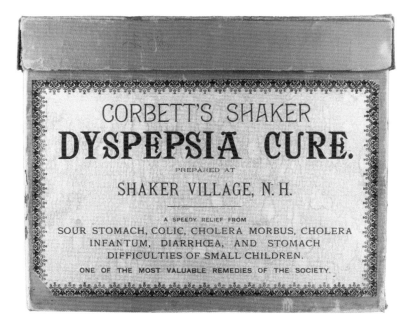

CORBETT'S SHAKER
DYSPEPSIA CURE.

PREPARED AT

SHAKER VILLAGE, N. H.

A SPEEDY RELIEF FROM

SOUR STOMACH, COLIC, CHOLERA MORBUS, CHOLERA INFANTUM, DIARRHŒA, AND STOMACH DIFFICULTIES OF SMALL CHILDREN.

ONE OF THE MOST VALUABLE REMEDIES OF THE SOCIETY.

The formula for "Wild Cherry Pectoral Syrup," a treatment for coughs and congestion, was patented by Canterbury in 1883. The medicine included the bark of the wild cherry tree, tinctures of antimony, Cicuta, bloodroot, ipecac, and morphine.[22]

ABOVE RIGHT: Black ink letterpress on yellow paper, pasted on aqua-colored glass, height 5½"; black ink letterpress on yellow paper (covering a bottle), height 5½". Canterbury, NH; BELOW RIGHT: Black ink letterpress on off-white paper, pasted on light blue paper-wrapped cardboard, 6" × 5¾" × 5½". Canterbury, NH. Courtesy of Canterbury Shaker Village, Inc., Canterbury, NH.

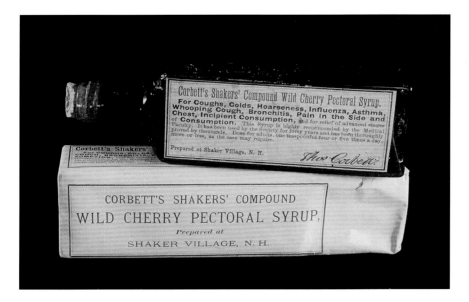

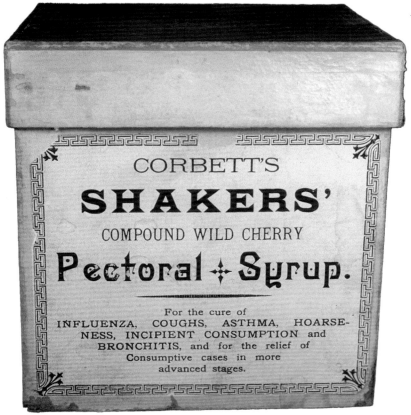

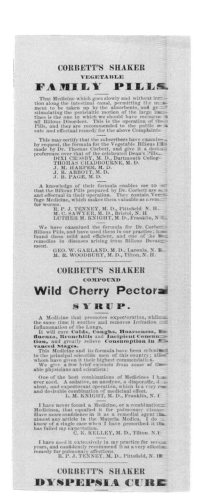

Nothing is known about the "Family Pills"; this package insert, probably for one of the other Corbett's products, is all that remains today. All three products seem not to have been very successful, but since the Shakers have left no sales figures for them, this is only speculation. Certainly none of the three was advertised the way "Syrup of Sarsaparilla" was. With the exception of many never-filled, embossed but unlabeled "Pectoral Syrup" bottles, plus the few items shown, virtually no evidence of these remedies is known to exist today.

LEFT: Black ink letterpress on off-white paper, 8¼" × 3⅛". Canterbury, NH, R-176.

In addition to the Corbett's products, the Canterbury Society made dozens of medicines that were *not* patented (in fact, all were listed in the U.S. Pharmacopoeia), formulating them beginning around midcentury. This group of labels and bottles represents but a small sample of them. All the bottles were removed from the infirmary at the community in the 1960s, by which time outside physicians were depended on for medical care and few homemade remedies were needed. It should be noted that no Shaker community made glassware; all of it was bought from the World over the years. This probably accounts for the fact that every example here has a different size and shape.

ABOVE RIGHT: Black ink letterpress on variously colored papers, 1⅓" × 3⅛" (Wintergreen) and 3" × 3½" (Rose Water). Canterbury, NH; BELOW: Black ink letterpress on variously colored papers, pasted on glass, height 3½" (Sassafras), height 10" (Rose Water). Canterbury, NH.

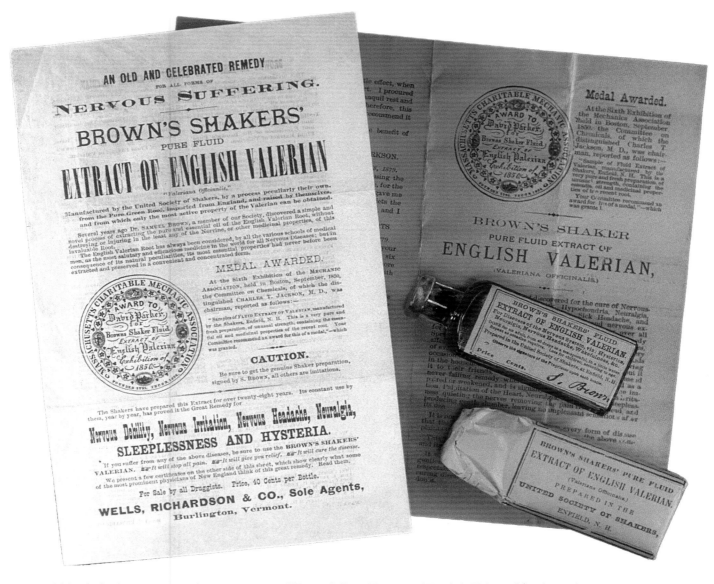

It would be difficult to overstate the importance of "Brown's Pure Extract of English Valerian" (and, to a lesser extent, "Shaker Anodyne") to the economy of Enfield, New Hampshire, toward the end of the nineteenth century.[23] Both remedies were based on an extract from the root of English valerian, *Valeriana officinalis*, one of three varieties of this plant that grow in the Northeast. Brother Samuel Brown, of Enfield, developed the formula in the 1840s, and although he died in 1856, the preparation carried his name for more than fifty years.

The valerian essence had to be extracted by means of heat, and this usually inactivated it. Brother Brown developed a technique, previously unknown in pharmacy, for keeping the extract potent, thus assuring the success of his preparation. The extract was known as a stimulant of the nervous system, and it was used for such disorders as "Lowness of Spirits [depression], Hypochondria, Neuralgia, Hysteria, and Restlessness." At times, opiates or henbane were added for their sedative or anodyne effect. Samuel Brown received many of the same types of endorsements that Thomas Corbett had and used them in his advertising in much the same way. He also was able to assure a large margin of profit by making the extract for $2.25 per dozen bottles and selling it for $3.75 per dozen. When one considers that as many as fifty thousand bottles were sometimes sold in a year, at a 67 percent profit, it is clear that the economic impact was substantial. The two-sided broadside on the left side of this group dates to the 1890s, when the extract sold for forty cents a bottle. The two bottles—one in its original wraps—lie atop an insert that, when folded, was enclosed with each bottle. These bottles are from the time when the business was in full flower, after 1880 and until about 1910.

ABOVE LEFT: Black ink letterpress (with wood or metal engraving) on white paper, 8½" × 5½", NIR. Black ink letterpress (with wood or metal engraving) on tan paper, 8" × 8⅝", NIR; TOP BOTTLE: Black ink letterpress on pink paper, pasted on light aqua-colored glass, height 3½"; LOWER PACKAGE: Black ink letterpress on yellow paper, height 3½". All Enfield, NH.

An interesting note on the reverse side of the broadside (opposite page) says: "Beware of all Anodynes, and similar compounds which contain opium. These invariably do more harm than good." The matter of opiates and similar additives is confusing, since at times both the valerian extract and "Shaker Anodyne" contained them. The main ingredients of both were alcohol (about 50 percent) and valerian, but as this handwritten formula for the anodyne shows, it also had vinegar, simple syrup (a saturated solution of "sugar water"), and *morphine*. The extract sometimes had opium and/or henbane added to it too. This author suspects that "Shaker Anodyne" was, at some point, made outside the community by licensing agreement. In an interesting side note, at the top of the formula someone wrote: "NB [note well] Please keep to yourself." Clearly, this formula was not meant for public knowledge.

RIGHT: Black ink manuscript on off-white paper, 8" × 5". Enfield, NH.

The two "Oil of Valerian" bottles and the wormwood bottle date to the 1880s. "Essence of Wormwood" was used as a topical preparation on wounds, for disinfecting and soothing them. The "Extract of Valerian" bottle is an early example of this remedy, pre-1870, before the time that it went into large-scale production and was packaged in short, square bottles. One final note is in order before we leave Enfield: the community grew huge quantities of an herb called yellow dock root and sold it to one of the largest proprietary drug makers in America, J. C. Ayer & Co. in Lowell, Massachusetts. The company used it in the manufacture of its very popular "Ayer's Sarsaparilla."

BELOW: Black or blue ink letterpress on off-white or tan paper, pasted on clear or aqua-colored glass, height 7½" (Wormwood). Enfield, NH.

In the 1870s, Sabbathday Lake, Maine, was feeling pressure from two quarters: the community was trying to recover from recent financial setbacks caused by dishonest and injudicious Trustees, and it was in need of a larger, brick-made dwelling. Into this void rode Brother Benjamin Gates in the summer of 1881 with a proposal the Sabbathday Lake Shakers could hardly refuse. His by-now benefactor A. J. White (whom we met in the section on soothing plasters) had developed a formula for a laxative that he asked Mount Lebanon to manufacture for him, but for unknown reasons the "Mother Church" passed it along to Sabbathday Lake. Called "The Shaker Tamar Laxative," it was a fruit-based product but will be considered here since it was, clearly, a medicine and not a food. Sabbathday Lake took up the challenge in hopes of changing its economic fortunes and, wasting no time, put up the first batch for sale in the fall 1881.

Tamar Laxative consisted mainly of dried tamarind fruit, prunes, and cassia bark. In addition there were hyoscyamine (a derivative of the herb henbane and a powerful narcotic) and flavorings—sugar and oil of wintergreen.[24] One machine

formed these ingredients into a roll, and another machine sliced the roll into disks or lozenges. These were dried and boxed. Unfortunately, no examples of the product or its packaging have survived. What has survived are a number of colorful display cards, the rare package insert, a few road signs, and this well-worn small packing box.

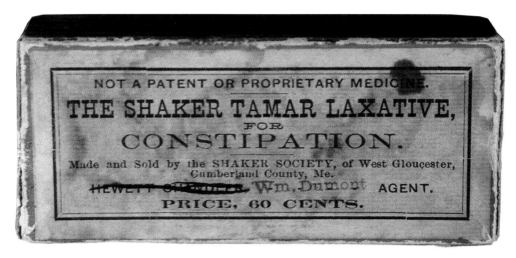

Writing about the industry in 1962, Sister Frances Carr of Sabbathday Lake said: "Stenciled signs advertising the preparation appeared discretely [*sic*] along the highways of southern Maine."[25] The box is interesting because the name of Brother Hewitt Chandler—who started the business but apostatized six months later—is lined out and the name of Elder William Dumont (who died in the faith in 1930) is added. The product sold all around Maine, south to Philadelphia, and west to Chicago between 1881 and 1890 but generated only a moderate profit for the community. Small batches continued to be made through the 1890s with the last one recorded in 1901. High hopes not withstanding, Tamar Laxative never achieved the success that the other A. J. White products did at Mount Lebanon.

PAGE 80 TOP LEFT: Color lithograph on off-white card stock, 11" × 8⅞". Sabbathday Lake, ME, NIR; TOP RIGHT: Black ink letterpress on tan paper, 8" × 4¼". Sabbathday Lake, ME, R-362; LOWER LEFT: Black and red paint on pine, 5½" × 14". Sabbathday Lake, ME; PAGE 81 ABOVE: Black ink letterpress on off-white paper, pasted on red paper-covered cardboard, 3¾" × 1⅝" × 2½". Sabbathday Lake, ME. Collection of the United Society of Shakers, Sabbathday Lake, Maine.

The Shakers' well-deserved reputation for being earnest, sincere, clever, hardworking, and trustworthy generally led them to be successful in their diverse business ventures. This next example, however, shows such traits were not always beneficial to the challenges facing the Shakers. In this case it was their trust in others that failed them. In 1879 a former member of the Pleasant Hill, Kentucky, community, along with the pharmacist she later married and a friend of theirs named T. K. Hardman—called, for some unknown reason, the "Indian Doctor"—came to the Shakers with a scheme whereby Pleasant Hill would produce a preparation called "Aromatic Elixir of Malt." There were a few "provisions," though; the three would provide all the raw material (barley), sell the necessary machinery for making the elixir to the Shakers, and also sell them "proprietary rights" for exclusive sales in (only!) four Kentucky counties. The Shakers took the bait.[26]

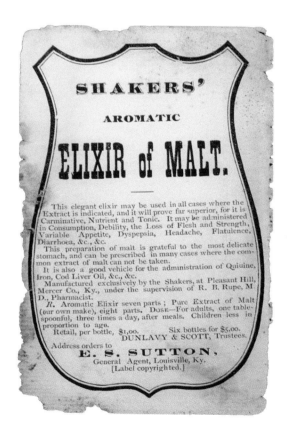

The claims made on the label are not out of step with those made for the nostrums of that age: "This elegant elixir may be used in all cases where the Extract is indicated, and it will prove far superior, for it is Carminative [i.e., causing expulsion of gas from the stomach and intestines], Nutrient, and Tonic"—a vague term, popular throughout the nineteenth century, for increasing tension or contraction of muscle or tissue.

The product was introduced in 1880, and only after a substantial investment of Pleasant Hill's capital and labor. Sales were so disappointing that by 1883 the business was discontinued altogether. This was certainly not the first or the last time that the Society would be taken advantage of, and yet, somehow, the Shakers' faith always moved them forward.

RIGHT: Black ink letterpress on off-white paper, 4½" × 3". Pleasant Hill, KY.

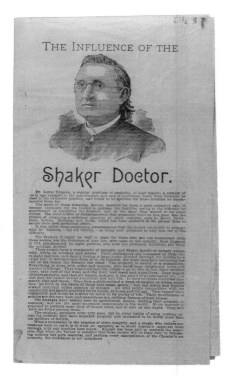

THE INFLUENCE OF THE

Shaker Doctor.

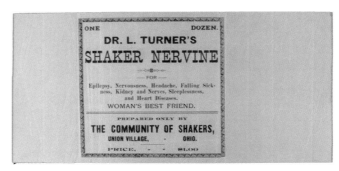

Union Village, Ohio, was the only western Shaker Society with a notable medicinal herb industry, but the accounts of its bottled products are a bit confusing because it is difficult to separate what the Shakers made themselves versus what was made using their name.[27] Three individuals are associated with the medicine business there: Elder Peter Boyd, Dr. Louis Turner, and Dr. Stewart D. Howe. Elder Boyd (1806–1889) served as a Trustee for Union Village in the mid–nineteenth century, the heyday of medicine sales, and was responsible for the whole herb enterprise.

Dr. Louis Turner, "a regular graduate of medicine, of high repute" (in his own words), was not a Shaker but a manufacturer of medicines in the World. His plant and/or offices were in St. Louis, Missouri; this was never specified. In his pamphlet *The Influence of the Shaker Doctor* he claims that his economic ties to Union Village stemmed from his previous inability to obtain sufficient quantities of raw material for his proprietary medicines. He goes on to list several preparations, including "Shaker Nervine," "White Wonder Soap," and "Shaker Wonder Herbs," that were made by the community. The Nervine, a carton label for which is illustrated here, is called "A Brain and Nerve Food, Which Soothes and Quiets the Nervous System." There is no information on its formula other than the assurance that it contains neither bromides nor opium.

Dr. S. D. Howe was also a non-Shaker medicine manufacturer; his company was located in Cincinnati, Ohio. Howe's claims were less extravagant than Turner's, and his "Shaker Sarsaparilla" was supposedly formulated "with the proper ingredients, as directed by the United States Pharmacopoeia." This broadside then says that "its most extensive use and application is in the treatment of secondary syphilis . . . chronic rheumatism, scrofulous [i.e., skin] affections [infections/afflictions?], and *other depraved conditions* of the body" (emphasis added). As a warranty of quality, Peter Boyd's signature was printed on this and on every bottle label.

This "Shaker Cough Syrup" broadside has been attributed to New Lebanon *and* Union Village but tradition, paper, typography, and the similarity to the last line of text of the sarsaparilla broadside all point to the latter. It states that in addition to wild cherry bark, squills (a tonic and expectorant then, a *rat poison* now), and seneca snakeroot (another expectorant), there is rhubarb, "a novel ingredient in a cough mixture." The only reference to the Shakers is an indirect one saying that the product has been "in use for a number of years among the several families of the Society of Shakers." This could mean almost anything!

ABOVE LEFT: Black ink letterpress on off-white paper, 9" × 5". Union Village, OH, R-416; ABOVE RIGHT: Black ink letterpress on blue paper, 6¼" × 23½". Union Village, OH; BELOW LEFT: Black ink letterpress on off-white paper, 11" × 9¾". Union Village, OH, R-419; BELOW RIGHT: Black ink letterpress on off-white paper, 10¾" × 7". Union Village, OH, R-312 and R-418.

Shaker Sarsaparilla.

For Sale by Druggists Generally.

SHAKER
Cough Syrup

For Sale by Druggists Generally.

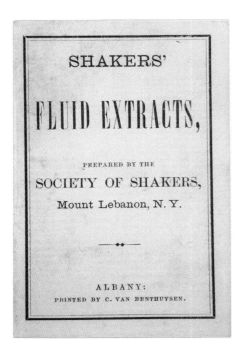

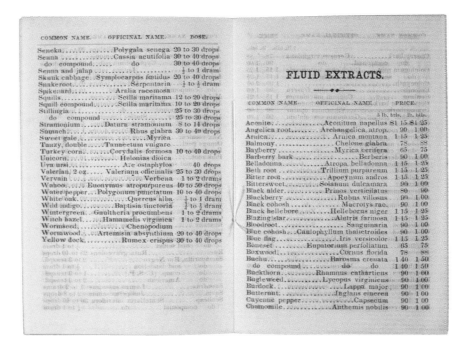

It would take a small book to fully explore the medicinal herb business at New and Mount Lebanon, but we will limit this section to a brief overview. This community was the seat of the Central Ministry, the ultimate authority for the entire movement up to the 1940s. It was also the major innovator among the eighteen long-lived Shaker Societies. One of its chief achievements was the successful integration of some aspects of established medical practice alongside some aspects of home-remedy medicine—and all in a communal setting. There was simply no precedent for this.[28]

At the beginning of the nineteenth century, New Lebanon had several "trained" physicians, although the extent of their training is open to question. Among these were Drs. Eliab Harlow and Isaac Crouch. In 1812, they started a "physic garden," raising herbs for their own use. Early manuscript records show that they used recipes that were brought from Europe, along with those of local Native Americans. In 1821, an Order of Physicians and Nurses was established, thus formalizing these roles within the community's organizational scheme.

By the 1830s, the early physicians had been succeeded by Drs. Garrett Lawrence and Barnabas Hinckley. When medicinal herbs evolved into an industry in 1830, it was Hinckley who took charge of it. Samuel Thomson's *New Guide to Health or Botanic Family Physician* had been published eight years earlier, and its influence was enormous. Thus, a demand for plant products had preceded the Shakers' ability to supply them.

In the late 1840s, an unschooled Shaker "chemist" named Alonzo Hollister introduced a technology to New Lebanon that revolutionized the medicine business there—the vacuum pan. For the first time extracts could be obtained in concentrated form, without deactivating them, by cooking them at a lower temperature in a vacuum. Thereafter, "prepared in vacuo" had a special cachet. In 1850, a four-story extract house (distinct from the herb house) was built. This pamphlet for fluid extracts, published in 1861 or 1862, packed a punch for its size. Not quite four inches high and only eight pages long, it lists 135 fluid extracts twice: first with the common name, then with the "officinal" [*sic*] (recognized by the pharmacopoeia) name, and dose, and then substituting price per bottle for dose. The interior view of the pamphlet shows how small the type had to be to accommodate all this.

ABOVE LEFT: Black ink letterpress on off-white paper, 3⅞" × 2⅝". Mount Lebanon, NY, R-299; ABOVE RIGHT: Black ink letterpress on white paper, 3⅞" × 5¾" (open). Mount Lebanon, NY, R-299.

This is the one-pound bottle of "Extract of Indian Hemp" with its cardboard container. Printed on both labels is "Prepared in Vacuo." There are actually three different and unrelated plants of this name: black, white, and foreign Indian hemp. Their properties, hence their uses, are also very different, and there is no indication which one this is. The Shakers, at some time, offered all three. This is an example of how empirical the "botanic" approach was and, therefore, of its inherent hazards.

RIGHT: Black ink letterpress on white and blue papers, pasted on clear glass and green paper-wrapped cardboard, bottle height 3". New Lebanon, NY.

This "Price List" from 1874 contains a staggering 402 medicinal preparations for sale on its three pages. Up to four forms are offered for each preparation: dried herbs, pulverized herbs, fluid extracts, and solid extracts. This is the final list that Mount Lebanon published, for they soon formed partnerships with Lyman Brown and A. J. White—from the World—and stopped producing these drug preparations. (We will soon see that the Shakers did put up some other "finished," or compounded, medicines in the 1890s.)

RIGHT: Blue and red ink letterpress on white paper, 10¾" × 8½". Mount Lebanon, NY, R-300.

Within a few years of starting its medicinal herb industry in 1830, New Lebanon was already putting up a few compounded and distilled products for sale. Illustrated here is the back page of its 1833 *Catalogue of Medicinal Plants and Vegetable Medicines*, where five products are described. Labels for each are shown (although it is noted that this Sarsaparilla label is for the "simple," not the compounded product). Sarsaparilla and Black Cohosh were syrups, Rose and Peach Water were distillates, and Slippery Elm was a finely ground powder that was quite popular at the time. It was dissolved in hot water to make a kind of tea that was supposed to be useful for "all inflammations of the mucous membranes."

LEFT: Black ink letterpress on variously colored papers, 6½" × 8" (open pamphlet) and 6¾" × 4¼" (Slippery Elm herb wrapper). New Lebanon, NY.

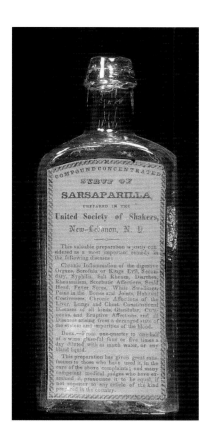

"Sarsaparilla Syrup" was a mainstay in nontraditional nineteenth-century medicine, as has already been discussed, and in this business New Lebanon kept pace with the societies at Canterbury and Union Village—as well as non-Shaker nostrum peddlers. All these bottles are embossed with "Shaker Preparation" on one side panel, "New Lebanon, N.Y." on the other, and all have the open pontil marks of early mold-blown glassware.[29] In 1855, two Brothers at New Lebanon reported that they had printed and trimmed *seven thousand* "Sarsaparilla Syrup" labels in one two-month period.

ABOVE: Black ink letterpress on blue paper, pasted on aqua-colored glass, height 6¾". New Lebanon, NY. Courtesy of Hancock Shaker Village, Inc., Pittsfield, MA.

These three labels that were used for dried herbs have several characteristics in common: all are members of the nightshade family, all are poisons in "high" doses, and all were sold only to qualified physicians and pharmacists. Deadly nightshade was used as an anodyne and sedative, henbane as a potent sleep inducer, thorn apple for asthma and nervous disorders. All were highly dose dependent, and so any of them could kill as well as cure!

RIGHT: Black ink letterpress on blue, green, and pink papers, 2⅜" × 4", 2⅜" × 3¾" and 2¾" × 4", respectively. New Lebanon, NY.

These two bottles typify the packaging of fluid extracts in the 1830s and 1840s. Since there is no community identification on them, and New Lebanon and Watervliet shared labels, their contents could have been made at either. Johnswort is commonly found in the eastern United States and was used either topically as an astringent or ingested as a sedative or diuretic. It was thought to be the best remedy for urinary tract infections in the century before antibiotics. Comfrey was recommended for digestive or menstrual disorders.

ABOVE: Black ink letterpress on white papers, pasted on light aqua-colored glass, approximate heights 6". New Lebanon, NY. Courtesy of Hancock Shaker Village, Inc., Pittsfield, MA.

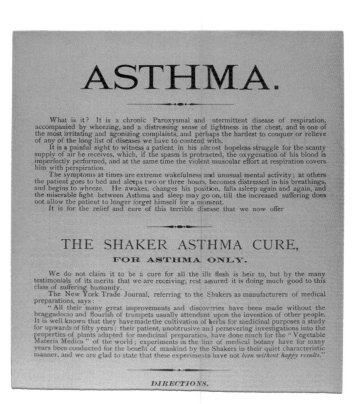

ASTHMA.

What is it? It is a chronic Paroxysmal and intermittent disease of respiration, accompanied by wheezing, and a distressing sense of tightness in the chest, and is one of the most irritating and agonizing complaints, and perhaps the hardest to conquer or relieve of any of the long list of diseases we have to contend with.

It is a painful sight to witness a patient in his almost hopeless struggle for the scanty supply of air he receives, which, if the spasm is protracted, the oxygenation of his blood is imperfectly performed, and at the same time the violent muscular effort at respiration covers him with perspiration.

The symptoms at times are extreme wakefulness and unusual mental activity; at others the patient goes to bed and sleeps two or three hours, becomes distressed in his breathings, and begins to wheeze. He awakes, changes his position, falls asleep again and again, and the miserable fight between Asthma and sleep may go on, till the increased suffering does not allow the patient to longer forget himself for a moment.

It is for the relief and cure of this terrible disease that we now offer

THE SHAKER ASTHMA CURE,
FOR ASTHMA ONLY.

We do not claim it to be a cure for all the ills flesh is heir to, but by the many testimonials of its merits that we are receiving, rest assured it is doing much good to this class of suffering humanity.

The New York Trade Journal, referring to the Shakers as manufacturers of medical preparations, says:

"All their many great improvements and discoveries have been made without the braggadocio and flourish of trumpets usually attendant upon the invention of other people. It is well known that they have made the cultivation of herbs for medicinal purposes a study for upwards of fifty years; their patient, unobtrusive and persevering investigations into the properties of plants adapted for medicinal preparation, have done much for the "Vegetable Materia Medica" of the world; experiments in the line of medical botany have for many years been conducted for the benefit of mankind by the Shakers in their quiet characteristic manner, and we are glad to state that these experiments have not *been without happy results.*"

DIRECTIONS.

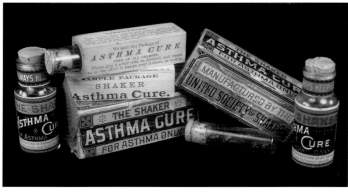

The "Shaker Asthma Cure" was manufactured in the 1880s and 1890s. The root cause or causes of asthma are not well understood or agreed on even today. "Four distinct, although overlapping answers have endured side by side . . . a primary disorder of the lungs, an allergic condition, a disease associated with environmental irritants, and a disease linked to emotional distress."[30] An estimated 15 million people in the United States are presently affected by asthma, and it is not a recent phenomenon. The Shakers never published their formula for this preparation, but most of the testimonials on the reverse side of this broadsheet speak of the asthmatic's newfound ability to sleep well. Therefore, it can be reasonably assumed that the pellets contained one of the three potential poisons discussed above, or lobelia—an antispasmodic herbal. The two smaller, plainer packages illustrated are sample sizes. (The offering of samples was a marketing strategy used in the World and adopted by the Shakers.)

ABOVE LEFT: Black ink letterpress on tan paper (detail), 14" × 6¾". Mount Lebanon, NY, NIR; ABOVE RIGHT: Color lithograph on paper, wrapped on wood, and black ink letterpress on off-white paper, wrapped on wood, lengths 3½" and 2¾". Mount Lebanon, NY.

The "Shaker Vegetable Remedy" made two strong claims for itself: pills (or "pellets") were sugarcoated, and they were "strictly vegetable." Both claims were probably justified, but the simple fact is that they were really one more in a long line of laxatives that filled drugstore shelves in the 1880s and 1890s. Both broadsides cautioned the public that this product "should not be confounded with the cheap [and] drastic cathartics with which the markets are flooded." Each vial was priced at thirty cents and enclosed in a brightly colored cardboard box.

RIGHT: Black ink letterpress on off-white and tan papers, 8½" × 5½" and 7¾" × 5". Color lithograph on paper, wrapped on cardboard, length 3". Mount Lebanon, NY, R-318 and NIR.

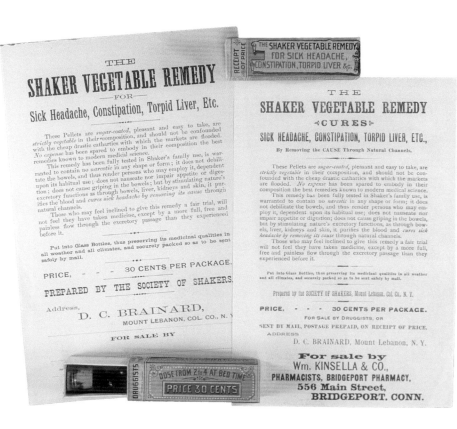

It might seem more appropriate to consider "Shaker's [*sic*] Pure Lemon Syrup" in the next chapter, which is devoted to foods—and this large broadside certainly promotes that aspect of the syrup—but it had another use. Lemon Syrup's early history is intertwined with that of "Imperial Rose Balm," discussed earlier. Both were the brainchildren of Brother Benjamin Gates. On the same business trip during which he bought material to start production of Rose Balm, he also bought "5 barrels of sugar, 6 gross of bottles & lemon oil & citric acid . . . preparatory to making Lemon Syrup for the [East] family to sell."[31] A month later, Elder Giles Avery—now in charge of production, and the recorder of this journal as well—writes of "starting it as a sale business."[32] While this 1861 broadside boasts that "one table spoonful of the Syrup in a Tumbler of Water, furnishes a Superior Lemonade at one-twelfth the cost of Lemonade commonly made at Hotels," there was the other, *medical* use for it. *The Shaker Manifesto* for 1881 states: "It [Lemon Syrup] is suitable to all stomach diseases; is excellent in sickness." No sales figures, and only this single bottle, are known to survive from what was likely a very modest venture.[33]

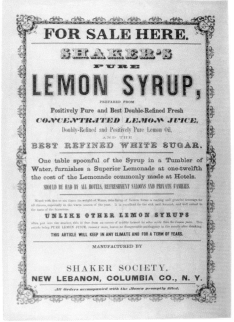

LEFT: Black ink letterpress on yellow paper, 18½" × 12¾". New Lebanon, NY, R-319; RIGHT: Black ink letterpress on yellow paper, pasted on clear glass, height 9¾". New Lebanon, NY. Courtesy of Hancock Shaker Village, Inc., Pittsfield, MA.

Of the last three remedies manufactured in large quantities at Mount Lebanon, "Norwood's Tincture of Veratrum Viride" (V.V.) was the first to be started and the last ended. In all, this drug had an *eighty-year* association with the community. The tincture was an extract from the commonly found white hellebore plant (*Veratrum viride*) in an alcohol solution. The main active ingredient was an alkaloid that depressed the respiratory and heart muscles. Since high fever was a common feature of many infectious diseases, some physicians believed that slowing the heart rate would lower this fever—and it often did. Of course this was at a time when there were no antibiotics to address the underlying *cause* of the fever—infection. The problem here was that V.V. was a poison in high enough doses and was, therefore, a dose-dependent remedy. In the nineteenth century, electrical stimulation to reverse severe bradycardia was unknown, and drug reversal was too slow, so the results of this "cure" were sometimes fatal.

Dr. Wesley C. Norwood (1806–1884) opened his medical practice in Cokesbury, South Carolina, in 1830, and became a vocal proponent of V.V. in medical circles throughout the Deep South. He began to bottle and sell the preparation himself in 1850, and in 1858 he contracted with the Church Family at New Lebanon to do this for him. A short time later the Civil War altered his life, and he served as a physician for four years in the army of the Confederacy (losing both sons in the conflict). When he returned home, he learned that the Shakers had kept an accurate accounting of the royalties that had been earned during his absence. As a result, he instantly became one of the wealthiest men in postwar South Carolina.

The Shaker account books show that by the early 1870s up to two thousand pounds of roots and five hundred gallons of 85 percent alcohol were processed in large vats that required sixteen days to "stand." This was enough to fill more than fourteen thousand four-ounce bottles of V.V. Sometime in the mid-1870s, and for reasons not recorded, Dr. Norwood granted full rights of ownership of his formula to the Shakers.

The 1906 Pure Food and Drug Act mandated changes to the labeling of all medicines, and many, especially those with *only* high alcohol content to recommend them, went out of business. The labels for V.V., however, clearly state that they contain 75 percent alcohol and also have the word "Poison" printed in diagonal red letters. A billhead in the author's collection shows that manufacture of V.V. continued into the 1940s. (Mount Lebanon closed in 1947.)

LEFT: Black ink letterpress (and manuscript) on white paper, 8" × 5". Mount Lebanon, NY, NIR.

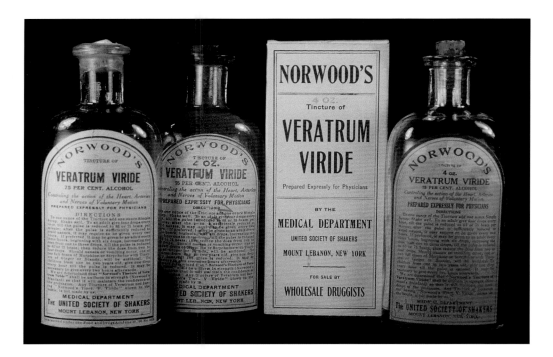

All three of these bottles, plus the box that came with the example on the right, date to sometime after passage of the 1906 Pure Food and Drug Act.

LEFT: Black (and red) ink letterpress on off-white papers, pasted on clear glass, height 5⅜", and black ink letterpress on tan cardboard, height 5½". Mount Lebanon, NY.

Dr. Norwood issued the first of three editions of *The Therapeutical Powers and Properties of Veratrum Viride* beginning around 1855. The one illustrated here is the third edition and was published in 1857. Next to it is the fourth edition, 1858, the first one issued by the New Lebanon Shakers. On the right is the twelfth and final edition from 1936. Over the eighty-year span, the format for these became increasingly sophisticated. The earliest one consists of a defense of V.V. plus many endorsements from other physicians. The last edition begins with a professional-looking "Table of Contents," followed by chapters on V.V.'s history, pharmacology, case reports, and only a few endorsements. One thing that *all* the advertising makes very clear over the years—this dangerous drug was sold only to physicians.

BELOW: Black ink letterpress on (respectively) heavy tan, blue-green, and gray papers, 7½" × 4⅝", 9" × 5⅝", and 8⅜" × 5¾". Wesley C. Norwood (*left*) and Mt. Lebanon, NY (*center and right*). NIR, R-1100, R-1097.

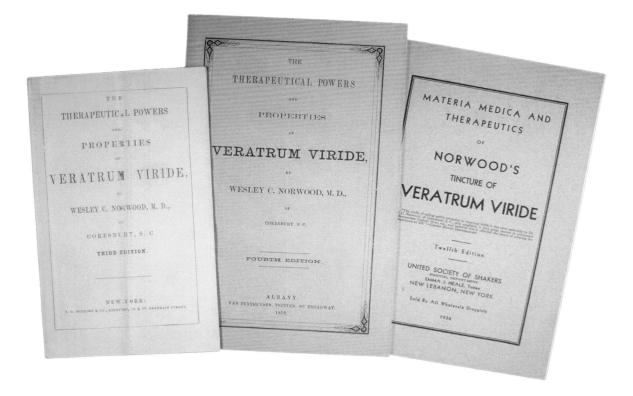

If the herbal medicine enterprise at New or Mount Lebanon deserves a book of its own, as I asserted earlier, then Lyman Brown and A. J. White surely each deserve their own chapter. Brown was a pharmacist by profession (and a Quaker by faith). He and White entered separately into agreements with the Shakers at Mount Lebanon to manufacture products that each man was responsible for, but the two men's lives and businesses were intertwined after 1875. This illustration of a letter from 1873 is the earliest known piece of ephemera from Brown's business, the making of "Seven Barks," which he claimed to have started in 1869. The letter reads: "Thou canst make thy remittance after the medicine is sold and if there is a refund I will refund to thee."

The early formula for "Seven Barks" claimed that it was derived from the seven different-colored layers of the bark of hydrangea, a formula devised by a Dr. Franz Gauzwein of Germany. This was almost certainly hogwash. The remedy was essentially a cathartic with muscle-toning, nerve-calming, skin-clearing, and expectorant properties. The Shakers used eight plant ingredients from their vast storehouse of herbs to make it: black cohosh, bloodroot, blue flag iris, butternut, goldenseal, lady's slipper, mayapple, and sassafras. It contained no alcohol. Also, Dr. Gauzwein was a fictitous character—common coin for nostrums.

In a curious aside to his medicine business, Elder Giles Avery noted the following in his journal in the fall of 1886: "Benjamin Gates goes to Pleasant Hill [Kentucky] . . . to assist the society there . . . to cancel indebtedness[.] He had some months since helped them to some $20,000.00 of Dr. [Lyman] Brown's money, of New York, secured to Brown by a mortgage of a valuable land tract [at Pleasant Hill]."[34]

RIGHT: Black ink letterpress and manuscript on white paper, 8⅞" × 5½". Lyman Brown, NY.

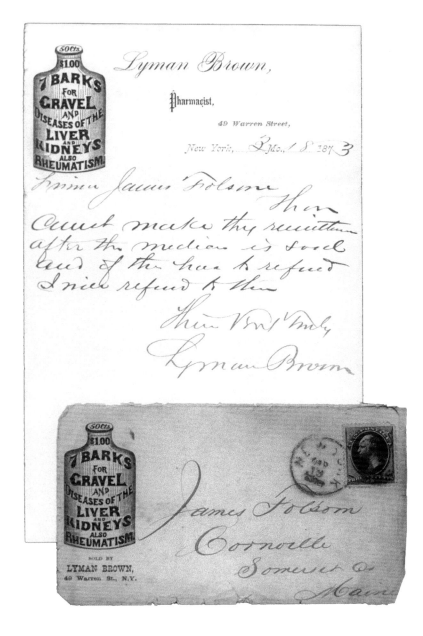

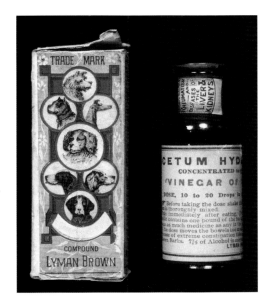

This is the style of box that was used throughout the marketing history of the product; the bottle label changed to "Lyman Brown's Compound" around the turn of the century. Brown died in 1906, the year that the Pure Food and Drug Act was passed, but since "Seven Barks" was not a poison and did not contain alcohol, it was not subject to those provisions. Each highly concentrated three-ounce bottle sold for sixty cents, and this price did not change for thirty years.

LEFT: Black and red ink letterpress on white paper, pasted on clear glass, height 3¼", and color lithograph on paper, pasted on cardboard, height 3¼". Mount Lebanon, NY.

This eight-page package insert is quite an elaborate affair for what it is. Along with instructions in English, German, and French it gives a brief history of the product—dropping now the bogus story about Dr. Gauzwein, "one of nature's noblemen." Yet there is humor here: "Seven Barks searches out the cause of that miserable dyspepsia which keeps you in bad temper, makes you wish you didn't have to eat to live, and takes the snap out of your muscles." The insert was printed in 1911. It is uncertain how long the remedy was made, but in the mid-1930s Brown's son was in charge of a business entity called "The Brown Herb Co., Inc."

RIGHT: Black ink letterpress on dark tan paper, 6½" × 8". Mount Lebanon, NY, R-310.

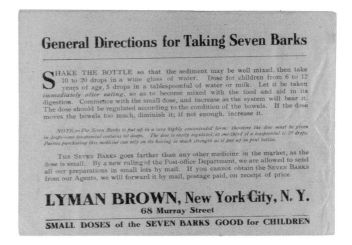

Lyman Brown issued an almanac almost every year between 1881 and 1905. None has yet been found for 1897 or 1899 or 1901–1904. These sometimes presented visual puns on the word "barks," showing seven dogs or seven sailing barques. They were typical of the almanac fare of the day: a monthly calendar with lunar cycles, fanciful looks at historical events or monuments, anecdotes, and—of course—advertising for Seven Barks with endorsements and testimonials. All were giveaways sponsored by Lyman Brown.

BELOW: Color lithograph on stiff papers, 4¾" × 3¼" (*upper left*) and 6¼" × 4½" (*lower right*). Mount Lebanon, NY.

When he died in 1898, Andrew Judson White left a conflicted legacy: scoundrel, impoverished peddler, man of the world, corporate success. Had he been more of a self-promoter, he also would have been a legend. Little is known about his early life, but by the time he met up with the Shakers, he had worked for several large proprietary drug firms in New York State, had stolen secrets from one and material from another, had been convicted of crossing state lines to avoid prosecution, and may have served time in jail (the court records burned many years ago).[35] In the late 1860s he appeared in lower Manhattan, where he tried to start a drug-making business. Soon he met Lyman Brown, who was a pharmacist in the same place, and "acquired" the title of "Dr." even though he had never received formal training in any profession. When Trustee Benjamin Gates visited him in the spring of 1875, White was working out of a tiny, shabby shop making a preparation that he called Mother Seigel's Syrup.

Mount Lebanon's Church Family had suffered a disastrous fire only months before, and Brother Benjamin was searching for a new source of revenue for the family and the community. A deal was struck between the two men: Mount Lebanon would produce White's medicine according to his formula, using material from its own herb gardens, and would bottle it; White would purchase all his finished product from them and market it. Moreover, Gates pledged two thousand dollars of "venture capital" in exchange for Seigel's Syrup being rebranded as The Shaker Extract of Roots. White's formula was supposedly developed more than twenty years earlier (and may have borrowed heavily from those used by the firms where he worked at the time) and consisted of sixteen ingredients. All these, except for aloes, borax, and salt, were found among Samuel Thomson's "botanicals"; the major herbs were black cohosh root, dandelion root, poke root, and sassafras. They were diluted in simple syrup, a saturated sugar solution, rather than in the more commonly used alcohol.

White's main claim for his product was that it purified blood that was tainted by dyspepsia. In other words, the "logic" was that constipation caused poisoning of the body by not allowing the elimination of waste products. It is no surprise, then, that the Shaker Extract was simply one more laxative in a market saturated with them.

Elder Giles Avery recorded that on March 15, 1876, less than a year after White and Brother Gates had made their agreement, Mount Lebanon "put up the 1st batch of Dr. A. J. White's medicine, a branch we are just launching into." In the months leading up to this the Shakers had invested another two thousand dollars "to fix up [extract] building, repair extract works, put in a new engine, new boiler, etc. etc. to enlarge capacity for working."[36] The community's optimism and faith in this remedy would be rewarded many times over in the years ahead.

At the time when production began, there were about ninety-four men and women living at the Church Family. By the time of White's death, in 1898, only forty-five remained, and most of them were younger than sixteen or older than sixty. Part of the irony of the White-Shaker connection is that while the fortunes of the former skyrocketed, those of the latter were in progressive decline. By 1890, when White could rightfully boast that he had sales agents in eighty-four countries, the Shakers had already closed three of their villages, and more closings were just around the corner.

One final bit of irony is that in the 1890s the Shakers had largely abandoned their herbal medicine trade everywhere *but* at Mount Lebanon, in favor of handcrafted goods. A. J. White's business, on the other hand, had grown to the extent that manufacturing plants for the extract were also flourishing in Canada, England, and France.

In the twentieth century, A. J. White, Ltd., underwent a succession of ownerships, the fortunes of each rising and falling with the world economy. The Shakers continued to ship barrels of the processed herbs used in the extract into the second decade of the twentieth century, and then the record fades. After about 1940 the extract was no longer a viable product, although its proprietary rights are still held—most recently by Smith, Kline & Beecham.

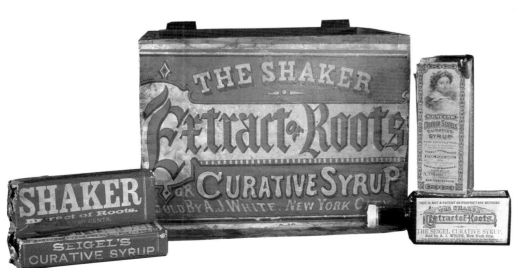

The packages and packing box illustrated probably date to the 1880s. The packaging changed little, in the United States at least, until the end of the nineteenth century.

Color lithograph (box) on paper, pasted on wood, 7½" × 9¾" × 8¼". Gold ink letterpress on red paper (*left*), wrapper on cardboard over glass, height 5¼". Black ink engraving on off-white paper (*right*), pasted on cardboard, height 5¼". Mount Lebanon, NY.

In contrast to the previous examples, these—from a slightly later period—show what the product packaging looked liked for sales outside the United States. For all sales abroad, White resorted to the moniker of Mother Seigel, a fictitious name based on an event that he had almost certainly invented and one that he had used, early on, to "explain" the special powers of his nostrum. He claimed to have met Frau Edith Seigel in Berlin, Germany, in 1868. This "gentle old lady" explained how she was herself cured of impurities of the blood many years earlier by a combination of locally picked herbs.

ABOVE: Color lithograph on white cardboard (*lower center*), height 5½". Mount Lebanon, NY.

Mother Seigel's Syrup also came to the world market in pill and tablet form, packaged in cardboard, metal, and glass containers.

BELOW: Blue ink lithography on off-white cardboard (*lower right*), 2½" × 2½" × 1¼". Mount Lebanon, NY.

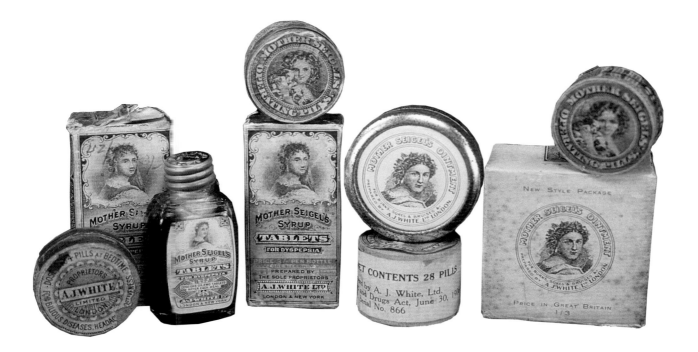

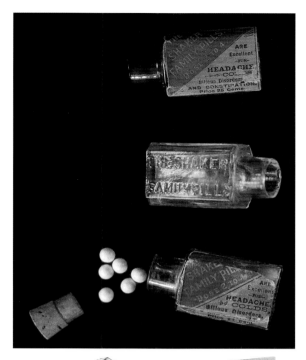

For the U.S. market White called the pill form of his extract Shaker Family Pills (although there is no evidence that Mount Lebanon was involved in making these). The pills were put up in small corked bottles that sold for twenty-five cents apiece. A colorful trade card was given away in hopes of stimulating interest in it.

ABOVE: Color lithograph on paper, pasted on amber and aqua-colored glass, height 2¼", and color lithograph on card stock, 5" × 3". Mount Lebanon, NY.

A series of annual almanacs along with a variety of other booklets were issued between 1875 and 1918. Some of them were printed entirely in French or German. In all, some sixty bound publications are known, along with a host of other advertising gimmicks ranging from tiny thimbles to large brass clocks, all with "Mother Seigel's Syrup" prominently featured. This is a tiny sampling of the almanacs printed for White's American clientele.

LEFT: Black ink and color lithograph on heavy off-white and blue papers, 6"x 4⅜" (lower center). Mount Lebanon, NY.

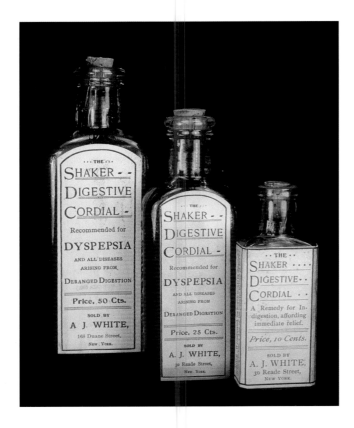

This paper was originally folded and packed inside the box or wrapper for a large bottle of Mother Seigel's Syrup. Instructions for its use are printed in sixteen languages, including Greek, Chinese, and Hebrew, demonstrating its worldwide sales.

ABOVE: Black ink letterpress on dark tan paper (detail), 9¼" × 27½" (full size). Mount Lebanon, NY.

Around the turn of the previous century the less assertive words "Digestive Cordial" were substituted for "Curative Syrup" in the United States. For foreign markets, the word "Curative" was simply dropped. These three bottles, priced at ten, twenty-five, and fifty cents each, were sold in paper wrappers in the United States.

LEFT: Blue ink letterpress on off-white paper, pasted on light aqua-colored glass, heights 4¼", 5¾", and 7". Mount Lebanon, NY.

Food Products

The Food Products Industry

No other shaker endeavor produced the astonishing range of goods that the food production industries did (and in the case of Sabbathday Lake, Maine, continue to do—although the range there now is a very narrow one). It goes without saying that every community was deeply committed to food production from the day that its Society was organized, since the societies were generally formed by the coalescence of several adjacent farms, each of which was *already* producing food. This is what farmers *do*. As large collective farm-villages, the Shaker communities simply figured out how to divide the work so that all Believers would be fed. Eventually, there was more food than was needed to meet their own needs and, as with garden seeds, the Shakers innovated in order to raise cash for their communities.

Converting a family (or here, Family) business into an industry was another matter entirely. The best available evidence indicates that the earliest effort in industrial food production occurred at New Lebanon, in 1828, and this involved dried sweet corn.[1] Corn had always been a vital grain crop for the Shakers' own sustenance, but when they began to prepare it in dried form for the retail and wholesale markets, a large-scale, coordinated effort was required. Edward Andrews, in his landmark 1933 publication, wrote: "At first the process consisted merely of boiling the cobs in great iron kettles, cutting the kernels off with hand knives, usually three-bladed affairs screwed to a vise [illustrated] and then drying them in the sun on large boards. A drying house was erected in 1840. Large

wheeled platforms [rolled] out of this house so that the corn, spread thinly over them, could be exposed to the sun at will. It was then raked at intervals to insure even drying . . . At a later period the process was mechanized by the introduction of steam-operated corn-cutting machines." Dried sweet corn was put up through all of the nineteenth century and into the first decade of the next (although it should be noted that the Shakers could not grow enough of their own corn to meet the needs of the industry and bought much of it from neighbors).

Another large industry, this one beginning around midcentury, revolved around apples (and used pomology, the scientific study of growing fruit). Nearly every Shaker village at some time in its history, usually for long periods, had apple orchards and sold apples—mainly as whole fresh fruit, sauce, or cider. Other orchards produced plums, pears, peaches, and quinces, and these, in turn, led to another industrial pursuit—jams, jellies, and sauces. The tradition continues at Sabbathday Lake, where thirty-five acres of apple orchards, with about ten thousand trees, are still harvested annually.

The history of the tomato in Shaker culture mirrors America's response to this then-exotic fruit. As a member of the nightshade family, superstitions abounded of its toxic potential, many of the fears crossing the ocean from Europe with early settlers in America. (Never mind that the tomato plant was brought to Europe *from* the Americas, which it is native *to*.) The Shakers first cultivated tomatoes in about 1830, at the same time that they started large-scale herb production, for their potential medicinal uses. In their first *Gardener's Manual*, issued in 1835, they note the tomato's culinary value for the first time: "We shall notice but two kinds, the large and the small, of which there is no material difference except in the size," and several paragraphs later: "There are but few who relish the tomato at the first taste; and few who are not extremely fond of it when properly cooked and they become accustomed to it." The idea of eating uncooked tomatoes does not make an appearance until much later. We shall soon see how the Shakers put this once-lowly plant to many uses.

This introduction barely scratches the surface of the food industry. Ahead we will look at a sampling of the products that came from Shaker farms, orchards, fields, kitchens, and even mills (ground flour) in an attempt to survey the enormous scope of the products drawn from those village settings. Yet, with all the impressive achievements that are associated with the Shakers, a few words are in order about one product that was a complete failure. Otherwise,

the myth of "Shaker perfection" is at risk of being further perpetuated. What sets the Shakers apart from most of us is not that they are or were perfect in any way, but that for more that two hundred years they have ceaselessly *strived* for perfection.

Toward the end of 1889, following closely on the heels of the collapse of the garden seed business at Mount Lebanon, several leaders at the Church Family decided to try something new. Elder Giles Avery made the following note in his "Ministry Journal" on November 21: "Eldress Harriet [Bullard] and Giles preparing Codfish for making codfish and potatoes for canning, it is an experiment[;] trying to start a business." The business died, however, even before it was born. It was never referred to again.

The reader should keep in mind, always, that the ultimate goal of the food industry, like all the other industries, was to provide an economic foundation upon which the spiritual edifice of the Believers could be built and maintained. At the same time it must be understood that profit, *rightly come by*, in no way conflicts with Shaker faith.

Early sugar corn seeds were first listed for sale on the first New Lebanon seed broadside of 1835, and this variety was also described in the *Gardener's Manual* issued that year. "The sweet or sugar corn is the best for cooking in its green state, as it remains much longer in the milk, and is richer and sweeter than any other kind." Illustrated here is an engraving from the 1877 seed catalog, where corn seeds are offered in traditional envelopes at six cents each, quart bags at forty cents, bushels at five dollars. While not mentioned here, these seeds were also available in *barrels* for twenty dollars.

LEFT: Black ink letterpress and woodcut on white paper (detail), 8¾" × 5¾" (full size). Mount Lebanon, NY, NIR.

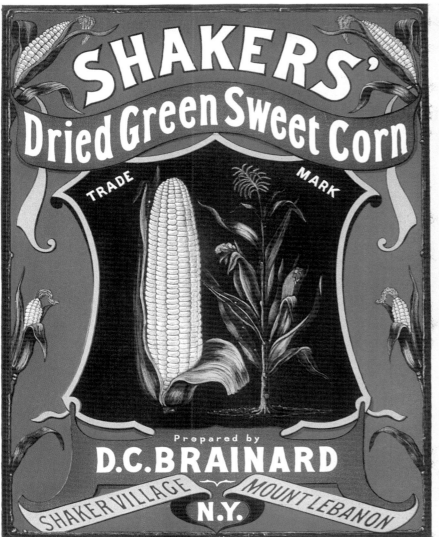

This colorful display card dates to around 1890. D[ewitt] C[linton] Brainard (1828–1897) served as the Trustee at this time and also oversaw the Shaker Seed Company until it closed in 1888. His name appears on various products put up by Mount Lebanon in the 1880s and 1890s. The community stopped selling Dried Sweet Corn in about 1910.

LEFT: Color lithography on card stock, 14⅛" × 11". Mount Lebanon, NY, NIR.

The Hancock community packaged its Dried Sweet Corn in cylindrical containers made from thin bentwood with tin reinforcing the lid and bottom. Instructions printed on the label direct the user to "Put the corn to soak for two hours previous to cooking, in warm water[, then] place it to cook [for] one hour before eating, in the same water."

RIGHT: Red and green ink letterpress on thin light green paper, pasted on wood, height 6¾". Hancock, MA.

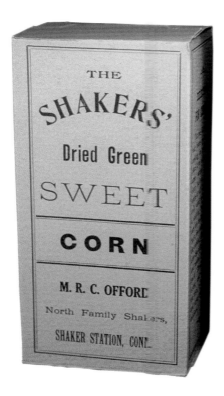

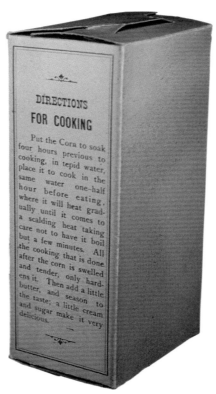

THE
SHAKERS'
Dried Green
SWEET
CORN

M. R. C. OFFORD

North Family Shakers,

SHAKER STATION, CONN.

DIRECTIONS
FOR COOKING

Put the Corn to soak four hours previous to cooking, in tepid water, place it to cook in the same water one-half hour before eating, where it will heat gradually until it comes to a scalding heat taking care not to have it boil but a few minutes. All the cooking that is done after the corn is swelled and tender, only hardens it. Then add a little butter, and season to the taste; a little cream and sugar make it very delicious.

Enfield, CT, packed its product in these cardboard boxes and offered them for sale into the twentieth century. (The community closed in 1917.) The "Directions for Cooking" are nearly identical to Hancock's, substituting "tepid" for "warm." What is unusual, probably unique, here is the name of the Trustee printed on the box. Miriam R. C. Offord (1846–1917) became Trustee in 1899, two years after moving there from Mount Lebanon. Normally there were two Trustees of each gender at each society, but by 1905 there were only eight males between the ages of sixteen and sixty at Enfield, and apparently none of them was qualified to serve in this position. Rarely was a female Trustee's name used on a product that was usually associated with the Brethren—such as this product of the fields—although, as we shall soon see, women's names were often used for crafts that involved textiles.

ABOVE   Blue ink letterpress on tan cardboard, 6¼"x 3⅛" × 2¼". Enfield, CT.

Apple culture was a major source of revenue for many communities. When journalist Charles Nordhoff toured the Shirley, Massachusetts, village in 1875, he noted: "their main business is to make apple-sauce, of which they sell from five to six tons every year."[2] This attractively printed display card is difficult to date because the Trustee named, L[eander] Persons, served in this position from the 1840s to the 1880s.

RIGHT: Black ink letterpress on yellow card stock, 5½" × 9¼". Shirley, MA. Courtesy of Fruitlands Museums, Harvard, MA.

GENUINE
Shaker Apple Sauce.

None Genuine unless marked L. A. PERSONS, Shirley Village, Mass,

FOR SALE HERE.

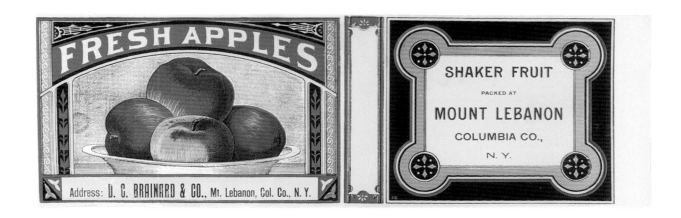

Mount Lebanon was another major producer of apples and their products: sauce, cider, vinegar, and butter. The community first sold applesauce in 1814, but this did not evolve into a coordinated industry until about 1830. Almost from the time that the villages were organized, a separate "order" of Brethren and Sisters was formed called Deacons and Deaconesses. It was their responsibility to oversee vital activities in their community: thus there were Farm Deacons and Laundry Deaconesses. At the Church Family of New Lebanon, an Orchard Deacon's position was created, showing the importance of this activity.

Illustrated here is a "strip label" or wrapper used on a tin or metal container of whole, fresh apples. It dates to the 1890s. In 1895, Mount Lebanon reported in the "Notes about Home" section of *The Manifesto*: "Abundance of early apples give amply [*sic*] employment for young [i.e., children's] hands in picking and sorting for market."[3] The wooden firkin, with its colorful label, held applesauce. It is a rare surviving example. Apples were not the only fruits under cultivation there; acres of plum, peach, cherry, and pear trees rounded out the orchard picture. A commercial lithographer provided the same "stock" labels for "Green Gage" plums and "Apple Sauce," and used letterpress printing to identify the different contents. This was common practice and economic necessity.

TOP: Color lithograph on paper, 6¼" × 19⅛". Mount Lebanon, NY; CENTER: Color lithograph on paper, pasted on wood, height 9". Mount Lebanon, NY. Courtesy of The Shaker Museum and Library, Old Chatham, NY. # 9324; RIGHT: Color lithograph on paper, 5½" × 9⅛". Mount Lebanon, NY.

At Canterbury (and perhaps elsewhere), apples were graded in three categories: "one" was the best and was for immediate sale; "two" was stored for later Shaker use; and "three" was good enough only for immediate drying and/or cooking. This community's recipe for applesauce was to simply cook the dried, peeled, and cored fruit with steady and moderate heat in a sweet cider, which itself was made by boiling down freshly pressed juice from four gallons to one. The firkins that were used to package the applesauce came in two sizes and were shipped six to a crate.

George F. Lane & Son, East Swanzey, New Hampshire, made the firkins used here as well as at Mount Lebanon, Shirley, Enfield, New Hampshire, and Enfield, Connecticut. Nowhere did Shakers make containers for packaging the products of their food industries: wood, glass, cardboard, tin, or ceramic.

ABOVE: Black ink letterpress on off-white paper, pasted on wood, height 6½". Canterbury, NH.

During the nineteenth century the apple orchards at Sabbathday Lake, Maine, were as extensive as they were esteemed. However, by the time Elder Delmer Wilson (1873–1961) took them over in 1910, they had gone through a period of neglect. Brother Delmer (as he preferred to be called) introduced newer scientific methods of orchard management known as "pomology" and also brought in new crossbred varieties of apples. By 1929 the business was much revitalized, with 160,000 pounds of apples harvested and sold in bulk wholesale. Those fruits consisted of three new favorites: McIntosh, Cortland, and Red Delicious. In 1953, with Brother Delmer the only male then at the community, the orchard business was turned over to non-Shakers. These trees are still producing today, and the Shakers at Sabbathday Lake still receive revenues from the sale of their fruit.[4]

LEFT: Black and blue ink letterpress on off-white card stock, 3" × 5" and 4" × 6". Sabbathday Lake, ME.

CATALOGUE

OF

FRUIT TREES, ETC.

RAISED IN THE

SHAKER NURSERY,

HARVARD, MASS.

POST OFFICE ADDRESS,

ELIJAH MYRICK,

SOUTH CROTON, MASS.

GEO. C. RAND & AVERY, PRS., BOSTON.

In 1837, Elder Grove Blanchard, of Harvard, wrote: "It is also agreed to commence the business of raising fruit trees for sale and to have 2 acres prepared . . . this was agreed to in [illegible] that it would be a Lucrative business and that we would prosper in doing so."[5] Indeed, that community proceeded to establish the only industry that raised not only fruit trees but stock for grape culture and a wide variety of berry bushes as well. This bifold pamphlet, from about 1850–1860, offers twenty-one types of apple trees and sixteen of cherry. The climate and topography of Harvard proved to be well suited to this industry.

Black ink letterpress (with wood or metal engraving) on off-white paper, 7½" x 4¾" Harvard, MA R-234v.

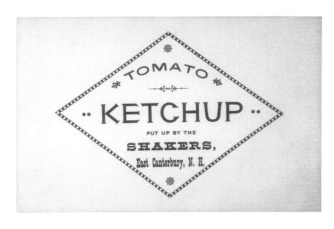

The Shakers at New Lebanon offered tomato seeds for sale as early as 1835, the same year that they printed advice in their first *Gardener's Manual* on how to plant them. They went on with this wry statement: "For the information of those not acquainted with the *tomato*, who may wish to try the experiment, we give the following directions for preparing and cooking them." They proceeded to offer a recipe for a sauce that we now call catsup or ketchup. From then until late in the century there was a succession of such recipes. The latest one that was printed in *The Shaker Manifesto* in 1882 read: "Cut tomatoes in pieces and between every layer sprinkle a thin layer of salt; let them stand a few hours, then add a little horseradish, garlic, pepper, and mace. Boil well and strain." They also say here, however: "Tomatoes . . . are not without defects as an article of food . . . they contain some obnoxious qualities. But they need not be thrown aside . . . nature has provided us with sufficient excretory organs that the obnoxious matter . . . is readily cast out."[6]

Earlier in the century, when tomatoes were grown primarily for the seeds that could be harvested for sale, the Shakers commented on how relatively easy this was to do and, therefore, how profitable it was. At the time that this recipe was published, in the 1880s, Mount Lebanon was dedicating two and a half acres, with an annual total of about ten thousand plants, just to tomatoes—so this was now a large, remunerative business. Mount Lebanon, Canterbury, Harvard, and Sabbathday Lake each put up catsup for sale, and labels from these communities are shown here. The Sabbathday Lake Shakers did not sell this or many other prepared garden products themselves but rather sold them wholesale to a firm in Portland, Maine, which then put them up in bottles for retail sale.

TOP LEFT: Black ink letterpress on yellow paper (center), 2" × 2⅝", and black ink letterpress on stiff, off-white paper (*top and bottom*), 1" × 4". New Lebanon, NY; TOP RIGHT: Red ink letterpress on white paper, 3⅛" × 4¾". Canterbury, NH; CENTER LEFT: Black ink letterpress on light pink paper, 2⅜" × 3¾". Harvard, MA; RIGHT: Color lithograph on off-white paper, pasted on clear glass, 3⅛" × 3½" (label). Sabbathday Lake, ME.

At Shirley Village, "Fresh Tomatoes" were probably sold in thin-sided wooden containers, as this is the style of label made for those. It dates to around 1875. This community was really not known for its vegetable output, so this is a bit of an anomaly.

ABOVE RIGHT: Multicolor letterpress on thin white paper, 4¾" × 6⅜". Shirley, MA.

This large label from Harvard dates to around the 1860s and was possibly wrapped around an open can or box. William Leonard (1803–1877) was an Elder after 1858 and not a Trustee, but at times he oversaw the business interests of the village.

BELOW RIGHT: Multicolor letterpress (with wood engraving) on off-white paper, 4¾" × 5½" (printed portion). Harvard, MA. Courtesy of Hancock Shaker Village, Inc., Pittsfield, MA, Box IX.

Watervliet, New York, put up canned tomatoes beginning at least by the 1880s, and from then into the twentieth century. This would have been among its last industries. This can has a label with the name of Eldress Anna Case (1855–1938). She was the last Trustee there, succeeding Josiah Barker in the 1920s. (She was also the last Eldress.) The community closed the year that she died.

LEFT: Color lithograph on paper, pasted on tin, height 6¼". Watervliet, NY. Courtesy of Canterbury Shaker Village, Inc., Canterbury, NH. # 1983.0841.0001.

Apiculture was a natural complement to the orchard business and was important for some flowering medicinal plants, such as poppies. While bees were essential for pollination, they also provided the communities with another source of income—honey. At Canterbury, the sale of honey took place between 1860 and 1896. Elder Henry Blinn (1824–1905) was famous for his prowess as a beekeeper there. The blue label comes from Canterbury. Sabbathday Lake's honey production spanned most of the twentieth century. The many-talented Brother Delmer Wilson was the bee-keeper there. This jar has a 1930s Art Deco motif in the glass but was probably used in the 1940s.

At Mount Lebanon the Shakers also put up honey in glass jars, and cans, and these sold for fifty cents and $3.50 respectively. Their honey was offered in either "extracted" or "comb" form. In 1899, a little more than one hundred pounds of honey was harvested, an indication that this was not a large-scale undertaking. The bifold pamphlet was issued in about 1906. Its craftsman-style cover was supposedly designed by a Rumanian émigré who lived at Mount Lebanon for a while. The photographic image was taken sometime before 1907 (when federal law directed that a vertical line had to bisect the reverse side of postcards, with the right-hand portion reserved for an address). It shows a Sister and Brother working side by side at one apiary, a scene not possible through most of the nineteenth century, when the two sexes were rigorously kept separate, both at jobs and in physical space.

ABOVE LEFT: Color lithograph on white paper, 3⅝" × 2"; multicolor letterpress on white paper, 3" × 1⅝"; black ink lithography on off-white paper, 7" × 10". Canterbury, NH; Sabbathday Lake, ME; Mount Lebanon, NY, R-340 (*right*); LOWER RIGHT: Photoengraving on card stock, 3½" × 5⅜". Mount Lebanon, NY. Courtesy of Hamilton College, Burke Library, Clinton, NY.

The canned vegetables industry was confined mainly to Mount Lebanon and Watervliet. This business began in the early 1880s and lasted into the 1930s. In 1884, Mount Lebanon recorded: "We prepare string beans for canning," up to five hundred cans in a day.[7] Five years later, Elder Giles Avery of that community perfected a "bean cutter," a simple mechanical device for preparing the beans for the "kitchen Sisters." It did not, however, remove the strings. "Nineteenth century varieties of green beans had tough strings down both sides of the pod that had to be removed [by hand] before the beans were cooked."[8] This can dates to around 1890.

RIGHT: Color lithograph on paper, pasted on tin, height 4¾". Mount Lebanon, NY.

Sister Lillian Barlow (1876–1942), sometime in the late 1920s, entered into a business arrangement with a division of Burpee Can Sealer Company to market Shaker-grown, Shaker-canned fruits and vegetables under the brand name of *HPA, Home Products Association*. Unfortunately, the community left no records of this endeavor, and all the Burpee Company's records were destroyed in 1956.[9] All that we have to recall this short-lived business are some color lithographed can labels, many of them "stock" labels that were overprinted for the Shakers.

ABOVE: Color lithograph on paper, 4¼" × 11¼" and 4⅝" × 14". Mount Lebanon, NY.

In the 1930s, several Sisters at Canterbury embarked on a very "New England" type of venture, selling baked beans and brown bread. The business involved preparing, packaging, and selling these products on a retail basis. The main dwelling house at the village was already outfitted with an industrial-size brick oven with revolving steel shelves that ensured evenly distributed heat. (Local lore has it that a Shaker there, Sister Emeline Hart, actually invented it.) Pea beans were generally used in a recipe that combined them with molasses, maple syrup, margarine, and onion, along with small amounts of salt, pepper, baking soda, and dried summer savory. After the beans were soaked overnight, six hours of baking at a moderate temperature was needed to fully cook the mix.

This photograph shows Sister Evelyn Polsey (1891–1955) ladling the prepared beans into cardboard containers from a large crock, circa 1940. The Shakers loaded these one-pound containers into a specially outfitted truck and sold them along the way to Concord, New Hampshire, and then in town. Several stores allowed the Sisters to set up sales tables inside when the weather turned wet or cold. The use for the label shown is unknown, but it includes the image of the [locally] famous Shaker-built brick oven as an unspoken symbol of Shaker quality—a marketing strategy we see used again and again.

TOP: Black ink lithograph on off-white cardboard, height 3¾". Canterbury, NH; CENTER: Photoengraving on card stock, 3½" × 5⅜". Canterbury, NH. Courtesy of Hamilton College, Burke Library, Clinton, NY; RIGHT: Black ink letterpress and photoengraving on off-white paper, 2⅝" × 4⅝". Canterbury, NH.

This shows the uppermost portion of a shingled "house" that was put in the bed of a pickup truck in the 1940s to bring the baked beans to town. The business ended in 1952, and this structure ended up at the Shaker Museum and Library.

ABOVE: Painted wood and asphalt shingles, dimensions of sign 7¾" × 66¼". Courtesy of The Shaker Museum and Library, Old Chatham, NY. # 4943.

In the 1830s, many Shakers moved toward the "reform" diet of Sylvester Graham (1794–1851), for many of the same reasons that they were attracted to the "botanical" medical practice of Samuel Thomson. For a group who already lived the ultimate "alternative lifestyle," these shifts were more evolutionary than revolutionary. Graham was a well-known, non-Shaker nutritionist who found the typical American diet of abundant meats—often fried in animal fats, accompanied by copious amounts of butter, cream, and eggs—appalling. He advocated a diet based on whole grains (especially breads) and fresh vegetables free from all added fats, sauces, alcohol, caffeine, and heavy seasonings. (Present-day cookbooks, filled with hundreds of recipes that the Shakers left us, would have been anathema to Graham.) This flour sack, from before 1860, attests to the marketability of Grahamian products.

RIGHT: Blue ink letterpress on white linen, 25" × 12½". Sabbathday Lake, ME.

The dietary preferences of individual members, and even of entire families or communities, varied considerably from one another. They also fluctuated widely with time. It is not possible to speak of an "average" Shaker diet. One area where the Shakers were completely in step with Graham, however, through all of the nineteenth century, was the matter of culinary herbs. Many villages sold these, but they all sold only four varieties: summer savory, sage, sweet marjoram, and thyme, and they were always packaged in small, cylindrical tin cans. (Some communities sold *seeds* for growing other varieties: caraway, coriander, dill, fennel, rosemary, sweet basil, and others.) Graham discouraged the *heavy* use of herbs for flavoring foods in favor of such things as honey, rose water, salt, and sugar. Before the twentieth century, the Shakers used culinary herbs sparingly themselves.

ABOVE: Black ink letterpress on pink and blue papers, pasted on tin, height 2⅛". New Lebanon, NY. Collection of the United Society of Shakers, Sabbathday Lake, Maine. # 95.1231 and 95.1232.

Sage was far and away the most popular sweet herb that was grown and sold by Sabbathday Lake. In 1876, a half acre was devoted to raising just this, and $270.00 worth of it was sold then. By contrast, in the five years from 1862 to 1866, Mount Lebanon sold nearly thirteen *tons* of sage. In addition to flavoring foods, sage could be made into a tea that was recommended for coughs, colds, sore throats, and fever. This tin dates to 1860s, when Charles Vining served as head gardener at Sabbathday Lake.

RIGHT: Black ink letterpress on tan paper, pasted on tin, height 3¼". Sabbathday Lake, ME.

Harvard had the largest culinary herb industry of all the Shaker villages, and it lasted the longest—by far. The names of Trustees on this "collage" of labels, designed as wrappers for herb tins, tell us part of the story of its longevity. Brother Simon Atherton served as Trustee for Harvard for fifty years, until his death in 1888. His name is on the two marjoram labels. There was a gap in trusteeship for a time, and a commercial distributor stepped in then, Bogle & Lyles of New York. (The same company also distributed canned vegetables for Mount Lebanon and/or Watervliet.) In 1908 Shirley was closed, and the Eldress there, Josephine C. Jilson (1851–1925), assumed the duties of Trustee at Harvard until *it* closed in 1918. The sage label with her name, one of three labels printed on the large sheet in the background, dates from between 1908 and 1918. Thus Harvard had a nearly ninety-year involvement in selling herbs of one kind or another.

ABOVE: Black, red, and blue letterpress on off-white papers, 1⅞" × 4¼' (Sage only), and 9½" × 8" (full uncut sheet of two Sage and one Thyme labels). Harvard, MA, NIR.

The herb industry at Sabbathday Lake had been moribund for nearly ninety years when Brother Theodore (Ted) Johnson arrived in the 1960s. From a modest beginning, it continued to expand until the arrival of Stephen Foster, a gifted gardener, in 1975. Foster stayed with the Shakers for only a few years, during which time the culinary herb and herbal tea business underwent a major revival and within a short time was offering up to eighty varieties for sale. The business continues today, with most sales by mail through the Sabbathdy Lake Web site. (The Shakers have *always* used the latest available technology, and this is yet another tradition that continues at Sabbathday Lake.) The tins and herbal tea labels illustrated are from about 1980. It is difficult to accurately date them since their design has changed little in the past thirty years. The typeface and decorative borders are unique, designed and cast specifically for the community's own printing press.[10]

ABOVE: Blue and red ink letterpress on off-white and yellow papers, pasted on tin, height 2½". Sabbathday Lake, ME; LEFT: Blue and red ink letterpress on variously colored papers, 1¾" × 9⅜". Sabbathday Lake, ME.

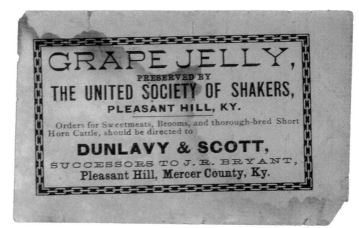

A list of preserved fruits, jellies, jams, and fruit-based sauces put up by the Shakers is a long one and includes the product names Barberry, Cherry, Citron, Crab Apple, Cranberry, Goose Berry, Grape, Peach, Pear, Pine-Apple [*sic*], Plum, Raspberry, Quince, Strawberry, and Tomato (in many variations). Canterbury, Harvard, New Lebanon, and Sabbathday Lake were the leading producers (in the East). In the West, Pleasant Hill and South Union, Kentucky, put up thousands of pounds of fruit preserves before and after the Civil War. The latter shipped three tons of these to New Orleans and East Texas by riverboat in 1856 and resumed selling large quantities again by 1869.[11] So little remains from these industries in the West that this small, stained label from Pleasant Hill will have to stand for them all. It dates to the period between 1872, when Elder Rufus Bryant was relived of his duties because of failing health, and 1886, when his successor, Elder Benjamin Dunlavey, died. (The fate of Dunlavey's co-Trustee, Elder Elhanan Scott, is unknown.)

ABOVE RIGHT: Black ink letterpress on light yellow paper, 1½" × 2¾". Pleasant Hill, KY. Collection of the United Society of Shakers, Sabbathday Lake, Maine. Box 1, # 2001.1.

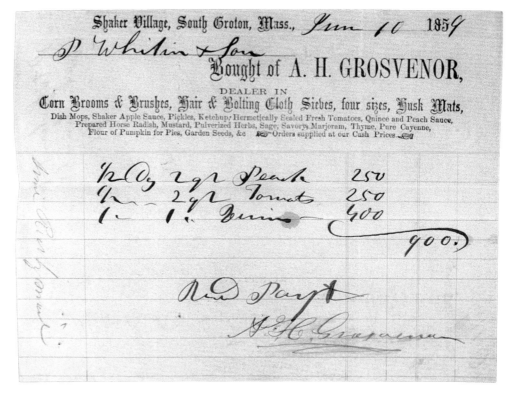

The billhead illustrated is from Harvard and is dated 1859. It records an order for a half dozen jars of Peach (Marmalade) and (Preserved) Tomato, along with a dozen of (Preserved) Quince. Elder Augustus H. Grosvenor (1807–1864) signed it. This is one small example of the array of printed material that was necessary to support all the industries, large and small.

RIGHT: Black and red ink letterpress, and black ink manuscript, on white paper, 5½" × 7". Harvard, MA.

This group of labels from Harvard was printed four to a sheet—a common printing practice—and the printer used either carved wood blocks or electrotypes, with gold ink, for the elaborate design. The Trustee's name on them was L[aban] S. Babbitt (1795–?). Brother Babbitt, part of a large "natural" family at Harvard, left the community in 1854.[12] (The Shakers credited one of his sisters, Sarah—called Tabitha—with inventing a circular saw. This unsubstantiated attribution is perpetuated in print to the present day.)

RIGHT: Gold ink letterpress on dark blue paper, 3" × 4" (printed portion of each). Harvard, MA.

In the mid–twentieth century the Sisters at Sabbathday Lake had only one Brother present (Brother Delmer, who died in 1961) and needed additional sources of income. They turned to their strengths in canning to develop a jam and jelly business. A century earlier, in 1849, a Deacon at Sabbathday Lake named James Holmes printed a book called *A Collection of Useful Hints for Farmers, and Many Valuable Recipes*. He described a process for making "Currant Jelly" (label in upper right): "Break your currants with a pestle and squeeze them through a cloth, put a pint of clean sugar to a pint of juice and boil it very slowly till it becomes ropy. This is an excellent article, especially in sickness."[13]

LEFT: Black ink letterpress on white paper, 1⅜" × 2" (Apple Butter). Sabbathday Lake, ME.

A curious business relationship developed in the late 1870s between the Shakers at Sabbathday Lake and a World's merchant, Edward D. Pettengill of Portland, Maine. One has to read a bit into this partnership because of a paucity of documentary evidence. We do know that the community supplied Pettengill with a variety of pickles, plus horseradish, relish, and catsup, in the early 1880s, but this author suspects that the relationship effectively ended around 1885. An affidavit sworn by Pettengill's widow, Sarah, in 1892 reads in part: "That said [Edward] Pettengill appropriated in his said business the word 'Shaker' [in 1885] as a trademark, which trademark he used exclusively for many years upon the goods manufactured and sold by him; that upon the decease of said Pettengill, I succeeded to said business and purchased all interests therein, including the right to use said trademark."

This collection of bottles, with colorful labels and of many shapes, comes from three distinct periods of time between 1880 and 1908. The left and center of three taller bottles date to 1893–1904, when the firm was called E. D. Pettengill Co. The bottle on the right is from 1880–1892, when the name was E. D. Pettengill & Co. Not shown is a bottle for "Shaker Brand Selected Queen Olives." This has the name E. D. Pettengill Sons Co., used between about 1904 and 1908. Of course the Shakers did not have olive trees, so the appropriation of their name is obvious but also was entirely legal—the result of Sarah's 1892 affidavit.

ABOVE: Color lithographs, pasted on clear glass, height 11⅜" (tallest). Sabbathday Lake, ME; BELOW: Color lithographs, pasted on clear glass, height 8½" (tallest). Sabbathday Lake, ME.

Candy making may not be one of the food industries that one readily associates with the Shakers, but from modest beginnings in the 1880s it became a rather steady source of revenue for three communities in the twentieth century: Canterbury, Mount Lebanon, and Sabbathday Lake. More that just a cottage industry, the manufacture of sweets involved a coordinated effort to gather the ingredients, ready them for the kitchen phase, prepare the finished products, package them in boxes that were printed, folded, and sealed specifically by type of confection, and market them.

Canterbury was the first of the villages to undertake this effort, beginning in 1882. Its earliest recipe was for Chocolate Cream Drops. After the turn of the century, the business moved into high gear with the sugaring of orange and grapefruit peel, nuts, and flag root (from the herb sweet flag—a spicy, lemony-tasting root that is sometimes substituted for ginger or cinnamon). The Sugared Butternut box (*upper left*) is the only one of these five from the nineteenth century and is a rare survivor.

ABOVE LEFT: Black ink letterpress on tan cardboard (Butternut) and black or brown ink letterpress (with red and white label pasted on Flagroot) on off-white cardboard, 2⅛" × 3¼" × 1⅛" and 2¼" × 4" × ⅞". Canterbury, NH.

These candy boxes from Mount Lebanon probably date to the 1890s, since candy making there did not extend very far into the new century. While some sweets were sold at the gift shops of each community, the larger amount went along with handmade goods for sale outside the communities. The boxes with black and white checkered paper on their sides (*center*) are actually recycled from a small clock-making company in Pittsfield, Massachusetts. This is a good example of the virtue that the Shakers saw in thrift.

ABOVE RIGHT: Black ink letterpress, pasted on paper-covered cardboard (two center boxes), 2½" × 2¾" × 1¾". Mount Lebanon, NY.

Sabbathday Lake's candy business began in 1883 and is still active. Every Sister who has been in charge of this kitchen industry seems to have taken particular pride in her position as the mantle of leadership passed from Elizabeth Noyes to Mary Jane Mathers to Mildred Barker. Today, Sister Frances Carr is in charge. The variety of box shapes and sizes in this small selection from the second half of the last century shows the variety of candies and weights available. Many boxes from Sabbathday Lake bear a sketch of the community's 1794 Meetinghouse—the oldest significant structure in the village and one that quietly expresses how the Shakers define themselves: a community of Believers.

BELOW: Blue ink letterpress on white and tan cardboard, 5½" × 8⅝" × 1" (lower center box). Sabbathday Lake, ME.

If a candy-making business comes as a surprise to some readers, the Shakers' wine business will probably be an even greater surprise to many. One of the common misunderstandings about the Shakers is that they shunned alcohol. While this was true for some members, it was not true for others, and it unmasks another, larger misconception: that the Shakers were, or are, all of the same mind and practices. The truth is that they are not and never were. There have been, at one time or another, about seventeen thousand people who have followed the faith—over a span of 225 years—so the path, while straight, has also been wide. (For example, many Shakers—men and women—smoked tobacco, and one of their *industries* was the manufacture of smoking pipes. Little is known about this industry, and nothing remains, so it will not be covered here.)

The production of wine for sale was a natural outgrowth of the Shakers' orchard and berry culture. When they found that more of these fruits were left after other needs were met, they turned the excess over to neighbors who had fermenting and distilling capabilities for the production of wine (and other spirits). This started at New Lebanon in the late 1850s and continued for the rest of the century. (Edward Andrews wrote that the first batch of ten gallons of wine was actually made by Sisters.)[14] At least sixteen varieties of wine were put up for sale during that forty-year period. One unusual variety was Metheglin (*lower right*), made from fermented honey and water. By 1893, the community was growing raspberry and blackberry bushes that extended for two-fifths of a mile, and most of this fruit went into wine making.[15]

ABOVE CENTER: (Blackberry) Black ink letterpress on orange paper, 4" × 3¼". New Lebanon, NY.

Dairying was a huge enterprise at every Shaker community. Not only were huge amounts of milk, cream, and butter produced for home consumption; huge quantities were also sold. This was no different from what was done on surrounding farms. What was different was the production of substantial quantities of cheese, something that required special skills, special facilities, and a good amount of time. Most of the Shakers' neighbors had none of these. A dilemma for this book is that the nature of this very important industry was such that few remnants survived: it sold locally so it was never advertised, no instructions for use were necessary, and the product was consumed!

Thus this butter wrapper from Canterbury, and an image of the creamery there, will stand for the entire dairy industry everywhere. It is interesting that while account books for the garden industries—garden seeds and medicinal herbs in particular—were assiduously kept, few records were made of the sale of dairy farm products. Perhaps this was because there was more interest in industries where the Shakers innovated and less in a traditional one that *everybody* participated in. In 1801, for example, Canterbury put up half a ton of butter and a ton of cheese. After this the record goes silent.

In 1905, Canterbury built a new creamery, and this postcard image dates to just after that. By this time the community was maintaining a herd of one hundred Holstein and Guernsey registered cattle. These cows were sold around 1920, and the industry ended.

ABOVE LEFT: Blue ink letterpress on thin tan paper, 12" × 8" (full sheet), and photoengraving on card stock, 3½" × 5⅜". Canterbury, NH.

The final word about foods goes to this can wrapper for mustard. At almost every large Shaker village there was at least one idiosyncratic food product put up that bore little resemblance to the rest. At Sabbathday Lake, it was dried mustard. Nothing is known about it except that a billhead from the early 1860s advertises it for sale and this wrapper, a rare survivor, remains. It is one of any number of oddities in the Shaker food industry that could be considered.

RIGHT: Black ink letterpress on orange paper, 2¾" × 9½", and black ink letterpress on white paper, 4⅝" × 8½". Sabbathday Lake, ME.

PART II

PRODUCTS OF THE HANDS

"THE EARLY SHAKERS were a pioneering people. Their immediate task was to sustain their institution in the interests of survival. They were conscious of a particular destiny, an aloofness from the world, a kinship with a divine plan, a fellowship of interests, but this consciousness was not at first refined into more than a general plan of how to live." So wrote the Andrewses in 1974.[1] We have already considered how from the beginning, as essentially large collective farms, Shaker villages did what all farmers did, selling farm products in order to be able to survive, as well as to purchase goods from the World that they could neither grow nor make themselves. Once the communities gained a foothold with subsistence farming—feeding themselves, which was the essence of the "general plan"—they rapidly expanded their operations into commercial farming. From there followed the natural, logical, and perhaps inevitable commitments to raising and selling garden seeds, herbs and medicinal preparations, and both fresh and prepared foodstuffs. From their beginnings, the Shakers were intimately tied to their lands, and for the first half of the nineteenth century the soil-based industries were the dominant paradigm.

Yet, from the time that the Shakers were first "gathered into order," in the 1780s, they made a variety of household and farm goods. Furthermore, almost from the time that they made these kinds of wares for their own use, they made others simply to produce income for their communities—dippers; oval boxes; tubs, pails, churns, and barrels; cheese hoops; hand cards; whips, tinwork, and forged iron-ware, just to name a few. While few of these items were produced on the scale of an industry, as some later would be, a craft tradition was established. After all, not every one of the early members had a farming background. Some were metalsmiths, leather workers, coopers, clothiers, mechanics, and artisans, and, along with their tools, they brought various levels of skill and experience as craftsmen into their communities. It is almost certain, for example, that New Lebanon made chairs for sale in the 1780s, at least eighty years before a "production chair" *industry* began there.[2]

In the mid–nineteenth century, internal and external forces well beyond their control conspired to alter the economies of all eighteen Shaker Societies. For a thoughtful consideration of the former, see Stephen Paterwic's essay in this volume: "Who Were the Shakers?" As to the external forces, the one that overshadowed all others was competition from the World. Large-scale seed companies, drug firms, and food-processing plants overwhelmed each community's ability to compete in the marketplace with its own soil-based products, and as a result these industries withered.

On the other hand, there *was* an arena where the Shakers could compete with the World: handcrafted goods. With the important exception of "sale" chairs and stools, Shaker crafted goods did not lend themselves to the factory model of production. Instead, many communities undertook labor-intensive work—employing for the first time women's hands in individual and creative ways—and found a niche in the World's marketplace that they were able to serve, and compete in, for another hundred years. (Had the Shakers not adapted in this way, their movement would almost certainly have ended before the twentieth century dawned.)

There will be only one example of craft work from any of the six villages in Ohio and Kentucky in the pages ahead. Although there was a craft tradition among the western Shakers, it was a very limited one. As far as we know, every community made brooms, and some made brushes. Union Village, Ohio, had a large textile industry, turning out palm-leaf bonnets and hats, and women's clothing. Watervliet, Ohio (not to be confused with Watervliet, New York), had a large textile industry in midcentury with whole buildings dedicated to dyeing, carding, and spinning wool—mostly for blankets. Unfortunately, no examples of any of the above can be positively identified. Union Village and the Kentucky villages also had a large silk industry, but while a number of Shaker-made silk scarves survive, it is not possible to identify the specific community of origin for any of them.

In the hundred-year period after the Civil War, the communities did not completely abandon their ties to the land, either for subsistence or for commerce. However, handmade work dominated, in much the same way that products shown in the preceding chapters did for the first seventy-five years. The following chapters will first look at a range of products that share one attribute: they are all made of wood. (For the purist, it will be conceded that almost all the handmade goods to be surveyed ahead used materials that *derived* from the soil: wood and its by-products, including paper; plant fibers, such as linen, cotton, and palm leaves.)

We will then proceed to survey the fancy goods trade, an industry that was vital to the few communities that survived beyond the 1920s. Textiles were also important to this select group of survivors, and some

of that output will be surveyed as well. Finally, several industries that defy easy categorization, but were economically too important to be called "miscellaneous," will be sampled.

In general, there is far more information available in secondary print sources for the products of Shaker hands than for the products from their lands. This is partly explained by the fact that handmade goods were intended to be used rather than consumed and were made to last. With utility and durability uppermost in the minds of their Shaker makers, relatively large numbers have survived. There is another factor that should not be overlooked. Unlike seeds or herbs or foodstuffs, Shaker-made goods are very collectible. Items that were once sold by the communities for a few dollars may now sell in the antiques market for several thousand dollars. Wherever possible, we will consider the economic impact of these products on the communities that *made* them—in other words, their value as industries—and leave matters of connoisseurship and present market values to others.

In the twenty-first century there is only one Shaker community remaining, Sabbathday Lake, Maine. It appears that the last traditional industry to survive there is not a craft but the selling of culinary herbs, a business that all but ceased at all the Shaker Societies a hundred years earlier. Some may see irony in this fact. This author sees instead the same pattern of necessity, and response to necessity, that has always guided and shaped the Shakers' world. Their amazing record of longevity is due not only to hard work, determination, and resilience but also to religious faith. If the economic foundation that supported their unique way of living for more than two centuries was their industries—and it was—the bedrock that this foundation was built on was, and remains, a profound and unwavering faith.

Woodenware

There are few crafted items that are as immediately recognizable as a product of Shaker hands as their oval-shaped boxes. These boxes were made in many sizes, all with "finger" or "swallowtail" laps forming the external joint. The reason behind this peculiar form of joinery is that wood expands and contracts across its grain, and such overlapping shapes allow for more of this dimensional change, thus preventing the wood from splitting. Finger laps were not a Shaker innovation; the Shakers simply elevated a vernacular form almost to an art form by making the sides of boxes very thin, carefully seasoning the wood so that the fingers would lie flat, and tracing uniform, symmetrical Gothic arch forms between fingers. (Straight laps were used on many other bent-wood pieces, most of them not made for sale, but again, the wood was carefully prepared.) It should also be remembered that no matter how attractive the fingered boxes may be to the eye, they were made for use and not as art objects.

The first oval boxes were made at New Lebanon and sold there in the early 1800s. By the mid-1830s, specialized machinery, such as a buzz saw for cutting out the pine tops and bottoms and a planer for finishing the maple sides, was brought in to speed up production. Sizes were also standardized and assigned a number, from no. 1 for the largest (15" across) to no. 12, the smallest. Thus an industry was born. David Meacham, Jr. (whose father was the first Trustee at New Lebanon and the source of the honorific D. M.), was in charge then. The Second Family was primarily responsible for this industry, which existed for about one hundred years. (Similar but smaller businesses developed at Canterbury, Alfred, Sabbathday Lake, Union Village, and Pleasant Hill later, each making oval boxes or related wares.) Few records of sales exist, but in 1854, for instance, New Lebanon made 840 oval boxes—like the four shown here from about that time period. There is little doubt that, overall, tens of thousands of oval boxes were made.[1]

Maple and pine, natural surface, lengths 10½", 12", 13½", and 15". New Lebanon, NY.

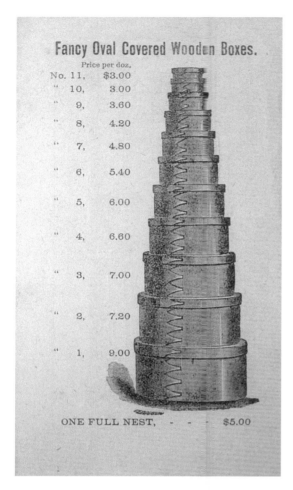

Fancy Oval Covered Wooden Boxes.

Price per doz.

No. 11,	$3.00
" 10,	3.00
" 9,	3.60
" 8,	4.20
" 7,	4.80
" 6,	5.40
" 5,	6.00
" 4,	6.60
" 3,	7.00
" 2,	7.20
" 1,	9.00

ONE FULL NEST, - - - $5.00

This illustration is of the only freestanding broadside that the Shakers issued to advertise oval boxes that were sold in graduated "nests." They were clearly intended for the wholesale market; all prices are "per dozen," and range from three to nine dollars. This broadside is actually a bifold, with three-quarters of it devoted to advertising Shaker chairs. It dates to around 1870. Soon after this Mount Lebanon ended the oval box industry.

LEFT: Black ink letterpress on off-white paper, 5⅝"x 3⅛" (folded). Mount Lebanon, NY, R-338.

From oval box to "carrier" was a short step, as the Shakers needed only to add a handle. The carrier illustrated was converted from an earlier box by adding shims to the sides—strips of wood that acted as spacers, allowing the wider lid to be removed without binding.[2] During the nineteenth century a carrier was no more specialized than a box with a handle to facilitate carrying it. New Lebanon made these for communal use only. Canterbury also made carriers—without lids—and sold many of them, but this was still a small business, not an industry. It was a Mount Lebanon carrier, however, that served as the inspiration for Brother Delmer Wilson to develop an industry at Sabbathday Lake.

BELOW: Maple and pine with dark red paint, length 10½". New Lebanon, NY.

Brother Delmer recorded the following recollections almost thirty years after the fact: "In 1894 Amanda [Stickney] and Sirena [Douglas] lined up two [Mount] Lebanon carriers which had been given to them and sent them to the Springs in August. It started a craze[;] accordingly other carriers were prepared and sold." The "Springs" referred to was Poland Springs, a large resort hotel where Sabbathday Lake sold up to 50 percent of its "fancy goods" annually to tourists. "Lined up" referred to the satin-woven silk lining that the Sisters placed on the inside of empty carriers, to which they added sewing accoutrements.

Brother Delmer goes on to say: "Finally, all spare oval boxes were picked up, some even had paint removed, and after I made bails [handles] for them . . . the carriers were lined and furnished."[3] The round carrier shown here dates to 1896, the first year that Brother Delmer made his own carriers rather than adapting those from Mount Lebanon. He made only thirty that first year, all with cherrywood sides, pine bottoms, and handles that swiveled on copper rivets. These were, in fact, the only round ones he ever made, so we can date this one with confidence.[4]

LEFT: Cherry and pine with blue silk, diameter 7½". Sabbathday Lake, ME.

It required only another short step for Brother Delmer to go from round to oval-shaped carriers, and he took it in 1897. Within ten years his output soared to more than one thousand in a year, as specialized forms called jigs and other kinds of tooling were developed to speed up the handwork. Shown (*lower*) is the second version of Sabbathday Lake's first *Catalog of Fancy Goods* from 1910. In it four sizes of sewing carriers were offered: no. 1, 11" long, $3.25; no. 2, 9½", $2.25; no. 3, 8", $1.75; and no. 4, 7", $1.50. By the time of the second (and last bound) catalog issued around 1920 (*left*), the largest size was dropped. The latest style of catalog (*right*) was issued under the guidance of Eldress Prudence Stickney (1860–1950). Once again four sizes were available and the prices had increased slightly, with the range being $2.00 to $4.00.

RIGHT: Black ink letterpress on white paper (*lower*), 5⅜" × 7¾". R-349. Black ink letterpress on heavy olive-color paper (*left*), 4½" × 5½". NIR. Black ink letterpress on off-white paper (*right*), 6" × 3⅜". R-351. Sabbathday Lake, ME.

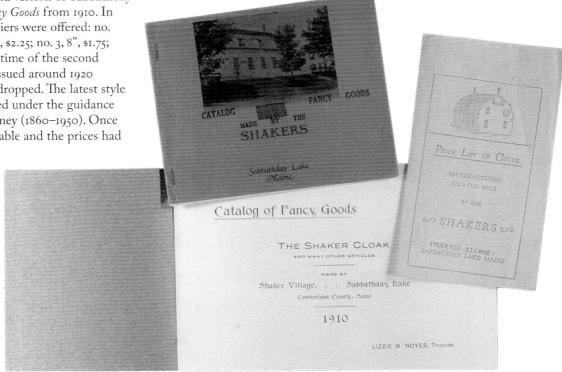

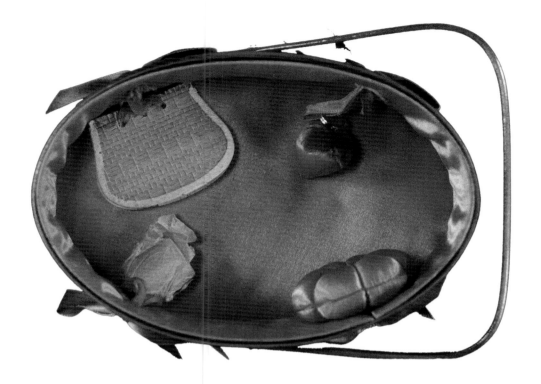

This is a typically outfitted sewing carrier with a satin-woven silk lining and four accessories: a strawberry-shaped emery (for sharpening needles), a tomato-shaped pincushion, a needle case of poplar-woven covers and felt leaves (for storing needles), and a cylinder of beeswax (for strengthening threads). All these were secured to the sides of the carrier with silk ribbons. Pink and rose-colored silks were the most commonly used colors; green, blue, and brown were also offered. Brother Delmer seemed to favor apple wood from his own orchards to construct the sides and handles of the boxes but also used maple, cherry, and quarter-sawn oak.

ABOVE LEFT: Oak and pine with pink silk, woven poplar, and wax, length 7". Sabbathday Lake, ME.

This photograph was taken of Brother Delmer in his workshop, amid machinery that he is credited with designing, in 1923. By late spring of that year he had finished making his annual supply of carriers for the summer tourist trade—1,083 by his own count. As each season progressed, Sisters lined and outfitted the boxes for sale. In 1903, this many-talented Brother designed and registered a trademark that was stamped in ink on the bottom of every carrier. In addition to the name of Sabbathday Lake, it used the initials "S C"—Shaker community. Long before Brother Delmer's death, in 1961, he was known by the sobriquet "Dean of the Carrier Makers."

Alfred, Maine, had an outfitted sewing carrier business that mirrored Brother Delmer's in almost every way. Its 1908 catalog offered only three sizes, "made from choice woods."[5] They matched the three larger sizes of Sabbathday Lake. There is one unusual feature found on many Alfred carriers (and oval boxes)—the fingers point to the left rather than the right. The reason for this is unknown.

LEFT: Photograph, 6½" × 4½". Sabbathday Lake, ME.

Sabbathday Lake was the alpha and the omega in the sewing carrier industry, followed by Alfred, but there were not the sole makers. In the 1920s and early 1930s, a talented Sister, Lillian Barlow (1855–1947), and a talented Brother, Elder William Perkins (1861–1934), both of Mount Lebanon, teamed up to produce their own style of sewing carriers. Four of them are pictured here.

The Perkins-Barlow line of carriers was never advertised, and this author knows of no production records. All the carriers of this style have these characteristics in common: they are made from gumwood, including handles (bottoms are pine); they are stained medium to dark brown and covered with clear varnish; they have swivel handles with flat, rounded shims separating them from the box; they have lids; they are fastened with shiny copper tack heads; and they are lined with brocaded silk.[6] Some are outfitted with the standard four sewing accessories and some are empty. The outfitted ones have ribbons either showing on the outside or hidden on the inside.

On rare occasions a gold-colored oval label was affixed to the bottom that reads: "Genuine Shaker Work; Mt. Lebanon, N.Y." Four sizes were available—from 7¼" to 10½". The standardization of sizes, styles, and materials, coupled with the relatively large number of surviving examples, indicate that this was, indeed, an industry.

ABOVE: Gumwood and pine with pink and blue silk, 7½", 8½", 9½", and 10½". Mount Lebanon, NY; RIGHT: Blue ink letterpress on gold paper, pasted on pine, ⅞" × 1½". Mount Lebanon, NY.

Shaker mills at a few communities produced several types of dry measures for sale, beginning early in the nineteenth century. These two examples, called dippers because of their long handles, date to around 1820–1830 and were made at New Lebanon. They are fabricated from three pieces of wood: a round disk of pine for the bottom, thinly planed maple for the sides, and turned maple for the handle. The joint or seam is of the straight variety, secured with straight rows of many copper tacks to prevent warping. An iron rivet was used to attach the handle and was then filed on its outer surface to conform to the concave shape of the handle. Usually no finish coat was applied. The dipper on the left has D. M. stamped on the bottom, a reference to Trustee David Meacham, Sr., whose initials were once again used as an implied warranty.

ABOVE: Maple and pine, lengths 13" and 10¾". New Lebanon, NY.

A completely different style of dry measure emerged from the hands of a Brother at Sabbathday Lake around 1877, Granville Merrill (1839–1878).[7] He produced forms and patterns from which a series of graduated measures could be made, ten in all. They ranged in size from twenty liters ("2 Deka") down to one-tenth liter. The largest and next to smallest are illustrated. In the 1870s, "Winchester" measures (quart, gallon, etc.) were the norm, but the metric system—authorized for use by Congress in 1832 and again in 1866—was regarded as quite progressive, the wave of the future. Metric measurements—a product of the French Enlightenment in the 1790s—were very much in keeping with the Shaker ethic of applying the latest, most scientific ideas to their own industrial culture. That this system never took hold was no fault of theirs. Brother Hewlitt Chandler took charge of this industry, since he already ran the Great Mill at Sabbathday Lake. Although the mill itself closed during the Second World War, there were many leftover parts so that measures were still assembled past midcentury.

FAR LEFT: Ash and pine, diameter 12", Sabbathday Lake, ME. Collection of the United Society of Shakers, Sabbathday Lake, Maine; BELOW: Maple and pine, 3", 3¾", 4½", 5¾". Sabbathday Lake, ME. Collection of the United Society of Shakers, Sabbathday Lake, Maine.

Coopering as an industry was confined to three societies: New Lebanon, Canterbury, and Enfield, New Hampshire. The earliest of them began at New Lebanon before the start of the nineteenth century and was pretty much finished in the early 1830s. After this date the Shakers there made pails, tubs, churns, barrels, and the like for their own use only. This pail was made in the first quarter of that century. The staves at New Lebanon were made with butt joints, meeting their neighbors with flat, unshaped edges. The Shakers did not have staving machinery until much later. As a result of this, the pail has slowly assumed a slightly elliptical shape because the staves have followed the dimensional change (across the grain) of the pine bottom. Shaping of the stave sides would have prevented this. (This present example once served as a wastepaper basket for Faith Andrews!)

ABOVE: Pine with iron bands, yellow exterior and white interior paint, maximum diameter 14". New Lebanon, NY.

Canterbury had a much larger cooperage business than New Lebanon, one that started early in the 1800s but depended much more on the use of machinery. This certainly accounts for the "look" of pails from here, true round and finely finished. To achieve the first goal the coopers used a staving machine that cut the clear pine staves into a V-shaped tongue-and-groove pattern, locking them together more effectively than butt joints. Then, once the staves were assembled and bound with iron hoops (whose ends were also clipped to a V shape), the whole piece was turned on a specially outfitted lathe. This resulted in a smooth, almost polished finish, inside and out.

There was so great a consistency of manufacture that it is not possible to date these red- and blue-painted examples. The former was most likely a gift to New Hampshire Ministry Elder Benjamin Harrison Smith; the initials BHS are painted on the bottom, outside and inside. The latter pail looks almost black but is actually deep oxidized blue, the color of the woodwork upstairs in the Canterbury Meetinghouse.

ABOVE LEFT: Pine with birch handle and iron, red paint, diameter 8". Canterbury, NH; RIGHT: Pine with birch handle and iron, dark blue paint diameter 10". Canterbury, NH.

Coopering at Enfield, New Hampshire, got into high gear only after 1850, but in the 1870s and 1880s grew to be very large, an important source of revenue for this village. It is probable that in total the Enfield Shakers produced more *finished* staved products than all the other Shaker societies combined. ("Finished" is emphasized because Sabbathday Lake, for example, produced tens of thousands of cask and barrel staves, "shooks," that required assembly by the buyer.) The recognizable characteristic of Enfield's cooperage is its tongue-and-groove pattern—its staving machine formed these edges into a square U shape.

The major output at Enfield was sap pails. Instead of a handle, these had a vertical metal strap that projected above the rim and had a hole that allowed it to hang from a nail hammered into a tree trunk. In northern New England, the collecting of maple sap in early spring was the first step in a big maple sugaring business, and the Shakers were the largest single supplier of sap pails in the region. They also made washtubs, and this illustration shows a never-used example of one. It was bound with brass bands, rather than iron, and covered with a protective coat of clear varnish. The bottoms were often stamped as this one was: "N[orth] F[amily] Shakers; Enfield, NH." The photographic image dates to around 1880; it shows a similar tub in use near a well at Enfield, New Hampshire.[8]

ABOVE LEFT: Pine and brass, clear varnish, diameter 20½". Enfield, NH; INSET: Detail of above; BELOW LEFT: Photograph (copied), original dimensions unknown (see note 6), Enfield, NH.

In the 1840s, Brother Thomas Damon (1819–1880) developed a type of table yarn winder at the Hancock, Massachusetts, Society that became the community's "signature" crafted item.[9] Earlier yarn winders were usually cumbersome affairs, resting on the floor and taking up a good deal of space. Brother Damon's "umbrella swifts," on the other hand, were clamped to a table or countertop and folded down to a compact piece when not in use. They were constructed of sturdy maple, with the slats connected in their centers by metal rivets and their ends tied to one another with string. They were often covered with a coat of yellow paint.

In use, a skein of yarn was placed over a partly opened swift, and then the sliding lower piece was raised and tightened with a thumbscrew, expanding the slats. As the skein was unwound, a ball was formed that was placed in the cup on top of the shaft. (A small number of swifts were made with a finial instead of a cup; the reason for this is not known.)

Brother Damon also developed a planing and shaping machine that he first used to prepare up to twenty thousand slats a year, enough for 830 swifts. By 1854, and for the next six years, an average of 920 swifts were being made. They sold for fifty cents apiece—wholesale. Five sizes were offered. Dedicated tools, producing interchangeable parts, in standardized sizes: these were hallmarks of a true industry.

TOP: Maple with metal rivets and string, overall heights 16", 18", 21" 23", and 25". Hancock, MA; BOTTOM: Maple with metal rivets and string, blue wool (from Sabbathday Lake, ME, ca. 1998), overall height 21". Hancock, MA.

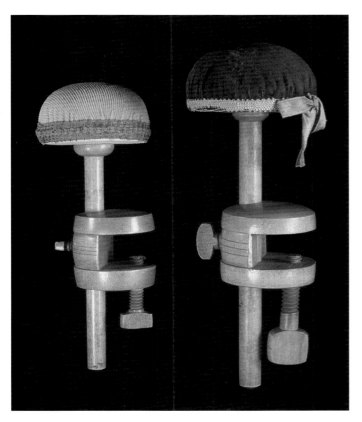

An apparent by-product of the manufacture of swifts was the making of table-clamped pincushions. While there is no manuscript evidence to support the connection, the same tools and jigs were apparently used for both, and only Hancock had them. Two pieces of maple were used, a clamp (with two thumbscrews), and a shaft surmounted by a cushion stuffed with wood shavings. The pincushions were available in two sizes, and if the number of surviving examples is any indication, not many were made. Unlike swifts, these were never advertised.

LEFT: Maple and fabric, overall height 8¾" and 10¼." Hancock, MA.

If one were looking for a way to define a "cottage industry," one could hardly do better than to point to these table-clamped pincushions made at Canterbury. No journal entries refer to them, but in the twentieth century Sisters called them "screwballs." Of the approximately sixteen examples that this author has seen, no two are alike! The bases and the cushion tops are of many dimensions, and the cushions use a variety of fabrics as covers.

The basic design and materials are always similar: two pieces of lathe-turned maple. One piece is the lower disk, and it turns up or down on a threaded shaft. The second piece *is* only one piece; it comprises a flat platform at the top to hold the pincushion, a sinuously shaped length of shaft, a second, heavier platform (which rests against the tabletop), and a long threaded shaft. The cushions were stuffed with wood shavings, covered with some type of wool, and finished with braiding (*center* and *right*) or rickrack (*left*).

Although the design appears simple at first glance—two pieces of wood, only one of them movable, the execution was anything but. The example on the left resulted from extraordinary skill at the lathe, combining beautifully graceful lines with knife-edge-sharp details in an exercise of inspired precision. All three were probably produced in the late nineteenth century and combined the talents of Brethren and Sisters.

BELOW LEFT: Maple and fabric, overall height (*left to right*) 10½", 6½", and 6½". Canterbury, NH.

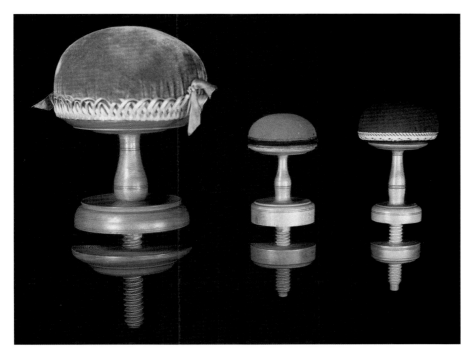

No manufactured Shaker goods approached the ubiquity of brooms and brushes. Every community from which records survive, through the nineteenth century, was heavily invested in these related enterprises. When one considers the Shakers' total commitment to spiritual and temporal cleanliness, this investment seems completely logical and natural, if not inevitable. Images of "sweeping" away sin appear in one of the most sacred expression of their faith—their hymns.[10]

Broom making probably started first at Watervliet, New York, around 1800. Two events coincided there: the Society purchased an island in the nearby Mohawk River where it could readily plant and harvest broomcorn, and a Brother—Theodore Bates (1762–1846)—invented a special vise that flattened out the bristles of the then-standard round broom, allowing heavy twine to bind the bristles in a flat shape. This gain in efficiency was a huge success with the World, and soon New Lebanon geared up for production too. This industry melded the Shakers' interest in agricultural production (broomcorn) with their proficiency in woodworking (lathe-turned handles).

We will never know how many brooms all the villages produced over time, but the total certainly ran at least into the tens of thousands. What we do know is that only a very few have survived to the present, perhaps two or three *labeled* examples. The broom illustrated here somehow escaped heavy use and is, with its paper label, largely intact. It was made at Mount Lebanon around the 1880s under the auspices of Robert Valentine (1822–1910, a Trustee from 1878 to 1896).

LEFT: Broom corn and pine, overall length 56". Mount Lebanon, NY. Courtesy of The Shaker Museum and Library, Old Chatham, NY. # 8578.

The four labels on the strip to the right bear the name Thomas Estes (1781–1863). He served as "agent" or supervisor for the industry at New Lebanon from about 1850 to 1860. The other two labels name Robert Valentine. Elder Giles Avery recorded the following in his journal in 1861: "manufacture of a parlor broom with a painted and varnished handle, all the undercoats of [broom]corn wound on the handle with a very strong cord & the outer coat wound on with wire, and then double sewed, & warranted not to get loose from the handle until worn out." The no. 6 broom then sold for $4.00 a dozen, wholesale.

LEFT: Black ink letterpress on thin yellow paper, 6½" × 3¾". New Lebanon, NY; RIGHT: Black ink letterpress on pink paper, 3¼" × 3⅝", and gold ink letterpress on dark blue paper, 3¼" × 4". Mount Lebanon, NY.

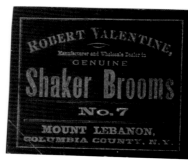

The Shakers at Shirley, to a larger extent than any other society, depended on broom making. The earliest journal entry for gathering broomcorn here was written in 1820. It is clear from their own manuscript notations that they could not grow enough broomcorn to meet their needs, and in 1872, for example, they bought a load from "the colored Shakers at Philadelphia." (This was a wholly black group that was an out-family of the Watervliet, New York, Society.) The final entry for broom selling there is dated 1898. This detail from an 1888 billhead records the sale of two dozen brooms at $2.25 a dozen. John Whitely (1819–1905) not only made this sale but may have also made the brooms. Although he had been an Elder since 1871, in his fifty-six years with the Shakers at Shirley he was also their main broom maker. Elder Whitely serves as a good example of the manual labor expected from Shakers at even the highest levels of authority in every community.

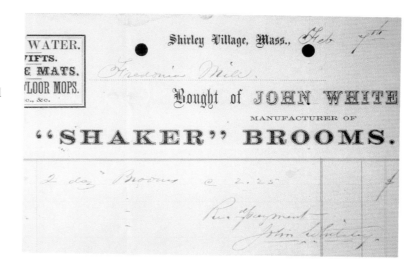

ABOVE RIGHT: Black ink letterpress and manuscript on white paper, 4½" × 8¼". Shirley, MA.

Brush making is far more difficult to document, because little was standardized in the way of shapes, sizes, and materials. Furthermore, little was specifically written about them in journals or ledgers, no special machinery was required to make them, and they were not marked or labeled.[11] The four examples here were selected mainly on the basis of their turned wood handles and how these compare to "documented" examples in public and private collections. In truth, there is some evidence of their being Shaker made, but no proof of this exists. The single brush shown *is* Shaker made, with cherrywood for its handle and natural horsehair for its bristles. The handle has wood-turning details that are distinctively "Shaker" but almost too small to show in a photograph. The communities of origin for all but "fancy goods" brushes (in the following chapter) are unknown.

ABOVE LEFT: Maple, birch, and cherrywood with natural and dyed horsehair, overall lengths 9½" to 10½". Communities unknown; BELOW: cherrywood with natural horsehair, overall length 14". Community unknown.

WOOL DUSTER, 40c.

11

Closely related to broom and brush making was mop making, and New Lebanon, Shirley, and Canterbury were its chief sites. Although no floor mops remain that are unquestionably the work of Shaker hands, a number of "wool mops" or dusters do. These were made at Canterbury and possibly New Lebanon. The Shakers turned lengths of maple with a small knob on one end (useful for tying a hanging string) and a thick button on the other. Coarse, dyed wool was attached to the thick end with color-matched yarn. Such dusters were made in the early part of the twentieth century—up to the time when there were too few Brothers to turn handles—and could rightfully be considered as one facet of the "fancy goods" industries. The illustration is from a Mount Lebanon catalog, *Products of Intelligence and Diligence* (1908). Readers should keep this fact in mind: the Shaker Societies bought extensively from one another, and in this case the appearance of these dusters for sale by Mount Lebanon does not necessarily mean that they were made there.

ABOVE: Maple and wool (dyed red and yellow), length 16½". Probably Canterbury, NH; LEFT: Black ink letterpress with wood or metal engraving on white paper, page size 7" × 4⅝" (p. 11). Mount Lebanon, NY, R-343.

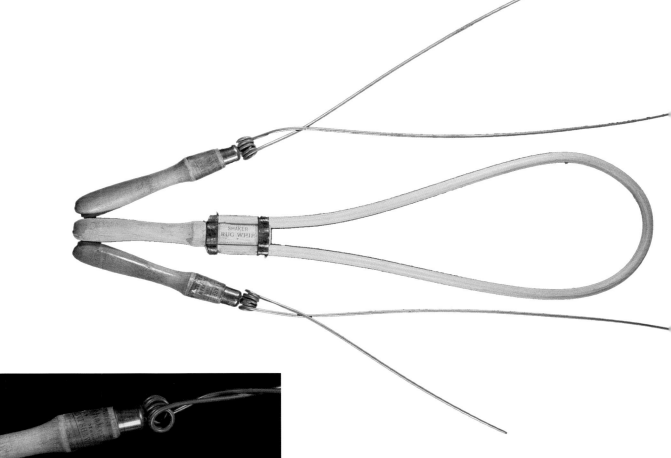

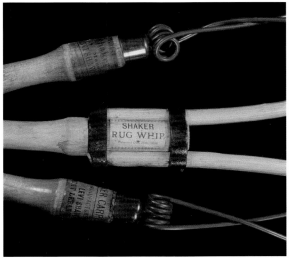

The New Lebanon Shakers (at the North Family) made carpet and rug whips from the mid-1890s to the first few years of the twentieth century. Brother Levi Shaw (1819–1908), the Trustee in charge of this business, produced up to five hundred pieces per day in 1898.[12] Two styles are shown; one (*center*) combined a simply turned softwood handle with a length of steam-bent willow wood. Strips of forged iron were used as fasteners. The Shakers were capable of making this style, and while the label on it says that these were patented in 1898, the Shakers were actually not the patentees. A non-Shaker by the name of Charles Comstock was granted the patent on October 25, 1898, and he assigned it to Levi Shaw—presumably in exchange for monetary consideration. He also went to Mount Lebanon to show the Brethren how to make both types of whips and may have supplied them with bent wire and brass ferrules for the two examples made in the other style.[13] These both have hardwood handles. The unattached label is one of several types used in this business.

TOP: Wood and metal, overall lengths 24" (*center*) and 31" (*top and bottom*). Mount Lebanon, NY; INSET: Detail of above; RIGHT: Black ink letterpress on yellow paper, 1½" × 3". Mount Lebanon, NY.

SHAKER CORRUGATED
Carpet and Rug Whip
LEVI SHAW,
Mt. Lebanon, N. Y.

Four villages made wool ("great") and flax (treadle) wheels for sale, all in northern New England: Canterbury and Enfield, New Hampshire, and Alfred and Sabbathday Lake, Maine. New Lebanon also made these plus yarn winder ("clock") wheels in the 1800s but did not develop them into true industries. The flax wheel shown was made at Sabbathday Lake, probably between 1830 and 1840. The initials of the maker, "J H," are stamped into the end of the horizontal table and stand for Deacon James Holmes. This wheel is constructed from oak and birch.

The photograph was taken at Mount Lebanon around 1915 and shows Sister Fanny Tyson (1836–1915) spinning flax into linen. Flax was one of the first crops planted by the Shakers here. They found that a quarter acre of the plant yielded about twenty-five thousand yards of linen thread, enough for four shirts, three pairs of trousers, and two bedsheets. This is certainly a posed photograph, perhaps made to honor Sister Tyson's many years of service, since all spinning and weaving took place indoors.

ABOVE LEFT: Oak and birch, natural patina, overall length 34½". Sabbathday Lake, ME. Collection of the United Society of Shakers, Sabbathday Lake, Maine. # 95.1043; BELOW RIGHT: Photoengraving on card stock, 5⅜" × 3½". Courtesy of Hamilton College, Burke Library, Clinton, NY.

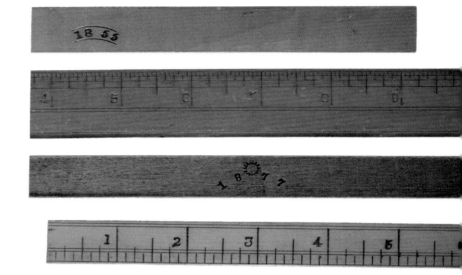

A little-known undertaking of the Shakers at Canterbury was making rulers of several types. Although not a single manuscript reference to these has been found, the physical evidence and provenance are compelling. (The reader was cautioned in the introduction not to draw conclusions about the size of an industry based on the quantity of surviving ephemera. Inferences based on surviving handwork, by contrast, are far more reliable, since these products were bought, used, and kept by many, while ephemera was kept by few and discarded by most.)

There is no reason to believe that ruler making was any more than an unadvertised, nonstandardized cottage industry. Yet rulers survive in large enough numbers for us to surmise that they were made in some quantity and were intended for sale. (It is possible that they were sold only to other Shakers, but there is no evidence to support this idea.) Of the more than a dozen examples in the author's collection, no two are alike. In this collection, however, is a series of ruler patterns—indicating that a degree of standardization was at least possible.

The rulers range in length from only six inches up to four and a half feet. A number of woods were used—maple, birch, and cherry along with seldom-seen elm. All the examples shown—three squares and four straight rules—rely on carefully seasoned woods to prevent warping and on meticu-

lously hand-stamped numbers. This is to be expected from conscientious craftsmen. What is surprising is how often dates and motifs are stamped on the back of both rules and squares. In the latter category are double arcs, six-pointed stars, and suns. The dates range from the mid-1850s to the mid-1870s. The significance of all this is presently unknown.

TOP RULERS: Maple and birch with clear varnish finish (unidentified wood under orange paint of longest rule), lengths from top to bottom 10" (1855), 12" (no date), 9" (1877), and 8" (1856). Canterbury, NH; LOWER RIGHT ANGLES: Elm (1862), birch (1855), and cherry (1862) (larger to smaller), clear varnish finish. Canterbury, NH.

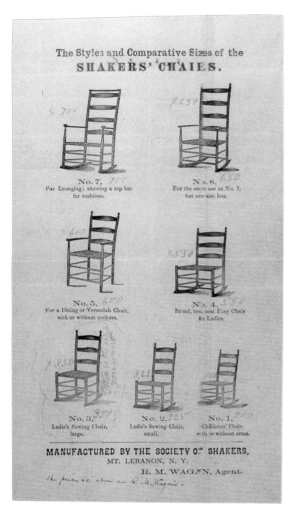

With few exceptions, the Shakers made furniture for their own use. The one notable exception—a huge one—was the manufacture and sale of chairs and stools at the South Family at Mount Lebanon.[14] The Shakers at New Lebanon (later renamed Mount Lebanon) were already making small numbers of chairs to sell by 1790 and continued doing so into the 1850s. In that decade, the pace of production picked up, and the first advertisement was printed.[15] In 1863, the South Family was split off from the Second Family, and this new unit was designated by the Central Ministry to be the production site for the fledgling chair *industry*. Soon Brother Robert Wagan (1833–1883, rhymes with "ray gun") was appointed Shop Deacon to oversee the business. In 1867, this illustrated broadside was issued—the first of its kind. It shows that sizes (and therefore parts) were now standardized, and this, along with an assembly-line method of production, meant that chair making had become a true industry. A dedicated chair factory was built in 1872 and is depicted in this cut from an 1874 chair catalog.

LEFT: Black ink letterpress (with wood or metal engravings) on white paper, 10" × 5¼". Mount Lebanon, NY, NIR; BELOW: Black ink wood or metal engraving on white paper, approximately 2½" × 3½". Mount Lebanon, NY, R-248.

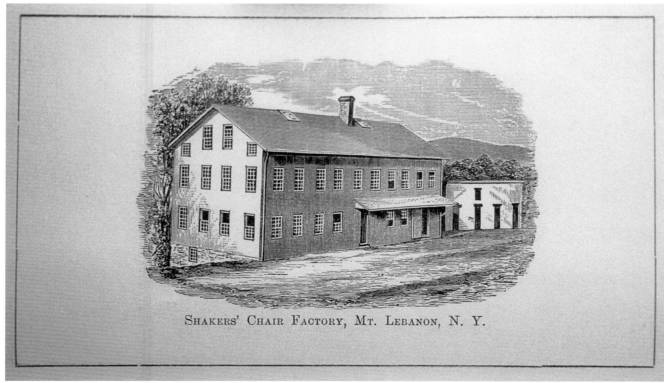

SHAKERS' CHAIR FACTORY, MT. LEBANON, N. Y.

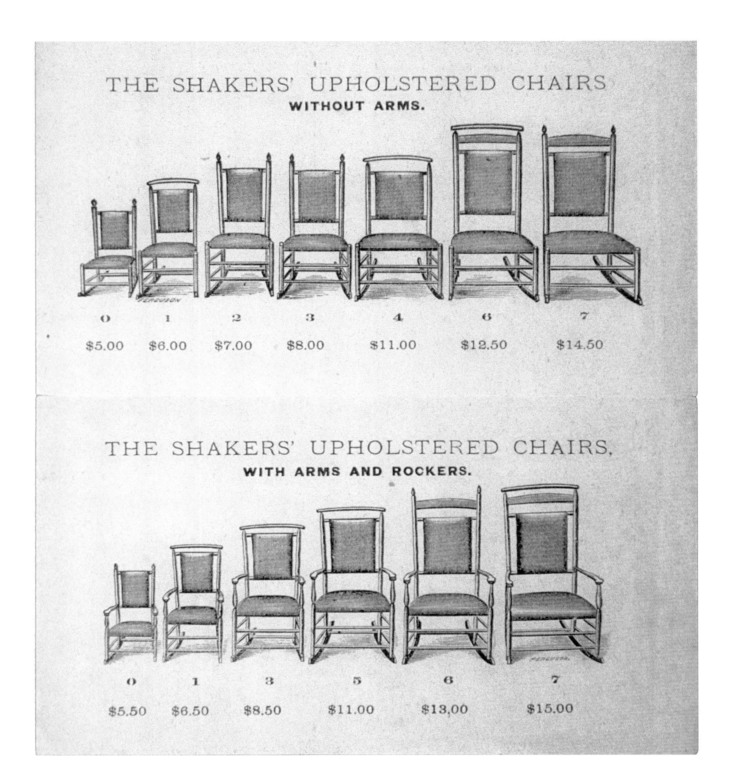

THE SHAKERS' UPHOLSTERED CHAIRS

WITHOUT ARMS.

O	1	2	3	4	6	7
$5.00	$6.00	$7.00	$8.00	$11.00	$12.50	$14.50

THE SHAKERS' UPHOLSTERED CHAIRS,

WITH ARMS AND ROCKERS.

O	1	3	5	6	7
$5.50	$6.50	$8.50	$11.00	$13.00	$15.00

The next broadside was printed on two sides (with oval boxes offered for sale on the reverse), and to judge from the prices, it was published sometime before 1874. It shows an array of upholstered chairs for sale, with and without arms. Neither a #2 nor a #4 size was offered.

ABOVE: Black ink letterpress (with wood or metal engravings) on off-white paper, 6⅜" × 5⅝". Mount Lebanon, NY, R-338.

The earliest bound catalog was issued in 1874, and between then and about 1880 eight more were produced. The formats for all of them were similar: many cuts of chair types with prices, descriptions of the many, many options available to the buyer, and occasional advertising for other products offered by Mount Lebanon such as footstools and even Dried Sweet Corn. An example of each catalog, in the run of nine (with two from 1875), is shown here. The one with blue wraps (*lower center*) was the earliest—1874.

ABOVE: Black and gold ink letterpress on variously colored papers, largest (red wraps, *lower left*) 6⅞" × 4⅛". *From left to right, bottom:* R-244, R-240, R-248, R-238, and R-242. *From left to right top:* R-239, R-247, NIR, R-245, and R-247. Mount Lebanon, NY.

If imitation is the sincerest form of flattery, the Shakers were indeed flattered: so much so that in 1875 they felt compelled to adopt a logo, which they said was trade-marked, to be affixed to all their products. Imitations of their chairs were already flooding the market at this early date, and they had a valuable product and reputation to protect. The back cover of their 1875 *Illustrated Catalogue and Price List* reads: "The above Trade-Mark will be attached to every genuine Shaker Chair."

RIGHT: Gold ink letterpress on heavy purple paper, 5⅛" × 3¼". Mount Lebanon, NY, R-247.

P. 3836.   PALM, FECHTELER & CO. NEW YORK & CHICAGO.

What was attached to each chair (and stool) was a gold-colored transfer decal. This is a detail from a full sheet of decals, fifty-five in all. They were printed in reverse because, after soaking and applying, they read correctly. There is no no. 2 on this sheet, a reflection of how scarce this size was, and nos. 4, 6, and 7 predominate, which corresponds with their dominance among surviving examples. Decals were placed behind the top slat on chairs or on the inside of rockers for rocking chairs. Stools had them wrapped around a leg.

Gold ink letterpress on clear substance on white paper, each approximately 1½" × 2", full sheet 10" × 24". Mount Lebanon, NY.

The Shakers set up a booth at the 1876 Centennial Exhibition in Philadelphia and won a Certificate of Award there. This cabinet card was issued in conjunction with that event and is the earliest known photographic rendering of Shaker "production" chairs. On the reverse side the word "Genuine" is emphasized; this was a steady theme for years to come, as the Shakers' hegemony in this arena was a constant concern.

Photograph on tan card stock, 3" × 5⅝". Mount Lebanon, NY.

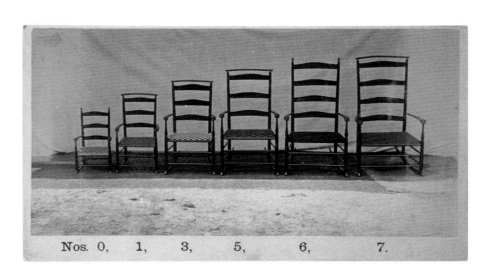

Nos. 0,   1,   3,   5,   6,   7.

This no 6 rocking chair appears to be identical to the one pictured on the card. It too dates from about 1875–1880. The seat material is a tape, made from fine woven wool, that surrounds a pad stuffed with wood shavings. In addition to choices of eight sizes, nos. 0–7, customers could choose a straight or rocking chair, with or without arms, slatted or taped back, and finial-topped posts or a cushion rail (often erroneously called a shawl rail; it was meant to attach the ties of a back cushion to). As if those choices were not enough, chairs were also available in a range of finishes, from "natural" (a clear varnish) to a dark ebony stain, and with a variety of tape colors.

ABOVE: Maple with wool tape, ebony stain. Overall height 42". Mount Lebanon, NY.

These chairs are both no. 5 size and date to sometime around 1880–1890. The styles of chairs varied little after the 1870s, but by the end of the century the laborious process of steam-bending the rear posts and turning the horizontal stretchers with a taper toward each end had given way to straight rear posts and dowel stretchers. The straight chair has an ebony stain finish, while the rocking chair has a brown-pigmented varnish. Both have replaced taped seats. The stool is the tallest of several varieties offered; its tapes are original. This gold transfer decal is on the back of the top slat of the straight chair.

ABOVE: Maple with cotton tapes, dark brown stain (*left and center*), light brown varnish (*right*). Overall heights (*left to right*) 36¼", 15¾", and 36". Mount Lebanon, NY; BELOW RIGHT: Gold ink transfer on wood (see armchair, above), approximately 1½" × 2". Mount Lebanon, NY.

FILLING CHAIR ORDERS   MT. LEBANON, N.Y.

Eldress Sarah Collins (1855–1947) was one of the last two Sisters to be engaged in the chair industry (the other was Sister Lillian Barlow). Sister Sarah was the one who wove the taped seats and, sometimes, backs. She is pictured in the 1890s doing just this. In the early years, these tapes were made from fine wool (as on the no. 6 chair illustrated on page 142), but once the business was in full production, cotton was the material of choice, because it was cheaper to make. Later in the century the Shakers bought commercial tapes or "listing" because there were not enough hands to weave it themselves. This had once been a responsibllty of the young girls in the community, and their numbers were in steep decline by 1890.

LEFT: Photograph on card stock 5¼" x 3½". Mount Lebanon, NY. Courtesy of Hamilton College, Burke Library, Clinton, NY.

This billhead, dated May 27, 1940, is among the last artifacts of the once-thriving chair industry. It records the sale of a "No. 6 and No. 3 arm rocker"[chairs] and a no.o stool. It is signed by sister Lillian Barlow (1876–1942). Having survived the death of its founder, Elder Robert Wagan, in 1883, and the complete loss of its factory to a fire in 1923, this chair business closed for good in 1941. The Mount Lebanon community closed in 1947.

RIGHT: Black ink letterpress and manuscript on tan paper, 8½" x 5½". Mount Lebanon, NY.

Mount Lebanon, N.Y., *May 27 1940*

Mrs. *Alvord.*

To **R. M. WAGAN & CO.**, Dr.

MANUFACTURERS OF THE GENUINE

☐ **SHAKER CHAIRS** ☐

Telegraph and Telephone Office :: West Lebanon, N.Y.

One No. 6 Arm Rocker - Slat-back - Rush - Seat - Old Maple .   15-

One No. 3 Arm Rocker - Old Maple, Garnet & rose .   11 00

One No. o. Stool Rush Seat   3

Received Payment Lillian Barlow. $29.00

Thank You!

Before we leave woodenware, it is important that we revisit oval boxes briefly since so little in the way of documented crafts from the western Shakers remains. This box, made at Union Village, was a developmental dead end in that it was not part of the sequence that led to a highly successful oval carrier industry in the East. In 1842, Micajah Burnett (1791–1879) came to Union Village and taught the Brethren how to make oval boxes using the latest in planing machines. This is the time that this example was made, and many more were made for sale in the decades that followed.[16]

The shapes of boxes varied slightly from village to village: those from Sabbathday Lake and Canterbury tend to be elongated ovals, while this one has a more rounded or squat shape. (This was simply a function of the shape of the wooden form around which the sides were steam-bent; the forms varied among communities.) As was customary, the sides are maple, and the top and bottom are clear pine. This box never had a finish applied.

Pasted inside the lid is a handwritten genealogy of the Miller family (no relation to the author). John (1770–1850) and his wife, Susanna (1778–1840), joined Union Village the year that it was organized, in 1805. They brought their seven children with them and, presumably, were divided within the community by age and gender. Lucy (1804–1869), the last born, wrote this family genealogy early in 1842. She had signed the covenant in 1841, just after her mother died, and at the time of writing this could not have known that her natural brother Craig would die later in 1842. The last words on this paper read, poignantly: "Lucy Miller was born the 13th of June 1804. *and yet living*" (emphasis added).[17]

ABOVE: Maple and pine, 5½" × 12½" × 9¼", with black ink manuscript on discolored off-white paper pasted on pine, 5¾" × 7¾". Union Village, OH.

Fancy Goods

This diminutive, octagonal-shaped workbox is among the earliest surviving remnants of what developed into a major Shaker industry after the Civil War: fancywork. It is also significant because it serves as a preview of the single most important aspect in that arena—poplarware. This box was made at Sabbathday Lake in the 1860s, where it still resides. It is constructed entirely of paper-covered cardboard but already shows the distinctive signs of the woven poplar cloth-covered boxes that will soon follow: rigidly geometric shape, meticulous handwork, and its intended use for the sewing arts.

ABOVE: Colored papers on cardboard with fabric, diameter 3⅜". Sabbathday Lake, ME. Collection of the United Society of Shakers, Sabbathday Lake, Maine.

An offshoot of small sewing-box making was fan making. Since these are considered "vanity" items today, it may surprise some that the business of making fans was a rather important and prosperous one for the Shakers. Many communities were engaged in fan production, and a wide variety of materials were employed: paper, woven poplar, palm leaf, and feathers—especially turkey and peacock feathers.

The partly opened, pleated paper example was bought by early collectors at Mount Lebanon but was probably made at Harvard.[1] The paper is attached to two flat, thin sticks with fine twine, and the wood is stained with an orange-tinted varnish.

ABOVE: Paper and wood, overall length 13½". Probably Harvard, MA.

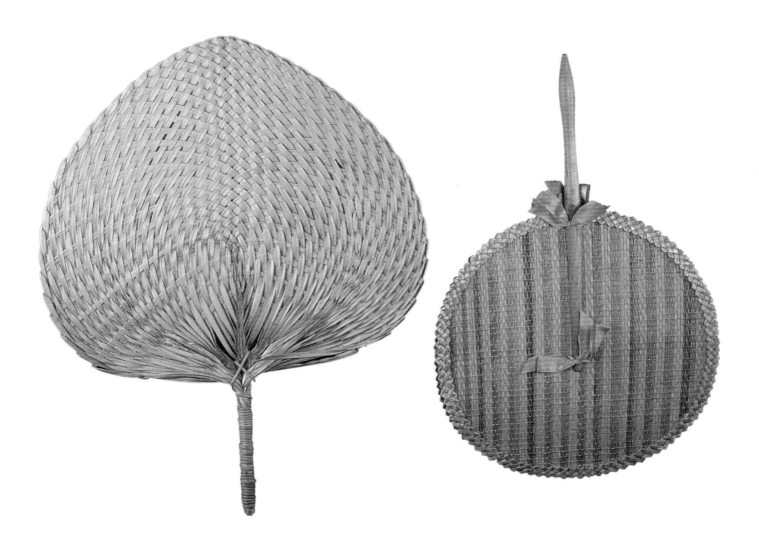

The woven palm leaf fan is made from a single frond, with the wrapped stalk forming its handle. Several communities, from Maine to Kentucky, have been cited as the source for these, with Sabbathday Lake a leading contender.[2] This village was known to have imported palm leaf for hat and bonnet making from Cuba (although other communities did as well).

More is certain about the origins of the woven poplar fan. It was the work of Sister Martha Wetherell (1855–1944). She had difficulty "fitting in" at any one village and moved among three or four in her life. She arrived at Canterbury in 1893 and is credited with introducing the woven poplar trade to them. One of her specialties there was dyeing poplar—thus we can positively attribute this fan to her during the time that she was there. It incorporates blue, pink, and brown strips, woven horizontally on the front face and vertically on the reverse. All this is fitted into a turned and slotted maple handle and finished with two silk ribbons. Similar fans were also made at Mount Lebanon, but this one was made at Canterbury, between 1893 and 1913.[3]

ABOVE LEFT: Palm leaf, overall length 14". Possibly Sabbathday Lake, ME; ABOVE RIGHT: Poplar, maple and silk, overall length 13". Canterbury, NH.

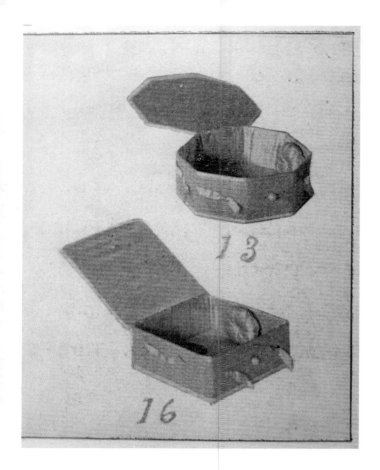

The most dominant format for fancy goods was poplar (sometimes called "popple" by the Shakers), cloth-covered sewing boxes.[4] These were made in a wide variety of shapes and sizes, outfitted in different ways. They were an important industry at Sabbathday Lake, Alfred, and Canterbury but were also made at Enfield, New Hampshire, and Mount Lebanon. The industry was a perfect fit for the Shakers since it played into several of their strengths: it combined an abundant natural resource, poplar trees, with two well-developed skills—weaving and handwork. The results were attractive, durable, and useful objects that found a ready, often eager, market in the World.

The craft developed first at New or Mount Lebanon around 1860. The Civil War disrupted supplies of other plant material, such as palm leaf, so it was natural for the community to use what *was* available. Brethren felled poplar trees, the wood of which was not useful for furniture making (except in drawers) or firewood, and they allowed sections to remain outdoors in winter. The frozen wood was more easily shaved into curled, paper-thin strips. These were flattened, dried, and then split into narrow strips only one-sixteenth of an inch wide. A loom was warped with cotton thread, and the strips of poplar were woven in using different weaving patterns. This cloth was glued onto paper to strengthen it, cut into pieces that wrapped around solid wood bases, and tacked in place. Edges of the poplar cloth were protected with a thin band of supple, white kid leather.

ABOVE LEFT: Photoengraving and black ink letterpress on off-white paper, image size 2½" × 5". Sabbathday Lake, ME, R-349; BELOW: Poplar cloth and silk, 2¾" × 6½" × 6½" (*bottom left*), 2" × 4¼" × 4¼" (*top left*), and 2½" × 6¼" × 5¾" (*right*). Sabbathday Lake and Alfred, ME.

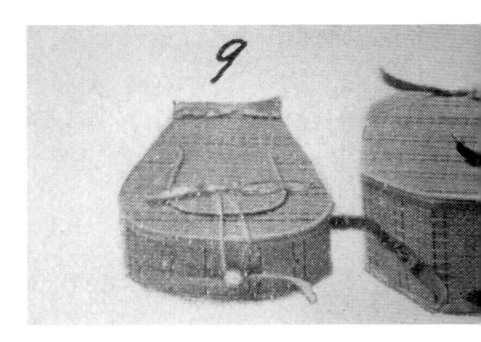

An array of colored silks were used to line the insides of the boxes, and matching silk ribbons were used as hinges for the lids and ties for sewing accessories. These latter were similar to what one finds in Shaker sewing carriers: pincushion, needle storage book, thread wax, and emery. The open page of the 1910 catalog from Sabbathday Lake shows six of the many types of poplarware boxes offered then. Two of those, nos. 13 and 16, are shown in the photograph (on page 150). The former (octagonal-shaped) sold for $1.50 and the latter (square-shaped) for $2.00. The third piece illustrated (above) is from Alfred and was called a "Bell shape Work Box" in Alfred's 1908 catalog. It was priced at $1.00. Both communities marked their pieces with a rubber stamp on the bottom. The one shown is the same that was designed by Brother Delmer in 1903 for stamping the bottom of his carriers. ("SC" stood for Shaker Community.)

ABOVE: Photoengraving and black ink letterpress on off-white paper, image size approximately 1½" × 1½". Alfred, ME, R-149; RIGHT: Black ink letterpress (stamp) on pink paper (bottom of square box), diameter 1¼". Sabbathday Lake, ME.

A postcard image shows the store at Sabbathday Lake as it appeared around 1912. Fancywork goods were sold to visitors there but were, to a far greater extent, brought on sales trips throughout New England and beyond. About half of the community's output of goods went just a few miles up the road to the Poland Spring House resort; most of the rest went to resorts on the coast and in the mountains of Maine and New Hampshire, and to local fairs.

RIGHT: Photograph, hand-colored, on card stock, 3½" × 5¼". Sabbathday Lake, ME. Courtesy of Hamilton College, Burke Library, Clinton, NY.

Canterbury was the other major center for poplarware production. It is unknown if this craft was undertaken before the arrival of Sister Martha Wetherell, in 1893, but in the first half of the twentieth century it probably outsold all other crafts there combined. Between 1930 and the end of the industry, in 1958, more than eleven thousand pieces were made. (After 1939, there were only Sisters and hired men at the village.) This postcard photograph shows Sisters Bertha Lindsay (1897–1990, *left*) and Lillian Phelps (1876–1973) at work making octagonal-shaped boxes from woven poplar cloth in the 1940s or 1950s. Sister (later Eldress) Bertha was in charge of the business from 1944 until it ended.

LEFT: Photograph on card stock, 3½" × 5¼". Canterbury, NH. Courtesy of Hamilton College, Burke Library, Clinton, NY.

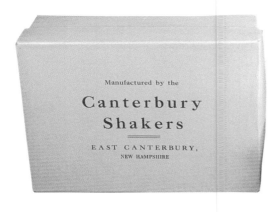

Eldress Bertha gave one of these octagonal boxes to a friend and early collector for Christmas—Mrs. Gladys Jordan. An enclosed note reads: "A simple token of my sincere affection, to add to your Shaker collection. (Woven by the Shakers.) Love from Bertha." Canterbury is the only community that packaged its poplarware in cardboard boxes such as this one.

LEFT: Poplar and silk, 2¼" × 6¼" × 4½". Canterbury, NH.

One of the styles of poplarware that was made only at Canterbury and the two Maine villages is this diamond-shaped piece called a "card tray" or, simply, a "tray." Although they were probably used most often to hold a woman's trinkets atop a bureau, the Shakers marketed them to accommodate the Victorian custom (among the well-to-do at least) of leaving calling cards for visits. They are described in catalogs as made of "poplar with satin lined bottoms[s]." What was called satin was actually silk, since satin is a weave (silk is a fabric). These trays sold for forty to fifty cents apiece, and the price did not change over a span of decades.

The undated photograph shows the gift store at the Trustees' office at Canterbury and includes some poplar trays. These offices served as the points of contact between the Shakers—at least the two women and two men Trustees—and the World. Every society had such an office located on the main road through its village.

RIGHT: Satin-woven silk, poplar cloth, and kid leather, overall length 7". Canterbury, NH; BELOW: Photograph on card stock, 3½" × 5¼". Canterbury, NH. Courtesy of Hamilton College, Burke Library, Clinton, NY.

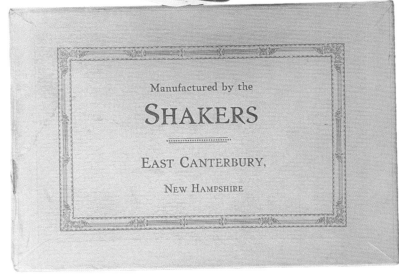

Manufactured by the
SHAKERS
EAST CANTERBURY,
NEW HAMPSHIRE

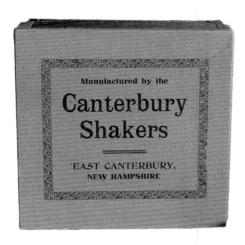

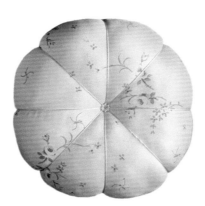

The production of freestanding pincushions was closely related to the poplar box business. This never-used example is still mated with the box that it was sold in. It was made at a relatively late date, probably the 1940s or 1950s, when boxes covered with white paper gave way to these simpler (and undoubtedly cheaper) ones of plainly printed cardboard.

ABOVE: Plain-woven, printed silk with silk thread, diameter 5". Canterbury, NH.

Canterbury and Sabbathday Lake both made these hat/clothing brushes as part of their fancy goods repertoire in the first quarter of the twentieth century. Virtually identical in appearance, the one feature that is said to distinguish which community they came from is the velvet "skirt" between the bristles and the handle: it was cut straight at the former and "pinked" at the latter. Sister Ada Cummings (1862–1926) was in charge of making these brushes at Sabbathday Lake, and they were no longer made following her death. A catalog issued there in 1910 says the following: "The hat . . . brushes are made of reveled horse hair cloth, strongly put together by winding in glue beside[s] being well nailed to the wooden handle." They were available in two sizes, selling for thirty and fifty cents apiece.

RIGHT: Horsehair, maple, cotton velvet, and silk, overall length 10¼". Sabbathday Lake, ME.

Several communities in the East made spool stands that looked like this, with only minor variations in the diameter of the base and in the shape and height of the shaft. Most versions have an emery-filled bag and a piece of beeswax attached to the pincushion on the top. This particular example was made at Canterbury and is accompanied by the type of box that it was originally sold in. (In this case, however, the box and spool stand were acquired separately.) Since other boxes of this size are unknown, it may be safely assumed that they were used for only a short time. In the 1930s, when this spool stand was probably made, they sold for $2.00.

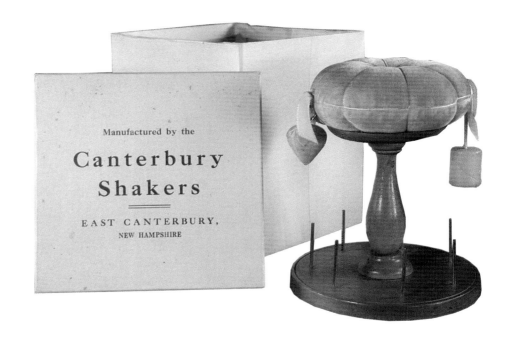

RIGHT: Maple and cotton velvet with silk, wax, and iron pins, overall height 5¾", diameter 4¾". Canterbury, NH.

EXHIBIT & SALE
BY THE
SHAKERS
From East Canterbury, N. H.
OF THEIR
Fancy Goods and Shaker Capes

This undated broadside from Canterbury was never used. It is shown here to represent all the sales efforts of the Maine and New Hampshire societies. As was mentioned earlier, very little fancywork was actually sold at the villages; the much greater part went "on the road." The Shakers organized annual sales trips to wherever tourists could be found, not only in New England, but also down the New Jersey coast and as far as Washington, D.C. In one instance, Elder Henry Green of Alfred made a forty-one-day sales trip that took him to Florida! This was in 1903.

The Shakers set up specially built folding tables at resorts, expositions, and fairs. At times, the routes of two communities crossed and caused friction; this was especially true at resorts in the White Mountains of New Hampshire. Nonetheless, the Trustees of those villages that were affected managed to talk through these difficulties with one another, and serious conflicts were avoided. The heyday of this activity was 1890–1920.

LEFT: Black ink letterpress on white paper, 12¼" × 9½". Canterbury, NH.

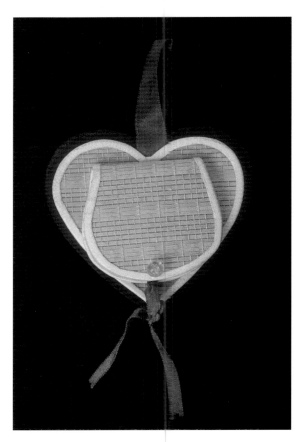

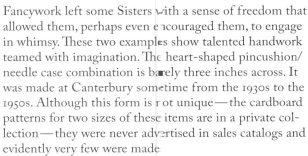

Fancywork left some Sisters with a sense of freedom that allowed them, perhaps even encouraged them, to engage in whimsy. These two examples show talented handwork teamed with imagination. The heart-shaped pincushion/needle case combination is barely three inches across. It was made at Canterbury sometime from the 1930s to the 1950s. Although this form is not unique—the cardboard patterns for two sizes of these items are in a private collection—they were never advertised in sales catalogs and evidently very few were made.

Sisters at the North Family at Sabbathday Lake, made the scallop shell cushion around 1880. These too were never advertised. Fancy goods were an industry that encompassed both organized *group* labor—seen in sewing carrier or cloak making—and the handwork of inspired *individuals*.

ABOVE LEFT: Poplar cloth with green velvet and silk, width 3". Canterbury, NH; ABOVE RIGHT: Scallop shells with russet-colored velvet, width 3". Sabbathday Lake, ME.

An unknown Sister at Canterbury made small numbers of outfitted, all-fabric sewing boxes around 1930. The stitching was both machine and hand done, while the embroidered felt displays fine handwork. This example is special owing to the painted flowers, probably the work of Sister Cora Helena Sarle (1867–1956). Sister Sarle is best known for two volumes of watercolor drawings of the flora at Canterbury. A handwritten note accompanying this piece reads: "Made by Shakers, given to me when I was 17 or 18 at Crawfords [resort, Maine] when I waited tables, by a guest."

RIGHT: Tan linen, blue silk, and off-white felt, overall length 11" (open). Canterbury, NH.

Textiles

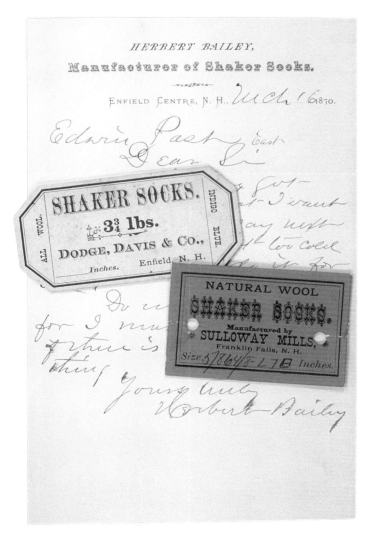

The story of Shaker-made socks in New Hampshire is a complex and convoluted one, but nonetheless too important a factor in the economies of Canterbury and Enfield to be ignored. The situation was similar at both communities, so only Enfield's enterprise will be considered here. A classic battle developed in the middle of the nineteenth century between man-made and machine-made goods. The New Hampshire Shakers used their talent for synthesis and sidestepped this issue of "either/or" by combining both. Around 1850, they found that the finest men's wool hosiery incorporated the benefits of circular (nonseamed), machine-knit foot and ankle sections with heavier, hand-knit toe and heel sections. Thus, the Shaker Sock was born.[1]

In 1851, the Enfield Shakers built a water-powered machine shop and bought either one or two newly invented circular knitting machines. Within three years an industry was under way. (Conflicting accounts say that the hand knitting took place within the society or by local townswomen. The true answer may be that both were involved.) Soon the community found that it suited them better to lease their old flannel factory (a label from which is illustrated) and sell their own processed wool to a Worldly manufacturer.

The first of these was Conant & Davis, later becoming Dodge, Davis & Co. (1873–1885, tag, *left*). Shortly after this, an Israel Sulloway (tag, *right*) opened a mill in town using the Shakers' innovation *and* appropriating their good name. He moved his operation in 1869 to a nearby town but kept the Shaker name.[2] A lawsuit filed by the Enfield Society dragged on for twenty years, with unknown resolution. Herbert Bailey (letterhead, *center*) bought Sulloway's

business and sold it in 1878. His relationship with the Enfield community is unclear. Suffice it to say that for at least thirty years the Shaker Sock was an important source of revenue for the community, with either its direct or indirect involvement.

ABOVE LEFT: Black ink letterpress and manuscript on white paper, 8" × 5½", black ink letterpress on off-white card stock, 1½" × 3⅜" (*left*), and black ink letterpress on blue card stock, 1¾" × 2¾" (*right*). Enfield, NH; RIGHT: Black ink letterpress on blue-green paper, 1¾" × 2¾". Enfield, NH.

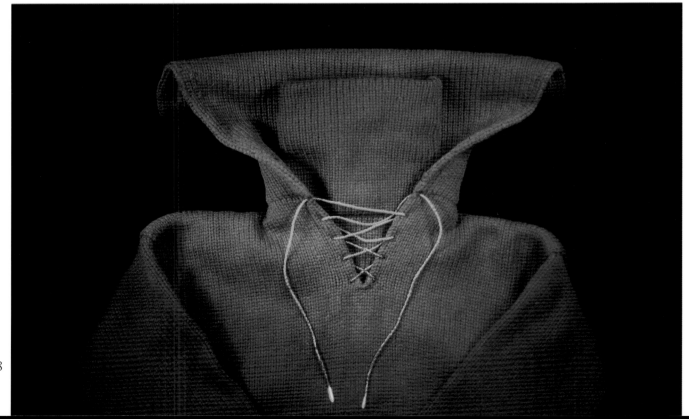

CANTERBURY SHAKERS

MANUFACTURERS OF

SHAKER ALL-WOOL SWEATERS

Address all orders to HART & SHEPARD

EAST CANTERBURY, N. H.

RETAIL PRICE OF SWEATERS

No. 0.	Extra Heavy Weight	$6.00
No. 1.	Heavy Weight	5.00
No. 2.	Medium Weight	4.35
No. 3.	Light Weight	3.35
	Jacket Sweaters	$1.00 extra
	Jacket Sweaters with pockets . . .	1.30 extra
	Turtle Necks	1.00 extra

COLORS

Harvard Red	*Navy Blue*	*Dartmouth Green*
Gray	*Black*	*White*

Shaker-knit sweaters did not originate with Land's End (which began in 1963). Some seventy-five years earlier, in 1886 to be exact, the Shakers at Canterbury started a modest business of knitting sweaters on a single flatbed machine. "Two types of sweaters were produced: a turtleneck pullover used as a letter sweater for Dartmouth [illustrated here in 'Dartmouth green'], Yale, Harvard, and Princeton; and a jacket or coat sweater [illustrated here in 'White'] manufactured for popular use."[3] Several styles of the latter type, in four weights and six colors, were available. Between 1887 and 1903, five Lamb knitting machines were purchased for Canterbury, and a variety of printed items—ephemera—was produced to support this full-fledged industry. In 1907, the community attempted to trademark the name "Shaker Sweaters": a court denied the request two years later for technical reasons.[4]

ABOVE: Black ink letterpress on off-white card stock, 3" × 4½". Canterbury, NH, NIR;
BELOW: Green wool with leather tie, overall length 33". Canterbury, NH;

This card (*opposite*), with a sample of no. 2 gauge knit—"medium weight"—dates from this period. In 1910, when the *Retail Price[s] of Sweaters and Coat Sweaters* (i.e., cardigans) was printed, 1,489 sweaters were made. The bifold pamphlet on the left records prices in the late teens; they had more than doubled since 1910, with the no. 0 going from $7.50 to $16.00. The last catalog (*right*) was issued just before all commercial knitting stopped and business closed, in 1923. A sweater of this same style and weight was now up to $18.00.

RIGHT: Off-white wool with mother-of-pearl buttons, overall length 28". Canterbury, NH; BELOW: Black ink letterpress on white paper, 4½" × 3½" (*left*), NIR; black ink letterpress on white paper, 6" × 4⅜" (*center*), R-165; black ink letterpress on white paper, 4½" × 3½" (*right*). R-164. Canterbury, NH.

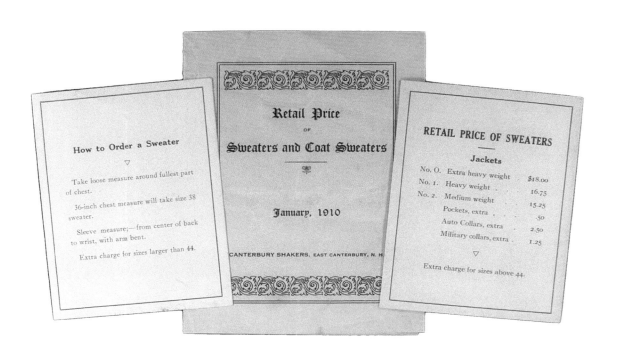

How to Order a Sweater

▽

Take loose measure around fullest part of chest.

36-inch chest measure will take size 38 sweater.

Sleeve measure;—from center of back to wrist, with arm bent.

Extra charge for sizes larger than 44.

Retail Price

OF

Sweaters and Coat Sweaters

January, 1910

CANTERBURY SHAKERS. EAST CANTERBURY, N. H.

RETAIL PRICE OF SWEATERS

Jackets

No. 0. Extra heavy weight		$18.00
No. 1. Heavy weight		16.75
No. 2. Medium weight		15.25
Pockets, extra		.50
Auto Collars, extra		2.50
Military collars, extra		1.25

▽

Extra charge for sizes above 44.

Canterbury is also where Shaker cloaks originated, but they were later made at Mount Lebanon, Sabbathday Lake, and Enfield, New Hampshire, as well. Eldress Dorothy Durgin (1825–1898) is credited with the inspiration for this industry, which was the sole province of the Sisters. "[Sister] Durgin based her unique design for the cloak on a raincoat she owned and found to be exceptional in design and function. An excellent tailor, she dismantled the coat to provide a pattern for a woolen cloak she made for herself."[5] This was in 1890. In 1903, "The Dorothy" was granted trademark protection. The cloak shown here, and sometimes referred to as an "Opera Cloak," was made at Canterbury. It is made from French wool broadcloth, dyed a deep purple, and has a brocaded silk lining and ties. Not visible are a full, pleated hood, arm slits, and inside pockets. This was the most expensive variant. In addition to this adult size, cloaks were available in children's and infants' sizes—even down to a "6 month size, hood lined" in white, pink, and blue! The full-size models varied greatly in price, depending on how much silk and handwork were required. By the time the business came to a close in 1942, the purple example above would have cost fifty-eight dollars.

RIGHT: Purple-dyed wool and brocaded silk, overall length 48". Canterbury, NH. Photograph courtesy of Canterbury Shaker Village, Inc., Canterbury, NH. # 2002.258.3.

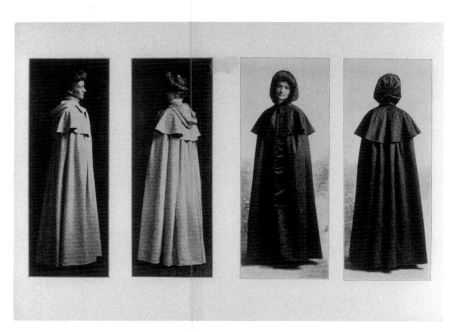

Cloaks formed an important portion of the fancy goods industry at Canterbury, accounting for some 25 percent of the total from sales trips, and the community promoted them in different ways. The four-panel photoengraving shown here is on the back of an order form. An employee at Kimball's Studios in Concord, New Hampshire, named Edith Green (not to be confused with a Canterbury Sister of the same name) posed for these views.[6] On the other side the text reads: "The 'Dorothy' Shaker Cloak supplies a long-felt want for auto, carriage, street or ocean travel, or in pastel shades for evening wear." It proceeds to enumerate the various options offered and instructs women on how to take measurements for their order.

LEFT: Photoengraving on white paper, 5¾" × 8". Canterbury, NH, R-161.

The postcard at the top shows the extent of sales trips: "The Shaker Sisters from East Canterbury [their postal address] will hold an exhibition and sale . . . [in] Washington, D.C., Dec. 18 and 19, 1911." The other card is a rare example of a Shaker advertising postcard. Its "divided back" shows that it dates to sometime after 1907. The bound catalog lists dozens of other fancy goods along with half a page devoted to extract of witch hazel. This product, considered earlier, was offered in sizes ranging from a half-pint to a full barrel.

RIGHT: Photoengraving and black ink letterpress on card stock, 3¼" × 5½" (*top*), black ink letterpress on tan paper, 6" × 4⅜" (*left*), R-154, and photoengraving on card stock, 5½" × 3⅜". Canterbury, NH.

Sister Mary Louisa Wilson (1858–1939) was appointed as Trustee in 1887 and guided Canterbury's textile industries in their later years. In May 1932, she wrote on this envelope: "Cloak and Sweater Labels and trade marks. Samples for ordering others. Please [do] not take. c/o MLW." The top labels were used on cloaks, the lower ones on sweaters.

LEFT: Woven silk (labels) and black ink manuscript on tan paper, 3⅛" × 5¼". Canterbury, NH.

NOTICE!

GENUINE HAND-MADE

SHAKER CLOAKS

· ADDRESS ·

EMMA J. NEALE

MOUNT LEBANON

Columbia County, N. Y.

Cloak making was an important part of the fancy goods trade at Mount Lebanon too. It is presumed that both the idea for developing this into an industry and the patterns for it came from Canterbury. Watervliet and Mount Lebanon had made woolen cloaks for their own use for some years before 1890, but the model that ultimately became the standard at Mount Lebanon was "The Dorothy." Sister Clarissa Jacobs (1833–1905), a talented seamstress, was in charge until 1899 and is credited with making the dove gray cloak worn by Mrs. Grover Cleveland at her husband's second inauguration, in 1893.

When Sister Emma Jane Neale (1847–1943) took over from Sister Clarissa, one of her first acts was to apply for a patent for "long cloaks" on behalf of the newly formed "E. J. Neale & Co. Mount Lebanon, N. Y." This was granted on November 26, 1901. (By now it is hoped that the reader has been disabused of the myth that the Shakers' altruism prevented them from seeking patent protection. This falsehood will be further exposed below when their inventions are considered.) This large display sign delivers its message simply but boldly. Once again, "genuine" is used as the Shakers' omnipresent warranty of quality. Cloaks were made into the 1930s; this sign could be from anytime between 1900 and then.

ABOVE: Black ink letterpress on white card stock, 14½" × 19½". Mount Lebanon, NY, NIR.

This photograph shows the Sisters' sewing room in the 1890s. A large "tailoring" counter (*left foreground*), sewing machine (*left background*), and "sewing desks" (*background*), were all essential to cloak production, as was the specially designed flat-top stove to accommodate pressing irons.

LEFT: Photograph on card stock, 3½" × 5¼". Mount Lebanon, NY. Courtesy of Hamilton College, Burke Library, Clinton, NY.

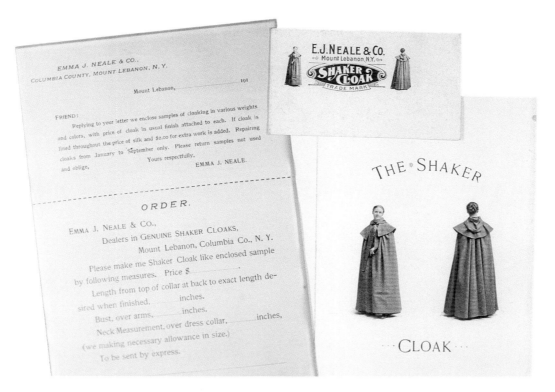

A variety of printed paper was needed to support this industry—an order form (dated 191_), circular, and business card (both undated) are shown here. The inside of the circular reads: "Respected Friend: We desire to call your attention to this Cloak, now so much used by the elite of society, and made exclusively by us." The Mount Lebanon Shakers must have meant the phrase "exclusively by us" to refer to their newly patented style, since other Shaker Societies and the World all made cloaks.

ABOVE: Black ink letterpress on (discolored) white paper, 8½" × 5½", NIR; photoengraving and black ink letterpress on off-white paper, 6⅞" × 4½" (folded), R-345; photoengraving and black ink letterpress on white card stock, 2¼" × 3⅞". Mount Lebanon, NY.

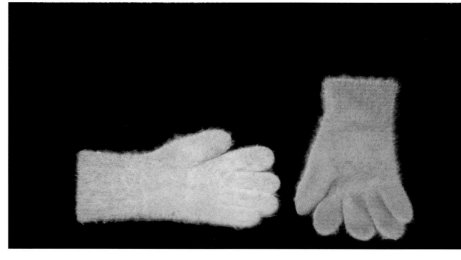

Another textile business developed by the Mount Lebanon Shakers—this one *was* exclusively theirs—was the manufacture of coonskin gloves. Actually it was the hair of raccoons, not the skin, that was used. The earliest reference to these was in September of 1884: "A large number of sisters [*sic*] are getting off the fur from Coon's skins for gloves and several Brethren also [are] engaged." Another reference appears four years later: "Br. Benjamin Gates goes to Michigan to buy Coon Skins to make fur gloves."[7] That summer the Church Family made three hundred pairs, and in 1898 they were still at it. The soft fur was combined with silk fibers and spun into yarn. "In 1891 one sister at the center family knit 47 pairs."[8] Shown here is a rare surviving pair, along with a linen label that would have been sewn inside and a paper label that would have been affixed to the packaging.

ABOVE RIGHT: Raccoon fur and silk, length 9", Mount Lebanon, NY. Courtesy of The Shaker Museum and Library, Old Chatham, NY. # 3327 a, b; LEFT: Black ink letterpress on off-white linen and on yellow paper, 2" × 4" (each). Mount Lebanon, NY.

A very small-scale business at Mount Lebanon in the early part of the twentieth century used chamois (probably deerskin), silk ties, and silk thread to make eyeglass and pen wipes. They were made by using a round steel punch (with sawtooth edges) that stamped out round disks of chamois cloth. A message was printed on the top of three leaves, a circle of thread was embroidered, and a silk ribbon was used to hold it all together. One of these sets reads: "Don't call an optician / To look at your eye; / Till you wipe from your glasses / The speck of a fly," the other, "In expense I'm a trifle / In service great worth; / For your pen I will clean / Anywhere on the earth." In 1910 these sold for twenty-five cents apiece.

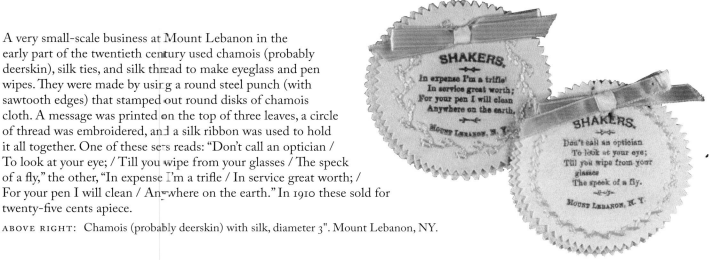

ABOVE RIGHT: Chamois (probably deerskin) with silk, diameter 3". Mount Lebanon, NY.

Textile manufacturing—wool, felted wool, linen, cotton, and silk—was a major undertaking at many Shaker communities in the first half of the nineteenth century, but it eventually gave way to competition from the World, which produced goods at much lower costs. Much of the Shaker output was intended for communal use, but a good deal was also sold. Unfortunately, nothing that can be documented of the latter remains, so this broadside and receipt from Sabbathday Lake will have to stand in to represent all of this early industry. Brother Ransom Gilman (1819–1886) was in charge of the newly built mill that carded wool for Shakers and non-Shakers when this broadside was printed (probably by Deacon James Holmes) in 1856. Later that year, Brother Gilman was released from his Trusteeship for putting the community deeply into debt. (A few years later he was removed to New Lebanon, where he lived out his life as a Shaker.) The receipt is dated 1864, a time when Brother Charles Vining was in charge of mill operations. He too put Sabbathday Lake in a precarious financial position, by speculating in the grain markets, and soon left the community for good. While these were two isolated cases of mismanagement and possibly malfeasance, they illustrate an important point: not all Shakers lived by the precepts of their Church and the terms of the Shaker covenant.

LEFT: Black ink letterpress on off-white paper, 12" × 9", R-367, and black ink letterpress on blue paper, 3¼" × 7⅝". Sabbathday Lake, ME.

The tradition of producing Shaker wool from Shaker sheep continues to the present. This sample card of colors dates to about 1975, while the skein of "Blue Denim" wool was put up in 2002. Inflation pushed a two-ply skein to $6.50 in 2005, but it was available in twenty-five colors.

ABOVE LEFT: Blue ink letterpress with variously colored wools, 8" × 3½" (card), and denim-blue dyed wool, overall length 10½". Sabbathday Lake, ME.

Legions of handmade textiles survive from Canterbury and Sabbathday Lake that can be traced to individuals. These few examples were selected because they speak to some special human dimension in the production of goods for sale. A note attached to the knitted cotton washcloth identifies it as the work of Sister Mary Maria Bassford (1842–1929), of Canterbury. What is especially poignant is this comment: "Sister Mary Bas[s]ford's last work just before she died. October 21st. 1929," possibly penned the very day that she died.

RIGHT: Off-white cotton with black ink manuscript on tan paper, 8" × 12". Canterbury, NH.

Pot holders were a favorite gift-store item throughout the twentieth century at both communities. This pair is special for its 1940 typewritten label: "These 'Holders' were made by Sister Myra Greene [1835–1942], at Canterbury, after she was more than 105 years old. All hand work." The Shakers were always known for their longevity—a fact that long elicited interest from the medical world—but Sister Myra is the record holder (so far).

LEFT: Printed cotton with typewritten paper, diamaters 5⅛" x 6⅜". Canterbury, NH.

Many Shakers remained in the faith for life, while others left after a stay of days or decades. Over a span of 225 years, approximately seventeen thousand people joined for some period of time, but how many of these died as Shakers and how many left is unknown. There was, however, another pattern of membership: those who came and went as their needs and circumstances changed. This sweater set represents this last, not uncommon aspect of Shakerism.

Sister Ruth [Perkins] Nutter was born in 1907 and placed at the Alfred community four years later. When Alfred closed in 1931, she moved to Sabbathday Lake with the remaining members of Alfred. In the 1940s, for reasons that are unclear, she left the Shakers and later was married for a brief time. In the 1970s, she took tentative steps to reconnect with the Believers at Sabbathday Lake, where she was received with great affection and acceptance. Over the following twenty or so years, Sister Ruth used her talents as a knitter to contribute a steady stream of goods for sale in the gift store at the community. She died in the faith in 1997. Shown here is the very last piece of knit work that she completed, a set of sweater, cap, and booties. The author's grandson, Jordan Robert Kates, modeled them when he was six months old.

RIGHT: White acrylic fiber with plastic buttons, overall length 11". Sabbathday Lake, ME. Photograph courtesy of Craig Rosenberg.

Other Industries

SILVER PENS,
Manufactured by the Society of Shakers,
Watervliet, Albany County.

SILVER PENS,
Manufactured by the Society of Shakers,
Watervliet, Albany County.

It is all but impossible to substantiate claims for Shaker inventions before about 1850, because documentation—in the form of written journal notations or eyewitness accounts, patent filings, plans, and working models—is simply absent. Also, the ever-innovative Shakers made constant improvements to the devices that were brought in from the World. Nonetheless, one early documented invention was the metal pen nib.[1] This was far more than a mere improvement on some existing model. While Watervliet and Mount Lebanon made these at a scale that qualifies as a small industry, there was never an effort to obtain a U.S. patent for the design. In 1819, the Shakers first rolled and trimmed a thin piece of silver—derived from melted coins—into a point and cut a fine slit into it. A small hole that was made away from the tip acted as a reservoir for the ink, which slowly made its way to the tip by capillary action. The tip was inserted into a wood and tin handle. The industry lasted until at least the mid-1830s. These labels are all that is known to have survived.[2]

Black ink letterpress on white paper, ¾" × 4½" (pair). Watervliet, NY.

In 1858, Trustee David Parker's (1807–1867) application for a patent on a commercial washing machine was approved, paving the way for a boost to Canterbury's economy. The machine was first designed at New Lebanon, for the community's own use, many years earlier. Parker improved it and started a small industry. Each of two units consisted of a large rectangular wooden box, mounted on legs and divided into three compartments. Each compartment had a set of vertically slatted "dashers" to agitate soapy water and laundry. A series of rods and levers connected these to a pulley that was, in, connected to the source of power by means of a belt. Hot water was piped in from above, and a series of drains on the bottoms of the tubs were all connected to a single lever arm for coordinated emptying.

The machines were intended for institutional uses: hospitals, schools, and hotels. The famous Willard Hotel in Washington, D.C., for example, had one or more installed. The machine won a gold medal at the Philadelphia Centennial Exposition in 1876. The pride that Canterbury took in these devices is evident in the use of a cut of one on billheads printed for decades following 1858. When this example, dated 1874, was printed, James S. Kaime (1820–1894) was the Trustee in charge of manufacturing and sales. Canterbury also made and sold soap after 1876 to support this product.[3]

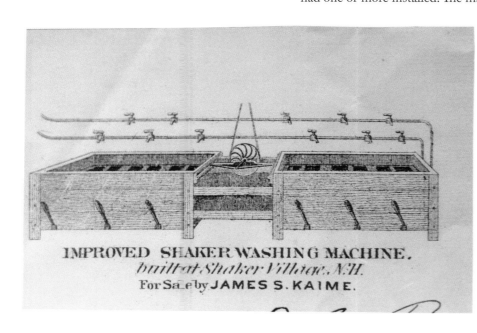

IMPROVED SHAKER WASHING MACHINE.
built at Shaker Village, N.H.
For Sale by JAMES S. KAIME.

TOP: Wood, painted dark red and metal, overall length 35½". Canterbury, NH. Courtesy of Hancock Shaker Village, Inc., Pittsfield, MA. # 62–781;
LEFT: Black ink letterpress (with wood or metal engraving) on white paper, 2¾" × 1¼" (detail). Canterbury, NH.

In 1865, Brother Hewlett Chandler invented a harvesting machine at Sabbathday Lake that was granted a U.S. patent.[4] The horse-drawn machine was called "The Improved Shakers' Maine Mower." Its innovation was a special arrangement of gear parts that reduced the friction of the cutting blades, allowing it to be pulled with less drag. The community's mill built as many as one hundred of these in a year. Unfortunately, none are known to have survived. What remains today is this single large broadside, dated 1866, and a simply constructed toolbox that was once meant to accompany each mower.

RIGHT: Black ink letterpress on white paper, 18½" × 12 '. Sabbathday Lake, ME. Collection of the United Society of Shakers, Sabbathday Lake, Maine;
BELOW: Pine, painted red, with stenciled black paint, 5" × 12" × 4". Sabbathday Lake, ME. Collection of the United Society of Shakers, Sabbathday Lake, Maine.

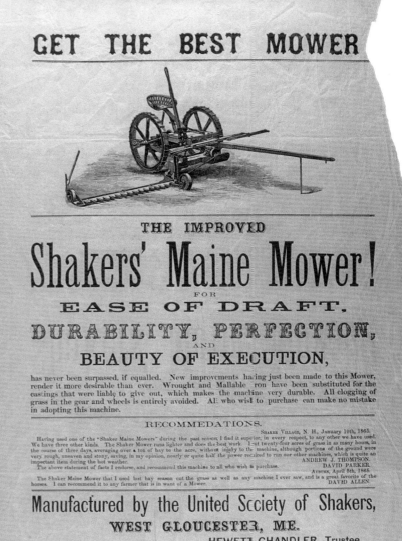

SHAKER SASH BALANCE.

Supercedes Weights & Boxes.

IS A PERFECT BALANCE AT ALL POINTS.

Is Simple, Neat, Cheap, Durable and Ornamental.

IS NOISELESS, AND OBEYS THE SLIGHTEST TOUCH—CAN BE ATTACHED TO ANY WINDOW WITH TWO SASH IN A FEW MOMENTS TIME.

SAMPLES COMPLETE BY MAIL FOR $1 50.

Samples may be returned and money refunded if not satisfactory. We continue to make this liberal offer, without ever having one returned to us. In ordering, cash must accompany the order, or satisfactory reference be given. We cannot ship C. O. D. to unknown parties without twenty per cent. accompanies the order, and the bill is for over $10. Without this assurance, in shipping to irresponsible parties we are liable to have our goods returned and charges to pay both ways.

In remitting please observe that your postoffice address, as well as your name, is plainly written, and, when convenient, obtain postoffice orders on Bowling Green or drafts on New York. If you send by express, prepay charges.

It needs no further comments to show that agents can make money rapidly with the "SHAKER SASH BALANCE," as there are so many buildings that have been put up without any balance, on account of cost, and the cheapness and simplicity of this makes them come within the reach of all, so that there is hardly any respectable house but what will take them. A gimlet and screw-driver is all that is needed to put them on with.

Address   W. J. McGOWN, Manager,
South Union, Logan Co., Ky.

We give herewith a few unsolicited evidences of its merits:

ABOVE LEFT: Black ink letterpress (with wood or metal engraving) on thin white paper, 11⅛" × 8⅜". South Union, KY, NIR; RIGHT: Black ink letterpress (with wood or metal engraving) and manuscript on white paper, 10" × 8". South Union, KY

"South Union, Ky., was the home of Sanford J. Russell, a Shaker, who invented and, strange to say, patented a sash balance, which without cords or pulleys worked perfectly, moved at a touch, locked at any desired point and, as *Scientific American* said of it, '. . . furnished the best ventilator known.'" This is what two Shaker Sisters had to say in their 1904 history about the final invention to be considered here, one that was also manufactured by the Shakers.[5]

Sanford J. Russell (1818–190?) was an "in and out" Brother, first at the Union Village, Ohio, community until 1861, when he seceded, then later at South Union, Kentucky, in 1873 (but Shaker status uncertain); he rejoined there in 1880 and, finally, died back at Union Village. The device that he invented was patented in 1872 and was "Improved and Perfected with a Cord-holder Attachment, Feb'y 1, 1875." Contrary to the opening quotation above, it *relied on* cords and pulleys in order to dispense with side-mounted counterweights. It was advertised for sale in *The Shaker Manifesto* through 1878.

The circular (with original mailing envelope) illustrates the device with the improved, ratcheted cord holder. An endorsement at the bottom from a dealer in Helena, Montana, A. M. Holter, is dated 1874. The letter, dated 1875, is from William J. McGown, the non-Shaker business agent for South Union, to the same Holter Company. In it he apologizes for overlooking another order from them but adds that he "took the liberty to copy a line or two of commendation from you." This neatly ties together these two pieces of ephemera.

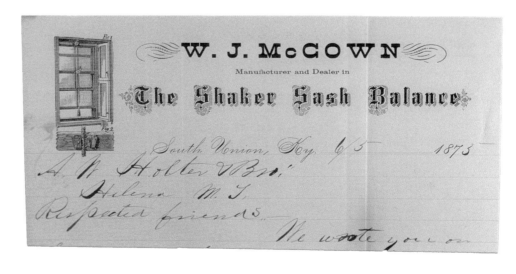

SHAKER SPRING WATER HOTEL OR RURAL HOME.

Is situated in the town of Ayer, thirty miles from Boston and one mile from Depot ; only one hour's ride from Boston, via Fitchburg Railroad ; eight trains each way daily ; it is on rising ground ; near the beautiful Sandy Pond ; good fishing and boating ; good driving ; good teams ; good stable ; first class accommodations for those wishing to bring teams. Telephone in the house connects with all surrounding towns and cities. This pleasant Summer Hotel will open for boarders June 1st. The celebrated Shaker Medicinal Spring Water will be free to the boarders.

RURAL HOME,

JOHN H. SPRAGUE,

MANAGER.

Ayer, Mass., Jun. 19 – 1890

L. H. Meade Esq

Hospitality is an underappreciated Shaker endeavor that, at times, approached the scale of an industry. At its most basic level many communities, if not most, served meals to paying guests. There were at least four villages, however, that had structures dedicated to guest stays: Harvard, Mount Lebanon, Enfield, New Hampshire, and South Union.[6]

Harvard's "Rural Home" was built in the 1850s to house that community's North Family, but by the time it was completed it was no longer needed, and its construction had put the Society into heavy debt. After the Civil War, Harvard leased the building to a veteran named John H. Sprague. He sought to attract a developing summer tourist trade and used the abundance of nearby "Shaker Medicinal Water" as a magnet. ("Moses smote the rock, This Water smites disease and death," reads an advertising card.) In the 1890s, the hotel was converted into a sanatorium; it is not known how much of a financial gain, if any, the Harvard Shakers ever realized from all this.

ABOVE: Black ink letterpress on white paper, 10½" × 8". Harvard, MA.

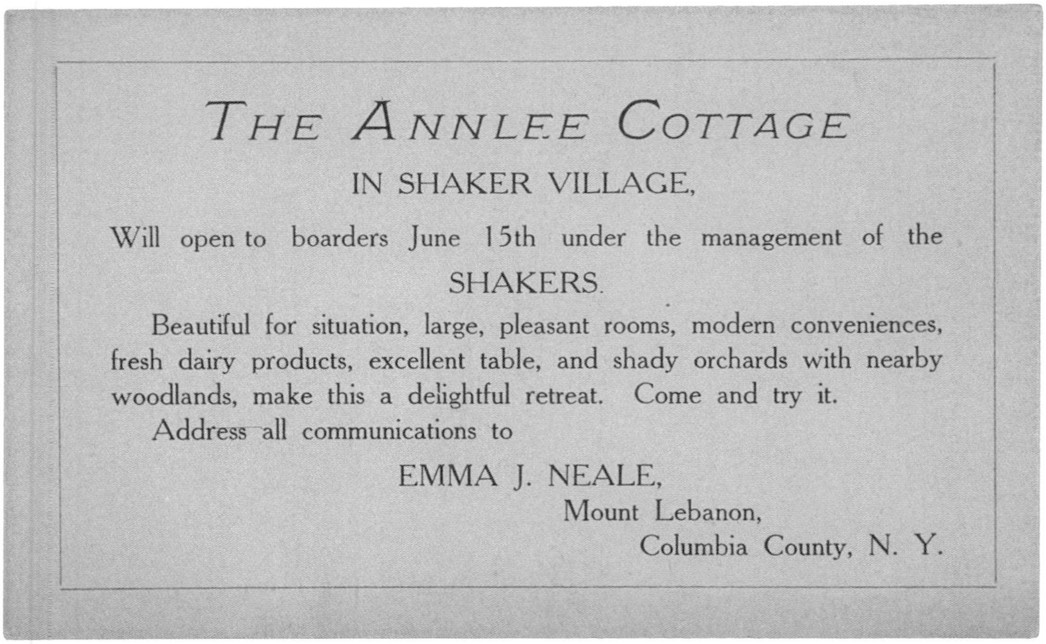

THE ANNLEE COTTAGE

IN SHAKER VILLAGE,

Will open to boarders June 15th under the management of the
SHAKERS.

Beautiful for situation, large, pleasant rooms, modern conveniences,
fresh dairy products, excellent table, and shady orchards with nearby
woodlands, make this a delightful retreat. Come and try it.

Address all communications to

EMMA J. NEALE,
Mount Lebanon,
Columbia County, N. Y.

In 1904, the Sisters at Mount Lebanon read the "handwriting on the wall" and reasoned that the future of their community rested on their ability to attract new members.[7] Census data for 1900 show that the total population was then 124, down from a high of 550 in 1860, with 41 percent now over the age of sixty. In 1904, two attempts were made toward recruitment: Sisters Taylor and White published *Shakerism: Its Meaning and Its Message*, and Sister Emma J. Neale (of the patented "Shaker Cloak" fame) opened the Ann Lee Cottage.

Sister Neale took an abandoned building from the Center Family (where she used to reside but had since been folded into the Church Family) and furnished it with unused furniture. The plan was for this summer guesthouse to be a source of revenue for the community and, of greater importance, a source of converts to the Shaker life. She failed on both counts. The cottage opened only for two seasons, 1904 (the time that this card was printed and distributed) and again in 1906. (In 1905, it served as a dairy and then an ancillary building during the Peace Convention.) The photograph was made sometime between 1904 and 1906.

ABOVE: Black ink letterpress on off-white card stock, 3" × 4¾". Mount Lebanon, NY, R-47; LEFT: Photograph on card stock, 3½" × 5¼". Mount Lebanon, NY. Courtesy of Hamilton College, Burke Library, Clinton, NY.

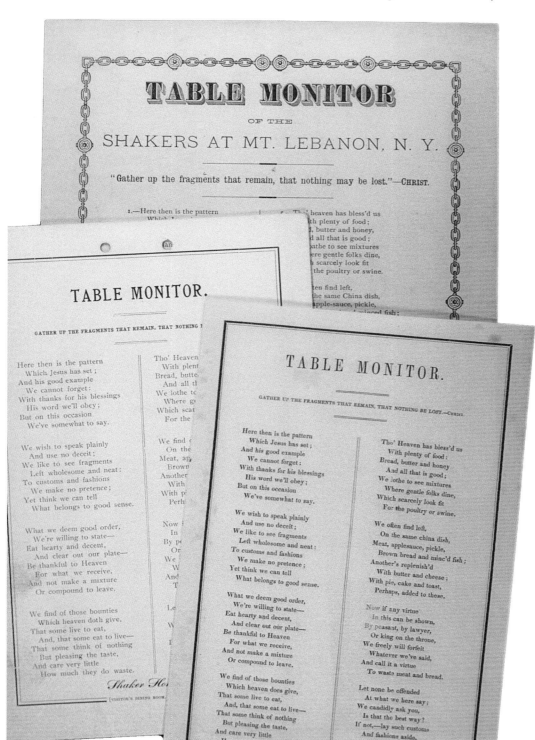

Along with the great volume of printing that they did themselves to support their industries, the Shakers also undertook printing as its own industry. Several examples will be considered that cover a range from the commonplace to the exotic and strange.

One group of printings intended for sale to the public was titled "Table Monitor[s]." These were copies of a poem composed by a Sister from Mount Lebanon named Hannah Brownson, who was placed with the Shakers at the age of five (1814–1886). She started with a quotation from the New Testament (John 6:12), "Gather up the fragments that remain that nothing be lost," and wrote eight stanzas of rhyme on the subjects of order and thrift. There were at least eight versions of it, printed between the 1830s and 1903, with most showing only minor differences in punctuation.

The three examples shown here were all printed at Mount Lebanon, but most other ones were done at Canterbury. The uppermost one, with the chain-link border, was printed in 1868. The lowermost one is very similar to that illustrated in Charles Nordhoff's *Communistic Societies of the United States* (1875). It is unusual in being printed on heavy paper rather than on card stock. The center copy is a 1903 Shaker reprint of the earliest version with holes punched at the top to facilitate being hung. It is the only example that survives in large numbers today.

LEFT: Black ink letterpress on off-white card stock (*top*), 10⅞" × 8½", R-125; black ink letterpress on white card stock, 10" × 6½", R-119 (reprint); black ink letterpress on off-white paper, 9½" × 6¼", R-121iv. All Mount Lebanon, NY.

Canterbury had a printing press early in the nineteenth century and a succession of talented Brothers to run it.[8] When Elder Henry Blinn (1824–1905) took it over around 1840, he transformed the small printing office into a virtual "job printing" shop whose output ranged from cards, labels, broadsides, and leaflets to music sheets and religious books. Of the latter, perhaps the most important was New Lebanon Brother Philemon Stewart's *A Holy, Sacred and Divine Roll and Book* of 1843.

The Shakers also had their own monthly publication that began as *The Shaker* in 1871 and, after several name changes, became *The Manifesto* in 1883. From then until publication ceased in 1899, it was printed at Canterbury (or in nearby Concord). Publishing *The Manifesto* was a true industry, for of the approximately five thousand subscribers, three-fifths were non-Shakers. Those from the World paid up to one hundred dollars annually apiece, providing the community with much-needed cash.

ABOVE: Black ink letterpress on white paper, 14" × 9¾" (*The Shaker*). Mount Lebanon, NY, and Canterbury, NH. Courtesy of Hancock Shaker Village, Inc., Pittsfield, MA.

At the lower end of the printing scale at Canterbury was the production of small gift and vanity cards such as those illustrated here. The Shakers bought lithographed blank stock and added names and/or religious messages. These were made and sold mainly in the period of 1870 to 1890. Both Elder Blinn and Sister Marcia Hastings (1811–1891) were actively printing at this time.

RIGHT: Color lithograph and letterpress on white and pink card stock, 4¼" × 3⅝" (card on left). Canterbury, NH.

Of all the endeavors surveyed in this book, surely one of the quirkiest was this one: the manufacture and sale of "Bible Charts." At approximately three by four feet, they were, by far, the largest printing project that the Shakers were ever involved with (although the actual printing was done commercially).[9]

It all began at the end of 1886, when two non-Shaker brothers from Ohio, Jacob and David Skeen, proposed that the Shakers underwrite the production cost of, and distribute, a two-part set of color lithographed sheets that combined some factual geography with a good deal of fanciful genealogy for the purposes of Bible instruction for children. The printed chronology on the chart begins with the birth of Adam in 4004 B.C. and ends with the life of Jesus Christ. The names of four communities—Mount Lebanon, Union Village, Pleasant Hill, and South Union—are listed in the inset (illustrated here), but only Mount Lebanon was actively involved.

In a journal entry for February 9, 1887, Elder Giles Avery said: "The Sisters are starting a new business, the backing with cloth, trimming and mounting Bible Charts for sale."[10] A month later, another Mount Lebanon Brother, Alonzo Hollister made a sales trip with the finished charts but evidently met with limited success. In all, 204 charts were assembled that year before the business was closed down.

BELOW: Color lithograph and letterpress on heavy off-white paper, 34⅛" × 16¼" (each sheet). Mount Lebanon, NY, R-1312a.

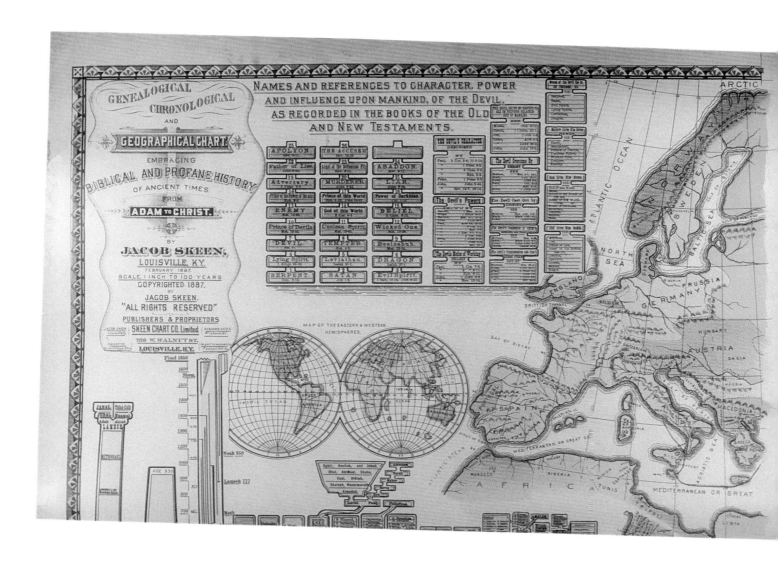

It seems fitting that the last industry to be surveyed here had roots in three areas of Shaker interest in the twentieth century: tourism/hospitality, fancy goods, and printing. It is also fitting that the multitalented Brother from Sabbathday Lake, Delmer Wilson, was at its epicenter. This industry was the making and selling of Shaker postcards.[11] While this may appear at first to be a marginal business, for these sold for no more than ten cents apiece, one must consider that in 1908—the year that Brother Delmer bought a camera specially designed for postcard production—approximately half a billion cards were produced in the World solely for the United States market.

In 1898, Congress passed the Private Mailing Card Act allowing for the private production of postcards. This was the year that Brother Delmer first began experimenting with taking and developing images for this purpose. By 1907, the year that federal legislation mandated the division of postcard backs, reserving the right side exclusively for the recipient's address, Brother Delmer was already printing "real photo" cards like the one on the lower right. Most of his images taken after this were sent to Germany for color printing. Until the First World War, when shipping was disrupted and dye factories (converted into munitions factories) were shelled, Germany was the printing center for the world. The two cards on top date from 1907–1915.

Once production shifted to America, in about 1916, means were sought to reduce ink costs. The solution was to shrink image size by framing the view in a white border. This practice lasted until about 1930, the time that the card on the lower left was made. Sabbathday Lake's sales of cards rose slowly but steadily from 2,600 in 1912 to 7,000 in 1922 to nearly twice that number in 1927. Then came the Great Depression, with an attendant steep drop in tourism. (The postcard collecting craze had already peaked some years before this.) We do not have precise sales figures for after 1927, but in all at least 272 different images were produced by Brother Delmer with the total output, up to the 1960s, reaching into the hundreds of thousands of Sabbathday Lake cards sold.

Photographs in black and white and color on card stock, 3½" x 5" (each). Sabbathday Lake, ME. Collection of the United Society of Shakers, Sabbathday Lake, Maine.

NOTES

Garden Seeds

1. Edward D. Andrews, *The Community Industries of the Shakers* (Albany: University of the State of New York, 1933), 67.

2. Ibid., 73.

3. "Ministry Journals" (1874–1890), New Lebanon, N.Y., NN, Shaker Collection, mss. no. 4, New York Public Library, New York, N.Y., microfilm, reel 2, #5–7, April 25, 1883.

4. Ibid., October 6, 1887.

5. Andrews, *Community Industries*, 73, 75.

6. Ibid., 73, 79.

7. Charles Crosman had been responsible for delivering the "western load," a seed route that followed the Erie Canal westward to at least Buffalo, New York, for many years. Only later did the Shakers realize that he had spent an inordinate amount of time in the city of Rochester. Within months of apostatizing in 1840, he was back there setting up a seed business with a partner. Crosman Bros., as it became known, specialized in selling seeds in bulk wholesale. More than 150 years later it is still in business. At least two of Charles's natural brothers, Daniel and Rufus, and a sister, Betsy, remained in the faith at New Lebanon for the rest of their lives.

8. The earliest known New Lebanon seed list is signed by John H. Dean and dated on the back, in manuscript, 1835. It is located in the Edward Deming Andrews Memorial Shaker Collection, Winterthur, Del., #SA 1452.

9. Andrews, *Community Industries*, 70.

10. Andrews, Edward D., and Faith Andrews, *Work and Worship: The Economic Order of the Shakers* (Greenwich, Conn.: New York Graphic Society, 1974) 60.

11. D. C. Brainard, *Rural Register and Almanac for 1874* (Albany: Weed, Parsons & Company, 1874), 33.

12. "Ministry Journals," January 1, 1885: "We are trying to revive the seed business by getting new boxes and bags printed in chromos."

13. "A History of 'Holy Land'—Alfred, Maine (Part II)," by Sister R. Mildred Barker, *The Shaker Quarterly* 3, no. 4, pp. 114–117. An Alfred seed list dated in manuscript 1856, is illustrated but no information is given as to its location.

14. *Let Us Sow with a Free and Liberal Hand: The Maine Shakers' Herb and Seed Industries.* This pamphlet was published by the United Society of Shakers, Sabbathday Lake, Maine, for an exhibition there of the same title in 1996.

15. Located at Harvard University, Cambridge, Mass., Graduate School of Business Administration. See R-187.

16. Galen Beale and Mary Rose Boswell, *The Earth Shall Blossom: Shaker Herbs and Gardening* (Woodstock, Vt.: Countryman Press, 1991), 36–44, and Deborah E. Burns, *Shaker Cities of Peace, Love, and Union* (Hanover, N.H., and London: University Press of New England, 1993), 73–78.

17. Enfield's tie to the southern market is indicated on this broadside by the added words: "For Sale by DAVID YOUNG, Seedsman, Americus, Geo[rgia]."

18. *Connecticut Courant*, Hartford, March 27, 1811. Also Burns, *Shaker Cities*, 73–78. This portion of a chapter provides about as much information as has been published (and Burns's book was *commissioned* for the bicentennial of the Hancock Bishopric).

19. Library, Fruitlands Museums, Harvard, Mass., 1820–1826, "Three Daybooks of Joseph Hammond": "Nathan ret[urne]d from seed journey . . . ," FM 1.10.

20. Library, Fruitlands Museums, Harvard, Mass., "1864 Diary of Grove Blanchard," March 18, 1864: "Dennis Pratt came home from a tour to Cape Cod, New Bedford, Nantucket, Martha's Vinyard [*sic*] . . . This was to settle up the seed rout[e] left by LDG in a very loose condition." LDG was Brother Lorenzo Dow Grosvenor. FM 31.4.

21. Library, Fruitlands Museums, Harvard, Mass., "1850–1852 Daybook . . . ," June 13, 1850: "plough the carrot field for dandelion." FM 31.1.

22. *Let Us Sow with a Free and Liberal Hand.*

23. Beale and Boswell, *The Earth Shall Blossom*, 40.

24. Mary L. Richmond, *Shaker Literature: A Bibliography* (Hancock, Mass.: Shaker Community, 1977) R-368–373.

25. Margaret Frisbee Somer, *The Shaker Seed Industry* (Orono: University of Maine, 1966), 11, n. 9.

26. Richmond, *Shaker Literature*, R-382–407, pp. 54–56. The Western Reserve Historical Society in Cleveland has all but one of the twenty-six seed catalogs listed here.

27. Amy Bess Miller, *Shaker Medicinal Herbs: A Compendium of History, Lore, and Uses* (Pownal, Vt.: Storey Books, 1998), 121.

28. Priscilla J. Brewer, *Shaker Communities, Shaker Lives* (Hanover, N.H. and London: University Press of New England, 1986), appendix C, table C.5, and Richmond, *Shaker Literature*, R-409, 408.

29. Burns, *Shaker Cities*, 73–74.

30. Dorothy M. Filley, *Recapturing Wisdom's Valley: The Watervliet Shaker Heritage, 1775–1975* (New York: Albany Institute of History and Art, 1975), 49.

Medicinal Herbs and Preparations

1. Andrews, *Community Industries*, 87.

2. Rita Buchanan, *The Shaker Herb and Garden Book* (Boston and New York: Houghton Mifflin Company, 1996), 98–104. This is a good overview of the subject with some of the antitraditionalists identified.

3. Amy Bess Miller, *Shaker Herbs: A History and a Compendium* (New York: Clarkson N. Potter, 1976), 114.

4. Buchanan, *Shaker Herb and Garden Book*, 123–124.

5. Ibid., 120.

6. A. B. Miller, *Shaker Herbs*, 68–72.

7. *Catalogue of Roots, Herbs, Barks . . . 1873*, Harvard, Mass., R-230, p. 1. "To preserve both Flowers and Leaves, the plan of compressing them, as practiced by the Shakers, answers a very good purpose; by this mode, many flowers and leaves are kept in a very efficient condition. R. Eglesfield Griffith, M.D."

8. Ibid., 1. "Neatly done up and labelled for the especial accommodation of the retail trade."

9. The name E. Myrick invites confusion. There were *two* brothers whose first name began with the letter *E*. Elisha started to work in the herb business in 1835, when he was only ten years old. He assumed charge of the herb house in 1850 but, in 1859, for unknown reasons, left the Shakers. Meanwhile, Elijah, a year younger than Elisha, was a Trustee for more than fifty years, the last seven of which he also served as an Elder. He died in the faith in 1890.

10. Miller, *Shaker Medicinal Herbs*, 137.

11. Sister Marguerite Frost (1892–1971) came to the Shakers at age eleven. She served as Canterbury's nurse and doctor in the 1940s. A photograph of her in the community's infirmary appeared in *Life* on March 21, 1949, p. 145.

12. Miller, *Shaker Medicinal Herbs*, 129, 156, 165.

13. *Harper's New Monthly Magazine* 15 (June to November 1857): 172.

14. Ibid., 164–177.

15. "Ministry Journals," March 26–April 27, 1861.

16. For an extended version of this story see "J. V. Calver

and Shaker Toothache Pellets" by this author in *The Shaker Messenger* 13, no. 4, pp. 5–8 and 19.

17. Richmond, *Shaker Literature*, R-432. Most of the surviving examples are located at the New York State Museum in Albany. The accession data for all of them show that they were given to the museum in 1931 by Sisters Emma and Sadie Neale of Mount Lebanon, New York.

18. *Catalogue of Medicinal Plants*, New Lebanon, N.Y., 1851, pp. 11–12, R-287.

19. Rita Buchanan, *Shaker Herb and Garden Book*, 128.

20. Beale and Boswell, *The Earth Shall Blossom*, 149.

21. A. Walker Bingham, *The Snake-Oil Syndrome* (Hanover, Mass.: Christopher Publishing House, 1994), 3–5. The author gives a succinct explanation of patent versus proprietary medicines. The former term, *in customary usage*, refers to a preparation whose efficacy is generally unproven and whose formulation is generally undisclosed. When the claims for such a remedy were extravagant and/or fanciful it was called a quack remedy. In the *legal* sense, a "patent" is a document of privilege granted to a medicine allowing exclusive rights of manufacture, for a specified period of time, in exchange for *not* keeping the formula secret. Few of the preparations that are examined in this book were patented; most were "proprietaries." The holder of the formula for a proprietary may *claim* the exclusive rights for manufacture, and that formula may or may not be a secret, but the law does not protect the formula.

Then there is the matter of trademark. A trademark that is registered at the U.S. Patent Office does grant legal protection to a *name*, irrespective of such matters as safety, effectiveness, or formula; any of these could be altered without affecting the trademark. It should be noted that many remedies *said* that they were trademarked, in order to dissuade competition, even if they were not. The law did not prohibit this. Several of the Shakers' remedies were trademarked, such as "Shakers Tooth • Ache Pellets," but it is difficult to determine whether or not the proper paperwork was ever completed for any of them. (I also wish to acknowledge William H. Helfand, an authority in this area, who helped to clarify this issue in a personal communication.)

22. Beale and Boswell, *The Earth Shall Blossom*, p. 243, n. 7.

23. J. Worth Estes, "The Shakers and Their Proprietary Medicines," *Bulletin of Historical Medicine* 65 (1991): 162–184, and Beale and Boswell, *The Earth Shall Blossom*, 151–154, are the best sources for information about medicines from Enfield, N.H. Dr. J. Worth Estes (1934–2000) was professor emeritus, Department of Pharmacology and Experimental Therapeutics, Boston University School of Medicine. He developed a special interest in Shaker medicines.

24. Estes, "The Shakers and Their Proprietary Medicines," 178.

25. Sr. Frances Carr, "The Tamar Fruit Compound: A Maine Shaker Industry," *The Shaker Quarterly* 2, no. 1 (Spring 1962): 39–41.

26. Estes, "The Shakers and Their Proprietary Medicines," 176.

27. Cheryl Bauer and Rob Portman, *Wisdom's Paradise: The Forgotten Shakers of Union Village* (Wilmington, Ohio: Orange Frazer Press, 2004), 192–194; Beale and Boswell, *The Earth Shall Blossom*, 139–140; and Estes, "The Shakers and Their Proprietary Medicines," 176.

28. These three sources were consulted repeatedly for information about this subject: Beale and Boswell, *The Earth Shall Blossom*; Buchanan, *Shaker Herb and Garden Book*; and Miller, *Shaker Medicinal Herbs*.

29. A few words are in order concerning bottles with labels on them that say New Lebanon. There are many examples of these in the antiques market, but few if any of them that appeared in the past twenty-five years are authentic. In some instances labels intended for other uses are pasted onto old bottles with no connection to the Shakers. In other cases the labels themselves are contemporary reproductions—counterfeits—and often for products that the Shakers never even made. As a basis for comparison, a substantial collection of authentic bottles is located at Hancock Shaker Village, Pittsfield, Massachusetts. Dr. Edward D. and Mrs. Faith Andrews placed them there in the early 1960s. In the author's opinion, they stand as the "gold standard" for labeled bottles from New Lebanon.

30. From a pamphlet for the exhibit "Breath of Life" at the National Library of Medicine, National Institutes of Health, Bethesda, Md., 1999–2001.

31. "Ministry Journals," March 26–April 27, 1861.

32. Ibid., 78.

33. *The Shaker Manifesto* 11, no. 4 (April, 1881): 91.

34. "Ministry Journals," October 15, 1886.

35. The best source for information about A. J. White's early adventures is Robert B. Shaw, *History of the Comstock Patent Medicine Business and Dr. Morse's Indian Root Pills* (Washington, D.C.: Smithsonian Institution Press, 1972). Another invaluable source as a general history of White's company and subsequent owners is an unpublished manuscript by Dorothy E. Ward, "History of A. J. White Limited and Menley and James Limited," written about 1980. The pharmacology of White's preparations is covered in Estes, "The Shakers and Their Proprietary Medicines," and J. Worth Estes, "Shaker-Made Remedies," *Pharmacy in History* 34, no. 2 (1992).

36. "Ministry Journals," March 15, 1876.

Food Products

1. Andrews, *Community Industries*, 82 (includes quote below). This work is one of the best sources for information about the food industries, but it should be kept in mind that Andrews had a decided bias toward New/Mount Lebanon since this is the community that he studied most and knew best. It may be that a true industry developed earlier at some different site, but this author has found no information to contradict Andrews's assertion.

2. Charles Nordhoff, *The Communistic Societies of the United States* (reprint, New York: Dover Publications, 1966) 194.

3. *Shaker Manifesto* 25, no. 10 (October 1895): 234.

4. *The Fruitage Will Never Fail*, a pamphlet published by the United Society of Shakers, Sabbathday Lake, Maine, in conjunction with an exhibit of the same name, 1999.

5. "Grove Wright Journal, 1836–1839," Western Reserve Historical Society, Cleveland, Ohio, November 1, 1837.

6. *The Shaker Manifesto* 12, no. 8 (August 1882): 189.

7. "Ministry Journals," August 19, 1884.

8. Buchanan, *Shaker Herb and Garden Book*, 72–73.

9. Letter from Burpee Co. to the author, 1983.

10. Sabbathday Lake Shakers, *The Shaker Herbalist*, number two (Sabbathday Lake, Maine: United Society of Shakers, 1975), unpaginated.

11. Julia Neal, *By Their Fruits* (Chapel Hill: University of North Carolina Press, 1947).

12. Magda Gabor-Hotchkiss (compiler and annotator), *Shaker Community Industries: Guide to Printed Shaker Ephemera in the Library Collections of Hancock Shaker Village*, volume IV (Pittsfield, Mass.: Hancock Shaker Village, 2003). This volume documents the ephemera holdings of this collection but is also filled with useful biographic information.

13. William Lawrence Lassiter, *Shaker Recipes and Formulas for Cooks and Homemakers* (New York: Bonanza Books, 1959), 209.

14. Andrews, *Community Industries*, 207.

15. *The Manifesto* 23, no. 10, p. 238.

Part II. Products of the Hands

1. Andrews and Andrews, *Work and Worship*, 137.

2. Ibid., 89–97. Another excellent, primary source of information about the early industries at New Lebanon is a journal written by Isaac Newton Youngs in 1856, "A Concise View of the Church," located in the Edward Deming Andrews Memorial Shaker Collection, Winterthur Museum, Winterthur, Del., #SA 760. The Andrewses used much of the information found in here, but there is still more to be mined.

Woodenware

1. June Sprigg, *Shaker Design* (New York and London: W. W. Norton & Company, 1986), and Andrews and Andrews, *Work and Worship* are two excellent sources for information about Shaker woodcrafts.

2. Illustrated in *Shaker: Furniture and Objects from the Faith and Edward Deming Andrews Collections Commemorating the Bicentenary of the American Shakers* (Washington, D.C.: Smithsonian Institution Press, 1973), 85 (right).

3. *The Shaker Quarterly* 15, no. 4, 1987, and 16, no. 1, 1988. A two-part article by John Wilson, including a quotation from Br. Delmer Wilson's "Carrier Notes," 1921.

4. Letter from the Shaker Society at Sabbathday Lake, Maine, to the author, 1997.

5. *Catalog of Fancy Goods made at Shaker Village, Alfred*, 1908, R-149.

6. Nancy and Herb Schiffer, *Woods We Live With* (Exton, Pa.: Schiffer Limited, 1977), 144–145. The authors

discuss the origins and uses of gumwood, one that the Shakers rarely used.

7. Gerard C. Wertkin, *The Four Seasons of Shaker Life* (New York: Simon & Schuster, 1986), 89.

8. Elmer R. Pearson and Julia Neale, *The Shaker Image: Second and Annotated Edition*, by Dr. Magda Gabor-Hotchkiss (Pittsfield, Mass.: Hancock Shaker Village, 1994), 88. (Every reasonable attempt was made to find the present holder of this image but without success. To anyone who may be a holder of this photograph: for future printings of this book you are invited to contact the author on behalf of the publisher.)

9. Jerry V. Grant and Douglas R. Allen, *Shaker Furniture Makers* (Hanover, N.H., and London: University Press of New England, 1989), 132–135.

10. Two songs—"Sweep as I Go," written by Elder Abraham Perkins of Enfield, New Hampshire, and "Sweep, Sweep, and Cleanse Your Floor," attributed to Sister Eleanor Potter of Mount Lebanon—are recorded in Edward D. Andrews, *The Gift to Be Simple* (New York: Dover Publications, republished 1962), 128, 125.

11. There is an illustration of a "brush vise," however, in Andrews and Andrews, *Work and Worship*, 88.

12. Andrews, *Community Industries*, 253.

13. Richmond, *Shaker Literature*, R-344.

14. A thorough examination of this industry may be found in Charles R. Muller and Timothy D. Rieman, *The Shaker Chair* (Winchester, Ohio: Canal Press, 1984), 169–232.

15. "Price List of Shakers Chairs" is located at the Western Reserve Historical Society, Cleveland, Ohio (R-249). This broadside, from 185_, lists chair sizes as "Large, Medium, Small," rather than by number, with Brother Jessie Lewis (1797–, left Shakers in 1867) and Brother DeWitt C. Brainard (1828–1897) in charge. It antecedes the *industry* of chair making by at least three years.

16. Bauer and Portman, *Wisdom's Paradise*, 172.

17. I am grateful to several individuals who provided information to me in 1997 about the Miller family: Dallas R. Bogan, Martha H. Boice, Dale W. Covington, and Mary Lue Warner. A few words should be said about an often-misunderstood Shaker document, the covenant. It was a written instrument of commitment that most, but certainly not all, members signed at some time. Beginning in the early nineteenth century, all applicants for membership over the age of twenty-one were required to sign a probationary covenant, stating that they were freely joining that community or family and would not seek compensation for work performed while living on trial there. After a suitable time, the applicant signed a family or church covenant. In *this* document the member ceded all assets to the "joint interest" of the community and pledged to live the Shaker life *in every way*. The form of these documents changed over time, with each revision designed as a response to legal challenges from former members or from the World. The final revision took place in 1832. Though repeatedly challenged, Shaker covenants have never been broken by the courts. I thank Steve Paterwic for providing the above information.

Fancy Goods

1. Esther Oldham, "A Shaker Industry—Fan Making," *The Antiques Journal*, September and October 1955.

2. Brother Theodore E. Johnson, *Ingenious and Useful: Shaker Sisters' Communal Industries, 1860–1960* (Poland Spring, Maine: United Society of Shakers, Sabbathday Lake, Maine, 1986), entry #131.

3. Richard C. Dabrowski, personal communication.

4. An excellent resource is Gerri Kennedy, Galen Beale, and Jim Johnson, *Shaker Baskets and Poplarware* (Stockbridge, Mass.: Berkshire House, 1992).

Textiles

1. An article by Richard M. Candee, "The 'Shaker Sock': A New Hampshire Contribution to Nineteenth-century Machine Knitting," *Historical New Hampshire* 52, nos. 3 and 4 (1997), examines all this in detail. I am also grateful to the late Wendell Hess, a scholar from Enfield, New Hampshire, for a series of personal communications between 1987 and 1989 on this subject.

2. The appropriation of "Shaker" for a host of products with no connection whatever to the United Society of Believers was common and continues today. "Shaker" salt, liquid paint, soap, and root beer are but a few examples. This, and look-alikes, were the reasons for the Shakers' use of "Genuine Shaker" on many nineteenth-century goods.

3. Scott T. Swank, *Shaker Life, Art, and Architecture* (New York: Abbeville Press, 1999), 195.

4. "Family Journal or Current Events: Compiled and Translated By Jessie Evans, et al. from 1901 to 1931," Canterbury Shaker Village, N.H., 94.

5. Swank, *Shaker Life*, 195–195.

6. "Family Journal or Current Events," 106

7. "Ministry Journals," September 27, 1884, and May 11, 1888.

8. Andrews, *Community Industries*, 252.

Other Industries

1. Andrews and Andrews, *Work and Worship*, 101.

2. Most of the surviving examples seem to have come from the sale of the collection of William L. Lassiter at Sotheby's, New York City, on November 13, 1981. Another interesting and unrelated facet of these pens is that in the *Millennial Laws*, put forth by the Lead Ministry at New Lebanon in 1821, Shakers were *specifically* forbidden to use or purchase such pens! This industry is further evidence of the extent to which these laws were sometimes ignored.

3. Elders Benjamin H. Smith and Nicholas A. Briggs bought the formula for laundry soap in 1876 from a Charles A. Guilmette. An original wooden soap box, with instructions for use, is in the collections of Canterbury Shaker Village, Inc. This product should not be confused with trade cards for a "Shaker Soap" that have some connection to Ohio but not to the Shakers.

4. Wertkin, *The Four Seasons of Shaker Life*, 90.

5. Anna White and Leila S. Taylor, *Shakerism: Its Meaning and Message, Embracing An Historical Account, Statement of Belief and Spiritual Experience of the Church from Its Rise to the Present Day* (Columbus, Ohio: Fred J. Heer, 1904). Their account subtly perpetuates the myth that the Shakers did not obtain patents for inventions but shared freely with the World.

6. There was a structure called the "Shaker Hotel" or "Mink's Shaker Hotel" near the Watervliet, New York, community that was run by a John A. Hills. This had no connection at all to the Shakers. On the other hand, the South Family Office at Enfield, New Hampshire, was converted into a "Shaker Hotel" in 1892, and it continued in business until at least 1899, under the guidance of Elder William Wilson. I thank Elizabeth D. Shaver, Shaker Heritage Society, Albany, N.Y. (and the late Wendell Hess of Enfield, N.H.) for providing me with the above information many years ago.

7. From the keynote address given by Stephen Paterwic at the Centennial Celebration of the 1905 Mount Lebanon Peace Convention on August 31, 2005.

8. Some of this information was taken from an unpublished manuscript by Tracey E. Adkins, "Printed at Canterbury, N.H.," 1995. A copy is located at Canterbury Shaker Village, N.H.

9. Much of this information about Bible Charts came from Jerry Grant, director of research, Shaker Museum and Library, Old Chatham, N.Y.

10. "Ministry Journals," December 1886 through April 1887.

11. Scott DeWolfe, "Brother Delmer Wilson and the Sabbathday Lake Post Card Industry," *The Shaker Quarterly* 17, no. 3 (Fall 1989): 97–100 and, *Wish You Were Here! The Postcards of Brother Delmer C. Wilson*. The latter is a pamphlet prepared by Michael S. Graham, curator, for an exhibit of the same title at the United Society of Shakers, Sabbathday Lake, Maine, in the summer of 2004.

SELECT BIBLIOGRAPHY

The information in this book was found in many places: in manuscript and in printed form, in imprints and in periodicals, in primary and in secondary sources. Often, the best information about Shaker products is connected with the product itself: labels, packaging, and advertising. Below is a short list of non-Shaker sources that were the most useful resources for the information found in this book.

Andrews, Edward D. *The Community Industries of the Shakers*. Albany: University of the State of New York, 1933.

Andrews, Edward Deming, and Faith Andrews. *Work and Worship: The Economic Order of the Shakers*. Greenwich, Conn.: New York Graphic Society, 1974.

Beale, Galen, and Mary Rose Boswell. *The Earth Shall Blossom: Shaker Herbs and Gardening*. Woodstock, Vt.: Countryman Press, 1991.

Brewer, Priscilla J. *Shaker Communities, Shaker Lives*. Hanover, N.H., and London: University Press of New England, 1986.

Buchanan, Rita. *The Shaker Herb and Garden Book*. Boston and New York: Houghton Mifflin Company, 1996.

Burns, Deborah E. *Shaker Cities of Peace, Love, and Union*. Hanover, N.H., and London: University Press of New England, 1993.

Estes, J. Worth. "The Shakers and their Proprietary Medicines." *Bulletin of the History of Medicine* 65 (1991): 162–184.

Gabor-Hotchkiss, Magda (compiler and annotator). *Shaker Community Industries: Guide to Printed Shaker Ephemera in the Library Collections of Hancock Shaker Village*, volume IV. Pittsfield, Mass.: Hancock Shaker Village, 2003.

Miller, Amy Bess. *Shaker Herbs: A History and a Compendium*. New York: Clarkson N. Potter, 1976.

Miller, Amy Bess. *Shaker Medicinal Herbs: A Compendium of History, Lore, and Uses*. Pownal, Vt.: Storey Books, 1998.

Muller, Charles R., and Timothy D. Rieman. *The Shaker Chair*. Winchester, Ohio: Canal Press, 1984.

Pearson, Elmer R., and Julia Neal. *The Shaker Image: Second and Annotated Edition* (annotations, appendices, and index by Dr. Magda Gabor-Hotchkiss). Pittsfield, Mass.: Hancock Shaker Village, 1994.

Richmond, Mary L. *Shaker Literature: A Bibliography*. Hancock, Mass.: Shaker Community, 1977.

Swank, Scott T. *Shaker Life, Art, and Architecture*. New York: Abbeville Press, 1999.

Wertkin, Gerard C. *The Four Seasons of Shaker Life*. New York: Simon & Schuster, 1986.

ABOUT THE AUTHORS

Stephen Paterwic is considered one of our most accomplished nonuniversity-based Shaker historians. With a formidable memory and no-nonsense style, Steve has lectured extensively on all aspects of Shaker history and in many places. A frequent contributor to *The Shaker Quarterly* and contributor to *Shaker Medicinal Herbs* (1998), he was the keynote speaker at the Annual Communal Studies Association Conference in September of 2004 and the Centennial Celebration of the 1905 Mount Lebanon Peace Convention in August of 2005.

United Society of Shakers, Sabbathday Lake, Maine, are part of a continuum of Believers who have lived at this community since 1794. The present group of four Shakers, two Sisters and two Brothers, closely follow the spiritual and economic traditions of their forebears. They still raise sheep and cultivate fields—for their yields of wool and culinary herbs—and still meet regularly for quiet contemplation, prayer, and song. In short, they continue to fully live "the life."

Gerard C. Wertkin is presently the Director Emeritus of the American Folk Art Museum in New York City. Gerry was Director there from 1991 to 2005 and Assistant Director from 1980 to 1991. Long interested in the spiritual dimension in American vernacular culture, he has organized exhibits and written extensively on the subject. He is the author of *The Four Seasons of Shaker Life* (1986) and, most recently, *Millennial Dreams: Vision and Prophecy in American Folk Art* (1999).

Dr. M. Stephen Miller is a retired periodontist who has collected items associated with, and studied various aspects of, the Shaker industries for more than twenty-five years. In 1988, he served as guest curator for "Marketing Community Industries, 1830–1930: A Century of Shaker Ephemera." Some seventy-seven thousand people saw this exhibit at Hancock Shaker Village, Pittsfield, Massachusetts. He also wrote, photographed, and self-published an annotated catalog of the same title.

In 2006, Dr. Miller cocurated (with Christian Goodwillie) the exhibit "Handled with Care—the Forms of Shaker Function" at Hancock Shaker Village. He also photographed and cowrote the accompanying catalog.

Dr. Miller has lectured on Shaker subjects from Maine to Mexico and has been published in numerous periodicals. Selections from his collection of artifacts have been included in more than a dozen books on Shaker material culture and history, including *Shaker Medicinal Herbs*, by Amy Bess Miller (1998). His ephemera collection includes more than sixteen thousand items from the community industries and is considered one of the most comprehensive gatherings of these materials.

In addition to his written and photographed contributions, he has served as copy editor for half a dozen books, including *The Shaker Image—Second and Annotated Edition* (1994) and all four volumes of *Guides to the Library Collections at Hancock Shaker Village* (2001–2003). He also wrote the foreword to volume IV (*Paper and Ephemera*).

He was interviewed for National Public Radio, Amherst, Massachusetts, in 1988 about collecting ephemera and appeared in the 1990 BBC documentary film *I Do Not Want to Be Remembered as a Chair*.

Objects from the Miller Collection have been lent to exhibits held at Hancock Shaker Village, Fruitlands Museums, Harvard, Massachusetts; the National Heritage Museum, Lexington, Massachusetts; the Whitney Museum, Stamford, Connecticut; and the National Library of Medicine, Bethesda, Maryland.

Dr. Miller served on the board of the Ephemera Society of America from 1994 to 1997 and was Chairman of the Board from 1995 to 1997. He also served on the boards of directors for Hancock Shaker Village (1992–2001) and Canterbury Shaker Village (1994–present).

Dr. Miller resides in West Hartford, Connecticut, with his wife of thirty-seven years, Miriam.

INDEX